THE CITY OF IBADAN

THE CITY OF IBADAN

EDITED BY

P. C. LLOYD
Reader in Social Anthropology
University of Sussex

A. L. MABOGUNJE
Professor of Geography
University of Ibadan

B. AWE
Lecturer in History
University of Lagos

CAMBRIDGE
AT THE UNIVERSITY PRESS
in association with the
INSTITUTE OF AFRICAN STUDIES
UNIVERSITY OF IBADAN
1967

Published by the Syndics of the Cambridge University Press
Bentley House, 200 Euston Road, London, N.W.1.
American Branch: 32 East 57th Street, New York, N.Y. 10022

© Cambridge University Press 1967

Library of Congress Catalogue Card Number: 67-18317

Printed *in* Great Britain
by *The Whitefriars Press* Ltd, London and Tonbridge

CONTENTS

List of Illustrations · vii

Foreword *by* Dr K. O. Dike · viii

I. The City

1 Introduction
 by Dr P. C. Lloyd, *Reader in Social Anthropology, University of Sussex* 3

2 Ibadan, its Early Beginnings
 by Dr Bolanle Awe, *Lecturer in History, University of Lagos* 11

3 The Agricultural Environment
 by Dr H. A. Oluwasanmi, *Vice-Chancellor, University of Ife* 27

4 The Morphology of Ibadan
 by Dr A. L. Mabogunje, *Professor of Geography, University of Ibadan* 35

II. Its People

5 Indigenous Ibadan
 by Dr Barbara B. Lloyd, *Lecturer in Social Psychology, University of Sussex* 59

6 Stranger Communities

 A. The Ijebu
 by Dr A. L. Mabogunje 85

 B. The Western Ibo
 by Dr C. Okonjo, *Senior Lecturer in Statistics, University of Nigeria* 97

 C. The Hausa
 by Dr A. Cohen, *Lecturer in Social Anthropology, School of Oriental and African Studies, University of London* . 117

7 The Élite
 by Dr P. C. Lloyd 129

CONTENTS

III. Life and Work

8 From Traditional Crafts to Modern Industries
   by Dr Archibald Callaway, *Research Associate, Centre for International Studies, Massachusetts Institute of Technology, Boston* 153

9 The Markets of Ibadan
   by Dr B. W. Hodder, *Reader in Geography, Queen Mary College, University of London* 173

10 Education Expansion and the Rise of Youth Unemployment
   by Dr Archibald Callaway 191

11 Government and Politics in Ibadan
   by Dr G. Jenkins, *Assistant Professor, University of Wisconsin, Milwaukee* 213

12 Religion in Ibadan
   A. Traditional Religion and Christianity
   by Dr E. B. Idowu, *Professor of Religious Studies, University of Ibadan* 235
   B. Islam
   by F. H. El-Masri, *Lecturer in Arabic, University of Ibadan* 249

IV. The Future

13 The Problems of a Metropolis
   by Dr A. L. Mabogunje 261

   Bibliography 273

   Index 277

LIST OF ILLUSTRATIONS

Maps

1	West Africa	2
2	Western Nigeria	4
3	The Oyo and Ibadan Empires	12
4	Ibadan: physical features	36
5	Ibadan: principal localities	43
6	Ibadan: residential areas, services and amenities	52
7	Oje	60

Plates

(between page 144 and page 145)

1 Chief Dele of Oje
2a Ibadan in the mid-nineteenth century: an artist's impression
2b Aremo compound, Ade Oyo
3a Central Ibadan and Mapo Hall
3b A shop in Agbeni
4 Hairdressing
5 The blacksmith's compound, Oke Are
6a A modern craft: sandal making
6b Gbagi motor park
7 The University of Ibadan
8a The Bodija housing estate
8b Élite wedding

ACKNOWLEDGEMENTS

Thanks are due to Frank Speed Esq. for permission to reproduce plate 7, and to the Western Nigerian Information Service for permission to reproduce plates 3a, 3b and 8a. Plates 2b, 5 and 6b first appeared in an article by Dr A. L. Mabogunje, 'Ibadan—Black Metropolis', *Nigerian Magazine*, no 68.

FOREWORD

This book attempts to provide an anatomy of present-day Ibadan, the largest *inland* African city south of the Sahara. Although many aspects and problems of the city's cosmopolitan and complex society are examined in this book by the twelve contributors, they do not pretend that their investigations are either comprehensive or exhaustive. They have revealed, however, the immense possibilities, the richness, and the challenge which the urban agglomerations in Africa have for scholars. This series of papers was presented to a seminar organized early in 1964 by the Institute of African Studies, University of Ibadan. The authors were then, for the most part, members or associates of the University.

Ibadan has a unique character of its own. It is instructive to note that many of Ibadan's characteristics, such as its ever-extending frontiers of built-up areas and farms, its cosmopolitanism and ever-swelling population, are rooted in the past, before the *Pax Britannica* was imposed on the city. Created largely by the upheavals which marked the disturbed last years of the Old Oyo Empire, Ibadan expanded and developed rapidly because of many factors. With its policy of discreet militarism, Ibadan became a refuge for industrious agriculturists and craftsmen, a place where careers were open to talent (rather than determined by kinship ties as in the rest of Yorubaland), and a nodal point for traders in the larger areas of Yorubaland and beyond.

The point made above is very important, in view of tendencies by uninformed observers to ascribe Ibadan's unusual growth and peculiar features to the establishment of British administration, the introduction of intensive European commercial effort and the development of modern communication systems. This is not to deny that all these agencies have aided Ibadan's modern growth and development. Indeed, they have brought into being new social, economic and political patterns and problems which, as revealed in the book, present a challenge to researchers, the Nigerian Government, religious organizations and the Ibadan City and District Councils. In my considered judgment this challenge is the basic value of this book and I have no doubt that those concerned will accept the challenge.

This book can fulfil yet another purpose: it can inspire a similar anatomy of other urban centres in Nigeria and Africa.

IBADAN
2 November 1965

K. O. DIKE
Director, Institute of African Studies

I. THE CITY

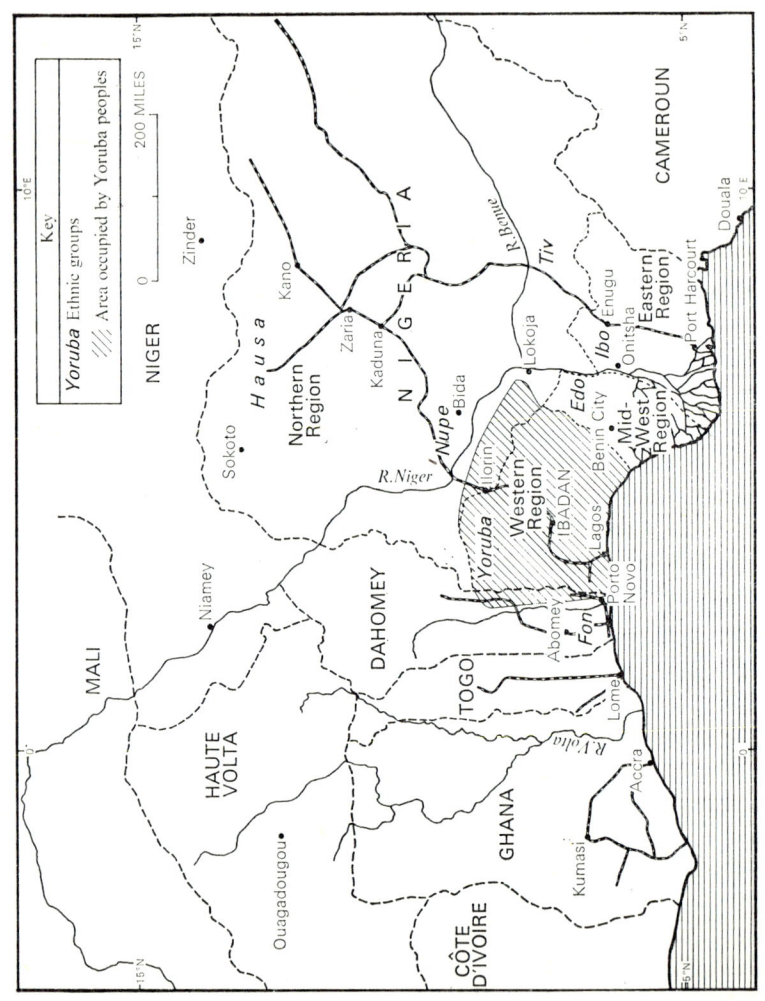

Map 1. West Africa.

1
INTRODUCTION

by P. C. LLOYD

Ibadan is a city-village. It is a city of a million inhabitants; the capital of a Region of eight million people and is a larger and more wealthy territory than many African states. Yet the core of Ibadan, settled in the nineteenth century, is peopled by farmers, traders and craftsmen living in large compounds organized on principles of common descent—a society more resembling the villages of Africa than the urban areas of the modern world.

The Yoruba towns are among Africa's ethnographic anomalies. Other ethnic groups have had higher densities of population and yet live in dispersed settlements; others again have had more highly developed political systems yet the capitals of their kingdoms have been small. Several existing Yoruba towns were in existence before the first Portuguese visits to West Africa—Ile Ife and Ijebu Ode are proven examples. But Ibadan does not belong to this group. Though, as the discovery of stone axes indicates, men have been settled in the area for centuries.

In the beginning of the nineteenth century, however, Ibadan was a relatively small town of the Egba people. This was destroyed in the fighting between rival kingdoms and the site occupied by an army, driven southwards by the collapse of the Oyo empire and Fulani incursions into Yoruba territory. As Bolanle Awe shows, from this war camp developed the town we now know. By the end of the nineteenth century Ibadan's population was already numbered in hundreds of thousands; it had grown larger than any other known Yoruba town. With Ijaye, twenty miles northwards, and founded in a similar manner, Ibadan was heir to the power of Oyo. In 1862 Ibadan crushed her rival and became supreme. Success attracted to Ibadan an increasing flow of immigrants though the other towns along the forest margins—Iwo, Ede, Oshogbo, Ogbomosho—were also enlarged by the southward-moving flow of refugees. In the second half of the century, Ibadan's population grew with the addition of domestic slaves seized in raids eastwards into Ekiti and Akoko.

Around the nineteenth century town the administrative, commercial and modern residential quarters have recently been developed. Most of Africa's capitals are towns of recent construction; the government buildings and the main shopping centres form the core, closely encircled by the homes of the new educated African élite and the expatriate community, with the settlements of the working population far on the outskirts. In Ibadan the sequence is reversed. Furthermore, indigenous Ibadan remains a largely rural settlement. Over half its total of adult males were, in 1952, engaged in agriculture; even a third of those

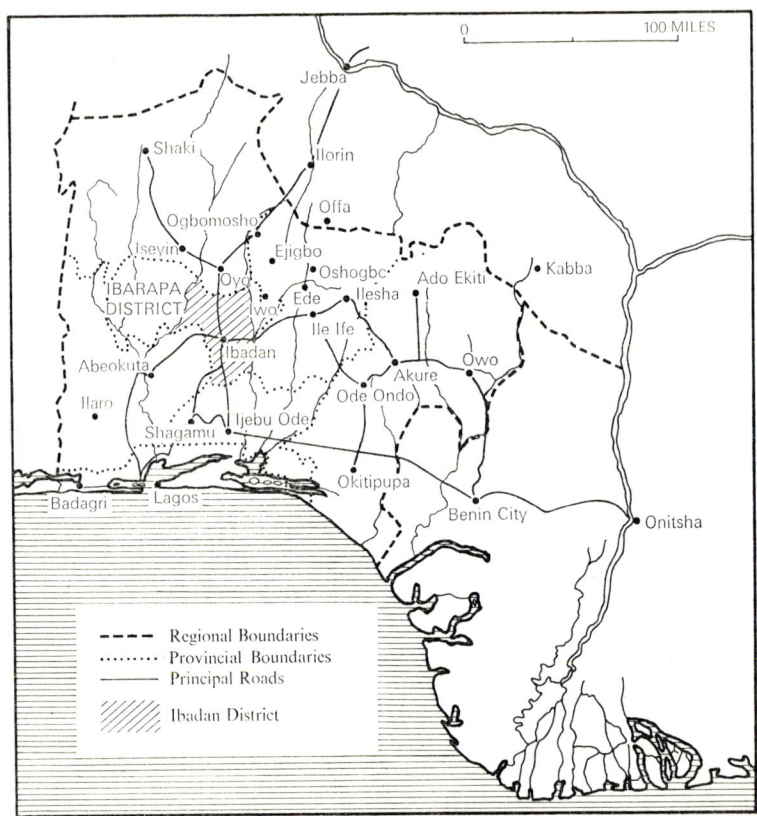

MAP 2. WESTERN NIGERIA.

resident in the city at the time of the census claimed to be so employed. It is of course difficult to define a farmer when all the members of the indigenous compounds hold rights to land and when many who are craftsmen, traders or clerks, work a small plot to help maintain their families. Those who are full-time farmers live for much of the year in one of the three thousand and more hamlets which lie on Ibadan land within twenty or thirty miles from the city. These, and their town-dwelling kin, regularly commute between compound and farm. At the

INTRODUCTION

times of major religious festivals the town's population swells; at the height of the farming season it shrinks.

Indigenous Ibadan is fairly typical, in its social structure, of most northern Yoruba towns. Our special interest lies in the relationship between the nineteenth century town and its twentieth century additions around it. To a large extent these remain separate settlements, the social life of one scarcely impinging on the other. Yet economically they are dependent on one another, and the fortunes of the older area are becoming increasingly associated with those of the newer.

Traditional Ibadan

Ibadan's people live in huge compounds, often containing several hundreds of inhabitants. In the past these were structures of a series of enclosed rectangular courtyards; today only one such intact compound remains in Ibadan—that of Aremo at Adeoyo. Modern buildings which tend increasingly to face towards the road have replaced the older structures, yet the pattern of co-residence and the concept of the compound remains. In a compound live, with a few exceptions, the descendants in the male line of one of the more powerful immigrants of the early or mid-nineteenth century, together with their wives, selected mostly from nearby compounds. A description of the composition of one quarter in Ibadan, that of Oje, is given below by Barbara Lloyd.

The lineage is a strongly corporate body of men and women. In it are vested rights, amounting to ownership, in both town and farming land. Its members elect from among the male members a *mogaji* who represents their interests in the traditional governing councils and who aspires to a chieftaincy title, setting him on the ladder towards the highest political offices.

Farming is characterized by a simple technology—the hoe, cutlass and axe are the main tools. There is a considerable variety of staple food crops, the rotation of which, together with the matching of soil to species calls for considerable skill. All the farming is carried out by men; their wives in the hamlets are engaged in gathering food for domestic use or in preparing manufactured products for the market. The great distance between farm and town compound, together with degree of specialization practised by the farmers, gives rise to the complex pattern of markets described by Hodder. A yam may pass through three or more markets between producer and consumer. Through the same series of markets the imported goods pass from the Ibadan merchants and wholesalers to their ultimate purchasers both in the city and at the farm. Craft industries were highly developed among the Yoruba. Many of these were, and still remain, hereditary occupations within certain lineages.

The traditional political system of Ibadan differs from that of other Yoruba towns. Ibadan has no sacred king or *oba*—a fact which may be explained by the peculiar origin and early growth of the town. Men, usually the *mogaji* of their lineages, are appointed by the chiefs to vacant titles of the lowest rank. As each chief dies, those ranked below him rise in theory one place, thus creating a vacancy at the bottom (in practice some leapfrogging of places is recorded). At the top of the ladder is the office of the Bale—since 1935, termed the Olubadan. Such a system results in the highest political offices being held by elderly men. In the twentieth century this is an undoubted handicap as it excludes from the traditional governing councils of the town those who are educated and of wider experience in contemporary affairs. The incompatibility between needs of modern Ibadan and its traditional system of government is a theme of Jenkins's chapter.

In his chapter on religion in Ibadan, Idowu has briefly outlined the principal traditional cults. To describe them in any detail or with any degree of completeness would require more than one book. Each lineage has its own cult, usually brought to Ibadan by the immigrant founder. Some of these are of the major deities of the Yoruba panthenon, whilst others are little known. All the lineages participate in the *egungun* celebrations—a type of ancestor cult. Ibadan's main festival is, however, associated with *Oke Ibadan*, a hill near the Eleyeile waterworks which legends connect with the founding of the town. To the Oke Ibadan deity is ascribed the function of creating fertility.

Modern Ibadan

As a major party in the wars of the late nineteenth century, Ibadan was politically important in the eyes of British consular officials. Yet it did not become an administrative centre until the late 1930s when the former Southern Provinces, with their headquarters at Enugu, were divided into Western and Eastern Provinces. Before 1951 Ibadan was not even a provincial headquarters for, being traditionally subordinate to Oyo, it had been placed within the administrative province which had almost the same boundaries as the ancient kingdom. It was, however, the headquarters of the largest Division of the Western Provinces—an area embracing the present Ibadan Province.

In the 1950s not only did the administrative machinery of the Regional Government grow rapidly, but government became much more highly centralized in the capital than in the colonial period. The Secretariat

INTRODUCTION

area has gained many new buildings. The senior civil servants, now almost all Western Nigerians, form the largest proportion of the new educated élite which overflows from the designated government residential areas into the privately developed suburbs. Only a small proportion of this élite is Ibadan born, though most are Yoruba. I have described some of the characteristics of the élite style of life. They constitute one of the most important groups in the town, for it is the educated élite which is creating the new patterns of behaviour and values appropriate to the modern world into which all Nigerians are being drawn.

Ibadan was an important commercial centre long before it became politically significant. The railway from Lagos reached Ibadan in 1901 and the major expatriate commercial firms and banks soon made the town their headquarters. As Hodder shows, the wares of their stores are distributed throughout the Region. Conversely Ibadan is one of the main centres for the collection of cocoa and palm kernels. It is only in Ibadan that Lebanese traders have been allowed to settle in any numbers. They were formerly engaged primarily in the retailing of imported cloth; they have now entered new fields—dealing in the provisions and electrical goods required by the élite.

The development of manufacturing industry in Nigeria is largely a feature of the past-colonial period. The Western Region government hoped that Ibadan would attract industries and it offered inducements to persuade them to come. It had the advantage of having a large, if unskilled, labour force and a network of good roads to all parts of the Region. But Lagos with its port facilities and other advantages has proved too strong a competitor for Ibadan.

Ibadan has been more successful in attracting the new social services. For many years its secondary grammar schools have drawn their pupils from all parts of the Region. In fact, in many of the leading schools, the sons and daughters of Ibadan men are in a small minority. An early suggested site for Nigeria's first university was Abeokuta, but Ibadan, offering a site of two and a half square miles to the north of the town was eventually selected; the University College admitted its first students to its temporary buildings (an ex-army hospital) in 1948. Since the Ibadan Native Authority hospital at Ade Oyo could not be recognized by London University as fulfilling the requirements of a teaching hospital, the University College built its own 500-bed hospital on the northern edge of the town. Although the doctors now trained at U.C.H. work in all parts of Nigeria, its patients are drawn predominantly from Ibadan. A small part of the land granted to the University College was used for the Ibadan branch of the Nigerian College of Arts, Science and Technology; the buildings of the latter college later became the Ibadan campus of the regional University of Ife. Thus, for a period, Ibadan has had two universities.

These economic and political developments have led to a substantial immigration into Ibadan from all parts of Nigeria. Unfortunately neither the 1952 census, nor that of 1963, indicates what proportion of the Yoruba residents in the town are from other parts of the Western Region. Of the 30,000 non-Yoruba, the Hausa and the Ibo (with Ibibio) each accounted in 1952 for 30 per cent of the total; other substantial minority groups are in decreasing order of size, the Edo, Nupe and Urhobo. Most of these non-Yoruba immigrants are resident in Ibadan city—yet even here they accounted for only 5 per cent of the total population normally resident. Only the Hausa are represented in any numbers in the rural area—they live in the principal market centres, engaged in the kolanut trade.

Of these immigrants only the Hausa, described by Cohen, are ethnically segregated—in Sabo (or Sabon Gari). Other migrants from Northern Nigeria tend to live together in Mokola, just across the road from Sabo. The Ibo and other southern Nigerian peoples are more widely dispersed through Ekotedo and Oke Ado quarters of Ibadan. For the Hausa the most important factor in producing cohesion as a community is the Islamic religion; they have no ethnic association based upon town or clan. Such associations are, however, extremely highly developed among other immigrants; many men and women have few close ties of friendship with any but members of their own ethnic group. The activities of one such association is described by Okonjo in his chapter on the Western Ibo of Ibadan. Even the Yoruba immigrants, as Mabogunje's description of the Ijebu shows, have their own ethnic associations and participate but infrequently in associations representing the total population of the town and thus having an Ibadan majority.

Within the past few years one particular form of immigration has attracted attention. Free—and it was hoped universal—primary education was introduced in the Western Region in 1954. In 1960 the increased numbers of scholars began to leave school seeking non-agricultural jobs, preferably as clerks or artisans. They began to come to Ibadan, seeing in this city not only the bright lights of a modern way of life but also the best opportunities for employment. But, as Callaway shows, these opportunities have not existed on the scale hoped for; the rate of growth of administrative organizations has slowed down, new industries have not been established. These youths, the 'applicants',

INTRODUCTION

stay in the town, living off relatives or in extreme cases by petty theft, until the hopelessness of their position forces them back to the provinces

The Impact upon Traditional Ibadan

The new offices, shops, factories and schools have almost all been built on the periphery of the old city. Yet the latter area is not without its changes. Cocoa farming, introduced to the Ibadan area quite early in the century, has brought a considerable cash income to the town. This is most easily apparent in the number of two-storey houses which have been built, usually within the owners' own compounds and thus scattered throughout the town, forming no single suburb of wealthier citizens. It is significant that of the occupations of Oje men those connected with building are so prominent. The new wealth, not only from cocoa but also from wage employment and trade, has contributed to the development of new craft industries. These are organized largely upon the guild principle and not within lineages. However important they may be in training men in rudimentary mechanical skills it seems, as Callaway suggests, unlikely that they could be developed into minor industrial enterprises.

Neither cocoa growing, wage labour, crafts nor trade, has resulted in a substantial change in the pattern of landholding within the nineteenth century town or in a marked displacement of population. And thus, in the second half of the twentieth century, we still find that the lineage and compound are the basis of social organization.

Furthermore, one has the impression that the people of Ibadan have failed to seize the opportunities presented to them. In 1953 only 20 per cent of their children were attending primary schools—one of the lowest proportions in the whole Region (cf. 70 per cent in Ijebu and Ekiti Divisions). Their traditional rivalry with the Ijebu was exacerbated when it was found that the latter were developing the margins of the city and realizing the profits from building houses for renting to the newly immigrant. Part of this conservatism of the Ibadan people may derive from their preference for basking in the fading glories of their nineteenth century dominance; some would assert that Islam, the faith of two-thirds or more of the indigenous Ibadans, has been partly responsible. For although Christianity, as Idowu shows, came to Ibadan in the mid-nineteenth century, Islam, as chronicled by El-Masri, was even earlier. One could well claim that life in Oje had changed no more in the present century than that in any other Yoruba town.

Ibadan is thus two towns—that of the indigenous people and that of the strangers. In the former men and women are organized in their lineages, in the latter in exclusive ethnic associations. The Ibadan élite of traditional chiefs, wealthy but often non-literate traders, a few local schoolmasters and officials of the City Council has few contacts with the educated, and regional or national élite, of senior civil servants, secondary school and university staff, and political leaders. Few associations unite the two groups. Thus in attending the churches nearest to their homes, Ibadan people belong to St. Peter's, Aremo or St. David's, Kudeti; while the strangers attend St. James' Pro-cathedral at Oke Bola. The division between the two communities impedes the flow of new ideas into the traditionally-oriented Ibadan society and is probably a serious brake on its development.

But however much divided in their social life, indigenous and modern Ibadan are but a single city—and moreover a capital city. Both Mabogunje and Jenkins, from their different viewpoints, discuss the problems of administering and developing such a metropolis. Conflict arises between the City Council and the Regional government over their respective areas of competence. Town planners, engineers, doctors despair of transforming the heart of Ibadan into an area which befits its status as the centre of a Regional capital.

2
IBADAN, ITS EARLY BEGINNINGS

by BOLANLE AWE

In the pre-colonial era, Yoruba country comprised a large number of kingdoms, the capitals of which were often towns of a substantial size.[1] The large kingdoms—e.g. Oyo, Ife, Ijebu, Ijesha, Owu—and the groups of smaller ones—e.g. Ekiti, Egba—gave their names to the ethnic subgroups into which the Yoruba people are divided. One of these kingdoms, that of Oyo with its capital at Oyo Ile or Old Oyo, grew to immense size, dominating the neighbouring kingdoms and acknowledging as equal only the kingdom of Benin. The power of this empire derived largely from its control of the trade route from the savannah to the sea and to its possession of an armed cavalry force. Internal dissension aggravated by external attacks by the Fulani led, however, to the collapse of the Oyo empire in the beginning of the nineteenth century. A new capital was built—the present Oyo—but much of the power of the empire passed to the newly founded town of Ibadan.[2]

For at least two hundred years before the nineteenth century, the existence of the Oyo empire had been one of the major factors making for stability within Yoruba country. Like the other semi-forest states of West Africa, the Oyo empire had no well-defined boundaries, but it incorporated within its frontiers a large part of northern Yoruba country east and west of the River Ogun, and it developed this area into a highly organized and culturally advanced state. With the rest of the Yoruba country it had arrived at a working arrangement to guarantee peace, partly through its army which was described as 'the scourge and terror of all its neighbours',[3] and partly through the claim to a common ancestor, Oduduwa, and a common cultural heritage.

By the beginning of the nineteenth century, however, the Oyo empire was on the verge of a decay which was to involve the rest of the Yoruba country. Internal strains then combined with external threats to

---

[1] Bascom (1955, 1957).
[2] Before the collapse of the Oyo empire in the 1830s, its capital was at Old Oyo (or Oyo Ile). A new capital thirty-five miles north of Ibadan was soon founded; this is the present town of Oyo. The people of the empire are known as Oyo and form an ethnic subgroup of the Yoruba, distinct from the neighbouring Egba, Ife, Owu, etc. Thus most of the people of the city of Ibadan are Oyo—though they may in certain contexts be termed Ibadan to distinguish them from the people of the present Oyo and its subordinate towns in Oyo Division.
[3] Norris (1789), p. 11.

THE CITY

bring about its collapse. Internally, the delicate balance of power between the ruler and his chiefs which had often been the means of ensuring that government was fair and just in Yoruba towns had been upset. The ruler of the Oyo empire, the Alafin, had, with the addition of new territories which came directly under his control, become too powerful, and consequently unpopular.

The revolt against him was led by Afonja, the Are Onakakanfo,

MAP 3. THE OYO AND IBADAN EMPIRES.

commander-in-chief of the imperial army. An ambitious man with some claim to royal blood, he was able to undermine the power and standing of the Alafin; he lived far away from the capital and was put in charge of an extensive area where he could easily build a rival power of his own. To strengthen his opposition to the Alafin, he invited the support of the Fulani, who, in the cause of Islam, had succeeded by the first decade of the nineteenth century in establishing their control over a large part of the present Northern Nigeria.[1]

[1] See Smith (1961), for the Fulani revivalist movements in general.

IBADAN, ITS EARLY BEGINNINGS

The onslaught of the Fulani into Yoruba country, coupled with the rebellion of the chiefs under the leadership of Afonja, brought the empire to its knees. The Fulani then entrenched themselves at Ilorin after an unsuccessful attempt to expel them had been made by Afonja, who now found their stay a source of great embarrassment.[1] From Ilorin the Fulani carried their raids into Yoruba country and by the 1820s their successes had set in motion the gradual dismemberment of the Oyo empire. Many of the towns in the northern part were deserted, and Old Oyo, the capital itself, collapsed *c.* 1837. Consequently, refugees from these towns first fled southwards to places such as Ogbomosho and Shaki and then, later, further south to those towns which were situated between the savannah and the forest region.

By the 1820s the southern part of the Yoruba country was also in a state of confusion; here the effects of the trans-Atlantic slave trade were just beginning to be felt. With the establishment of the Fulani at Ilorin, free access to the north, which was formerly the main source of slaves, was seriously interrupted. The Yoruba therefore turned on themselves to meet the demand for more slaves.[2] The Ijebu, whose country bordered the coastal areas, were the middlemen in this trade, and they soon started to encourage their neighbours, the Ife, to engage in slave raiding.

The immediate consequence of this was the Owu war fought between the Ife and their Ijebu allies on the one hand, and the ruler of Owu, the Olowu, who tried to prevent their slave raiding expeditions against his subjects, on the other. The Oyo refugees joined this struggle as allies of the Ife and Ijebu, and together they soon destroyed Owu.[3] With the collapse of the Owu kingdom, the disintegration of the southern part of Yoruba country also began. The allied forces attacked next the Egba towns, particularly the Egba Gbagura; there was no united resistance here, and most of the Egba towns extending from present Oyo almost to Apomu were destroyed.[4]

Many of the Oyo refugees then either settled in neighbouring towns, such as Ile Ife, Odunabon and Ipetumodu, where they were easily absorbed, or later created their own towns such as the present Oyo, Ijaye and Eruwa. But the allied army did not disband immediately; instead they chose Ibadan, an Egba village which was still habitable, as their camp *c.* 1829.

---

[1] See Hogben (1933), p. 153, for account of Afonja's attempt to dislodge the Fulani.
[2] The old Spanish and Portuguese colonies in South America had just won their independence during this period and were in dire need of slaves to work their plantations.
[3] See Johnson (1957), p. 206–10, for an account of the Owu war.
[4] Biobaku (1957), p. 13, gives an account of the destruction of the Egba towns.

Ibadan is Founded

Ibadan was at this time a small village on the less elevated southern extremity of a ridge of hills running from the north-west to the south-east, around the present Mapo Hall. Its position on the edge of the grassland, and the protection which it was afforded by the large expanse of lateritic outcrop in the area, made it an ideal place of refuge from the Fulani cavalry attacking from the north, and from the hostile Egba in the neighbourhood.

What was intended primarily as a camp, therefore, soon became a permanent settlement where these wandering soldiers from Ile Ife, Ijebu and the Oyo empire made their home. The Oyo and the Ife settled around the present Oja Iba and Mapo Hall and their leaders, such as Oluyole and Olupoyi from the Oyo empire, and Labosinde from Ile Ife, built their compounds here. The Ijebu settled at Isale Ijebu to the south-east in the area closest to their own country, whilst the remaining Egba settled at Iyeosa.

It was, however, a settlement not without growing pains. Its heterogeneous nature, as well as the insubordinate spirit bred by the wandering life of those who had been soldiers of fortune, made peaceful settlement difficult. Moreover the leadership was not clear-cut and Ibadan therefore became the scene of frequent civil wars in the continuous struggle for leadership.[1] At first, the Ife, being the host army, succeeded in establishing some kind of ascendancy over the other groups. With the continuing influx of the Oyo fleeing from the northern part of their empire, however, they grew in number, and their Ife allies were finally worsted with the help of other Oyo, particularly those from Ijaye.[2]

With the success of their kinsmen, many more Oyo refugees came to settle at Ibadan. Since the new settlement was primarily a military camp and did not observe the customs and traditions which restricted life in an ordinary town, it attracted in particular those who were daring and adventurous. These came, as the settlement grew, not only from among the Oyo, but from all parts of Yoruba country; indeed, a survey of the various compounds in Ibadan indicates that almost every Yoruba town had a son in Ibadan. As a new town, unbound by any traditions, it offered more scope for achievement than the traditional Yoruba

---

[1] A common Yoruba saying about Ibadan up to the present day is *Aki wa aiye ki a ma l'arun kan lara, ija igboro l'arun Ibadan:* 'We all have our defects; Ibadan's shortcoming is its constant civil war.'

[2] Oyo forces inflicted a crushing defeat on the Ife soldiers under their captain, Maye at Gbanamu Hill with the help of Kurunmi, the Oyo Yoruba ruler of Ijaye.

towns. Ambitious young men eager to achieve success, craftsmen looking for better opportunities for their trade, and rich men bored with life in their own towns came there. Later in the century, a handful of Sierra Leoneans and Brazilians, descendants of those formerly carried into transatlantic slavery, and now finding their way back to the Yoruba country, arrived in Ibadan.[1]

Often these newcomers settled in groups according to their place of origin and there are still areas in Ibadan which have been colonized by people from particular towns. By 1851, according to David Hinderer, the first European Anglican missionary in Ibadan, the town could boast a population of between 60,000 and 100,000.[2] It is not surprising therefore that it soon expanded and by then covered an area of nearly 16 square miles, 'beginning with the closely packed houses ... spreading over the slopes of the hill on which the old town was built, and continuing into the plains below where the houses are less crowded, and are interspersed with gardens in which flourish the orange, plantains, bananas....'[3] The town soon expanded beyond this hill and settlements grew around the other hills, notably Oke Are to the north. It embraced many of the nearby deserted Egba towns.

Town walls, which were estimated to be about 10 miles in circumference in 1857, surrounded the whole settlement. There were four main gates in these walls, leading to Abeokuta, Ijebu, Oyo and Iwo. Some small farms were within the town walls, but the main farms were outside them; these stretched in 1858 as far as Lalupon and beyond to the north-east, and as far as the town of Apomu in the south-east. Indeed, they were sometimes as far as 30 miles away and embraced more deserted Egba townships such as Ojo, Ika, Iroko, Ikeye, which then became Ibadan farm villages.

As Ibadan grew in size, so it grew in commercial importance; its geographical situation between the coast and the interior made it a convenient meeting place for traders from all parts of Yoruba country. As the destruction of the Oyo empire had meant a shift in the direction

[1] The early 1830s saw the return of Yoruba men and women who had been sold into Atlantic slavery, but had fortunately been recaptured by British naval vessels and settled in Sierra Leone. Most of these emigrants had settled at Abeokuta and Lagos but a few found their way to Ibadan.

[2] Much of the evidence for the early history of Ibadan is based on David Hinderer's journals and letters; these have not been published and are now kept in the archives of the Church Missionary Society, London. Hinderer spent many years in Ibadan and could speak and understand the Yoruba language. He was also on very friendly terms with the chiefs and therefore had access to information about developments in Ibadan. His wife, Anna, also started a school and ran a boarding house, which were attended by the children of the chiefs, missionaries and others.

[3] Hinderer (1872), pp. 58-59.

of trade within Yoruba country from the north to the south, Ibadan became increasingly important. To serve the ends of trade, therefore, a number of small market places were founded in front of their compounds by important chiefs such as Ibikunle and Dele, who established Ayeye and Oje markets respectively.

The main market in Ibadan, which had become the focal point for traders from all over Yoruba country, was, however, Oja Iba, sited in the oldest part of the town.[1] It was named after Oluyole, one of the most distinguished of the early Oyo immigrants. According to eye witnesses, it contained all types of local produce and 'all kinds of European goods which have yet been imported'.[2] Here Egba and Ijebu traders from Lagos and Badagry brought imported goods such as textiles, guns and ammunition, salt, cutlery and mirrors, which they gave in exchange for the hand-woven cloths, livestock and foodstuff of Yoruba merchants from Ijaye, Oyo and Ogbomosho, as well as for the slaves, leatherwork and ivory of Hausa and Nupe merchants from the North.

Indeed Ibadan's trade and its policy of accepting all newcomers combined to make a large town with a large heterogeneous population. But in this new town, the Oyo were in the majority, and their first leaders were men such as Oluyole, Elepo, Olupoyi and Oluyedun, who came from the heart of the Oyo empire. Because of the dominance of the Oyo group, Ibadan came to be regarded as an Oyo town whose inhabitants were the subjects of the Alafin of Oyo and whose status within the political hierarchy of the Oyo kingdom could only be that of a daughter settlement looking to Oyo as its metropolis and acknowledging its dependence on it. For example, its chiefs could only be installed with the consent of the Alafin, who sent a representative to cap a new chief with the *akoko* leaves—the sign of chieftaincy in Oyo country. Ibadan was also expected to present each year, through the Babayajin, the Oyo chief who acted as spokesman for Ibadan in Oyo, the customary tribute expected of all Oyo towns. Its fate like that of other towns in the Oyo kingdom was bound up with that of Oyo.

This semi-dependent relationship with Oyo had great implications for Ibadan's history and development, and for the fate of Yoruba country as a whole. It was to affect both the internal and external development of Ibadan, and to shift the emphasis in its development from the internal aspect to its external activities. Indeed, so important

[1] Oja Iba is not to be confused with Oja Oba or King's market, the central market in most Yoruba towns. Ibadan had no king, and Oja Iba is really Iba's market, Iba being the shortened form of (I)Bashorun, the title taken by Oluyole.
[2] Hinderer's Journals, June 7th, 1851.

was its foreign policy and its standing in Yoruba country to be that all through the century its internal development would be geared to what was happening outside its borders.

The reason for this development is to be found in the state of Yoruba country during the nineteenth century and the inability of the new capital of Oyo to fulfil its role as the new metropolis of the Oyo community. Right from its foundation it was subjected to trials.

Rivalry for Power

Although the Oyo had left their old homes to escape the onslaught of the Fulani, peace could still not be guaranteed in their new homes. The Fulani, from their new post at Ilorin, still constituted the greatest menace to Yoruba country; they had succeeded in bringing under their control those parts of the country, such as the Igbomina and Ibolo districts, which were formerly under Afonja's jurisdiction, and were carrying their expeditions to settlements, such as Ede and Iwo, with large populations of Oyo immigrants. Their aim was not so much the propagation of Islam as the desire to carve an empire for themselves in Yoruba country. If Yoruba country was not to be completely overrun and brought under their imperial control, an effective check had to be put to their raids and expeditions. Since most of their incursions were primarily directed against the areas of Oyo settlement, this responsibility fell squarely on the Oyo. In such a situation, involving the whole kingdom, the initiative for action lay with the metropolis and the Alafin.

The Alafin at Oyo was Atiba, a royal prince from Old Oyo who had succeeded in founding a new dynasty in Oyo. He had tried to create in this new capital a court worthy of the descendants of the Oyo empire; he had revived most of the pomp and splendour of the old empire, and had surrounded himself with as much ceremony and ritual as had former rulers. But although by so doing he had given much prestige to Oyo, and had achieved recognition as the spiritual head and ruler of the Oyo, he had not the resources, particularly the military power, to protect his new domain.

Military power, which had formerly been shared between the Are Onakakanfo and the Eso or 'praetorian guards' at the metropolis, was distributed between several men;[1] the soldiers of the Alafin were now at Ibadan whilst others had joined Kurunmi the new ruler of Ijaye. Indeed in recognition of the fact that responsibility for defence lay

---

[1] These were the 70 captains who were resident at the capital of the Old Oyo empire and formed the nucleus of the Oyo imperial army.

primarily with these two towns, the Alafin conferred on their leaders the most important titles in the old Oyo empire. Kurunmi of Ijaye became Are Onakakanfo, or Commander-in-chief to the Alafin while Oluyole of Ibadan became the Bashorun. Kurunmi was to be responsible for the defence of Ekun Otun, which had been the western district of the former Oyo empire, whilst Oluyole in Ibadan was to look after Ekun Osi, which had been its eastern district.

The responsibility for saving Oyo country from Fulani attack was, however, to lie mainly with Ibadan. Alafin Atiba was never for long on good terms with Kurunmi and therefore leant increasingly on Ibadan's advice and support.[1] Moreover, Kurunmi had succeeded in establishing a dictatorship in Ijaye only after driving away the Egba inhabitants. With his death in 1861 and the consequent removal of his guiding hand, the political fabric and the military power which he had created, collapsed. The existence of Ibadan prevented the disastrous consequences which this would have had for the rest of Oyo country.

It was this external factor which shaped to a large extent the political development in Ibadan. To combat the Fulani threat, Ibadan had to evolve a political system geared to a state of continuous warfare. The military nature of its political system was therefore to become its most notable and distinguishing characteristic in the nineteenth century. During this period it was on its military strength that its reputation among other towns rested.

Ibadan's origins as a war camp gave it a unique opportunity among other Yoruba towns for developing a military potential. Since the first settlers were all soldiers, the tradition for exalting the military aspect of life had been established. Even its myth of origin attributed the founding of the first two settlements at Ibadan to restless warriors who were regarded as the ancestors of the nineteenth century inhabitants of Ibadan. The chief religious festival, the worship of Oke Ibadan, also helped to infuse in the inhabitants the war spirit.[2] It stressed the endurance of the first settlers in Ibadan who, after defeat, fed on whatever they could find on the hill where they took refuge.

Moreover, the fact that Ibadan had acknowledged the Alafin as its ruler made it possible and easy to evolve a new system of government without the strains and restrictions which kingship imposed on traditional Yoruba towns. Ideas were borrowed from wherever they could be

[1] Atiba and Kurunmi were contemporaries and soldiers of fortune together, and Kurunmi, an arrogant and imperious character, resented Atiba's overlordship; moreover Atiba, in an effort to build up his power, tried to lure away from their allegiance those towns which were under Kurunmi's control.
[2] See Parrinder (1951), pp. 54–58.

found and many new titles were created.[1] The problem of hereditary succession to leadership was also avoided since no one could establish a better claim than another, and all, moreover, were subordinated to the kingship of the Alafin.

By 1851, government in Ibadan was divided into two spheres, the military and the civil, and there were four main lines of chiefs.[2] At the top of the main military line was the Balogun, and at the top of the main civil line was the Bale. Below these men were subordinate chiefs bearing titles which signified their positions beside their leaders on the battlefield, and their order of sitting at meetings. The younger men, with less experience, who still had to prove themselves had a separate and third line, headed by the Seriki, a young warrior who was, in most cases, marked for greater distinction. The fourth line of chiefs was also civil and was to represent women's interests. The Iyalode, described by Anna Hinderer as 'a sort of queen, a person of much influence and looked upon with much respect', headed the line of female chiefs.[3]

These were the most important lines of chiefs in Ibadan, and the titles differed from those of other Yoruba towns in some notable respects. None of them was hereditary. Competition for them was open to all freeborn residents in Ibadan. For the three male lines, the most important qualification was a man's merit as a soldier, for it was by bravery in war that a man could render the greatest service to the town. Even the main civil line headed by the Bale was made up largely of retired soldiers.

To ensure that the chiefs gave their best to the cause of the town, no one was ever allowed to attain the highest title on taking office. There existed instead, within these lines, a system of promotion from the lowest to the highest title. Promotion again depended primarily on a man's valour, the available vacancies and the political interest of those in a position to influence the choice of chiefs.[4] There was no definite order of promotion, but the existence of opportunities for advancement attracted to Ibadan the best soldiers from all parts of Yoruba country

---

[1] For example, Sarunmi and Mọgaji are titles borrowed from the Hausa-Fulani, whilst Baba Isale, Agbakin, etc. were new creations.

[2] The 4 lines of chiefs are as follows:

Bale	Balogun	Seriki	Iyalode
Otun Bale	Otun Balogun	Otun Seriki	Otun Iyalode
Osi Bale	Osi Balogun	Osi Seriki	Osi Iyalode
etc.	Ashipa, etc.	etc.	etc.

Ọtun and Osi indicate the right and left and so second- and third-in-command respectively to the Balogun, the commander-in-chief.

[3] Hinderer (1872), p. 110.

[4] For example, Bale Orowusi, 1870–71, was in favour of age and experience, whereas Are Latosa, 1871–85, being himself fairly young, preferred the daring and bravery of youth.

and encouraged them to do their best in the service of the town. When indeed they had achieved a title, they also had another incentive to give further of their best. Ibadan gave public recognition to the services of such men by conferring the title of *mọgaji* on their heirs and recruiting new chiefs from these *mọgaji*.[1]

Actual leadership rested in theory with the Bale as head of the civil line, and political decisions not involving war were to be made by civil chiefs. In the actual conduct of political affairs, however, the Bale and civil line of chiefs were often overlooked and power rested mainly with the military chiefs. Indeed throughout the nineteenth century, because of the particular role which Ibadan had to play as defender of the Oyo community, the military chiefs took the most prominent part in Ibadan politics; also because of their military inclination, they gave Ibadan's politics a definite military bias even after the menace of the Fulani had been removed.

With this governmental set-up, Ibadan was in a position to check the inroads of the Ilorin Fulani in Yoruba country. About 1840, Ibadan forces inflicted a crushing defeat on them at Oshogbo and checked their attacks on the Oyo country. This, however, did not put an end to their activities in other parts of Yoruba country; they now turned their attention to the north-east and the Ekiti, whose separatism had always made them prey to external invaders.

Imperial Ibadan

Ibadan too had moved beyond its original position of defending Oyo country to that of building a sphere of influence for itself and of becoming a power to be reckoned with in the Oyo community. The spirit behind this new move was Ibikunle, the Balogun of Ibadan from *c*. 1851 to 1862. He saw in the Fulani attack on the Ekiti an opportunity to carve an empire for Ibadan. Since Ekiti was part of the Yoruba country, Ibadan would still be able to secure the support of the Alafin and the Oyo community in expelling the Fulani from that area. Therefore in the 1850s he carried a series of successful expeditions into the Ekiti country, at first ostensibly to check Fulani aggressions but finally to bring the country under Ibadan's control.

Ibadan's successes in Ekiti country were of great significance. It meant that Ibadan now had under her control a number of towns from which it could derive a great deal of benefit. In each conquered town, a resident representative, the *ajẹlẹ*, was left to ensure that the conquered

---

[1] The *mọgaji* or heir is not necessarily the chief's son, but one of the oldest and most respected members of his patrilineage.

towns remained loyal and paid their yearly tribute to Ibadan. Moreover these towns were expected to send a quota of soldiers to Ibadan's army in time of war.

But more important than this was the prestige which these newly acquired territories gave Ibadan. With such extensive resources to draw from, Ibadan became one of the most powerful and outstanding towns in Yoruba country. Its only rival for effective leadership in the Oyo country was Ijaye; Ibadan's spectacular successes, however, gave it more potential power than Ijaye, whilst its close association and friendship with the Alafin of Oyo strengthened its hand. A head-on collision was virtually inevitable, and was precipitated by an alleged insult to the Alafin of Oyo, by Kurunmi of Ijaye.[1] Ibadan, under the active leadership of Ogunmola and with the support of the Alafin, brought almost all the resources of the Oyo community to bear against Ijaye, which was finally destroyed in 1862.

With the elimination of Ijaye, Ibadan became the leading town in the Oyo community; it commanded the resources of the Ekiti country and of a large part of Oyo country; also for further prestige, it had the backing of the Alafin of Oyo, whose supremacy it still acknowledged. Its ascendancy, however, brought great uneasiness to Yoruba country. Other Yoruba states, particularly the Ijebu and the Egba of Abeokuta, feared its increasing power; they regarded its military constitution and its declared military potentiality as a threat to their own safety.

These two states had, so far, succeeded in maintaining their independence; the Egba had put a check to any aggression on Ibadan's part after Ibadan's unsuccessful attacks on them in 1832 and 1835, whilst Ibadan leaders, particularly Ibikunle, had found it a wise policy to keep on friendly terms with the Ijebu, who controlled one of their routes to the coast and the source of their guns and ammunition.[2] With the new increase in Ibadan's power and its new status in the Oyo community, the Egba and Ijebu now felt that the balance of power, which had existed in Yoruba country and in which no one state had really been powerful enough to hold the others to ransom after the collapse of the Oyo empire, was being upset. Nor were their fears allayed by the ambitions of Ibadan's leaders, particularly Ogunmola and Latosa in the 1860s and 1870s.

This fear of Ibadan's growing power prompted the Egba and Ijebu

---

[1] It was alleged that Kurunmi's soldiers intercepted the soldiers of the Alafin, who were sent to punish a recalcitrant subject of the Alafin at Oke Iho. See Johnson (1957), pp. 331–32, for an account of this incident.

[2] Both at the Owiwi War in 1832 and the Arakonga War in 1835, Ibadan failed to crush the Egba.

to help Ijaye; but with Ijaye's defeat and the strengthening of Ibadan's position, they felt that they had to take measures which would check further growth in Ibadan's power. Since Ibadan's power depended on its military strength, and this in turn depended to a certain extent upon the availability of guns and ammunition from the coast, they decided that the most effective way of checking its growing ambition was to prevent the passage of ammunition to Ibadan from the coast. Indeed they were both ideally situated for this move, which would lead not only to a set-back for Ibadan's military ascendancy, but also to its economic strangulation. They were both situated midway between Ibadan and the coast, and the Ijebu in particular acted as middlemen between Ibadan and Lagos. Because of their policy of not allowing strangers through their country, the Ibadan traders met for the exchange of goods at Oru, one of the Ijebu market towns on the way to Lagos.[1] It was upon the routes passing through these two countries that Ibadan depended, not only for obtaining its ammunition but also for selling its own products to Lagos and receiving in return imported commodities.

Indeed Ibadan's economic stability owed a great deal to this trade with Lagos. Apart from trading with various parts of Yoruba country, it acted as clearing house for a district rich particularly in palm oil, which was, with the British emphasis on legitimate trade in the nineteenth century, a very important commodity for export.[2] It was mainly from Ibadan that the palm oil from the surrounding districts went to the coast.

One of the most effective measures towards checking Ibadan's growing power was therefore to close its trade routes to the coast; this both the Egba and the Ijebu intermittently did for the rest of the century. The effectiveness of this course of action was, however, undermined by the representatives of the British government in the colony of Lagos.

Freeman and Glover, 1861–72, the two most active Governors of the Colony, saw in the move of the Ijebu and the Egba only an attempt to monopolize the trade between the coast and the interior and to cut Ibadan off from this trade; in their anxiety to stimulate trade with the interior and to make Lagos self-supporting from the customs revenue of such a trade, they adopted a policy of friendship towards Ibadan, whom they regarded as the object of victimization by these other powers.

[1] The traditional saying about Ijebu Ode is, *Ajeji ko wo; bi ajeji bawo larọ, nwon afi s'e bọ l'alẹ:* 'A town forbidden to foreigners; if a foreigner entered it in the morning, he was sure to be sacrificed in the evening.'
[2] After the bombardment of Lagos by British naval vessels in 1851, it was decided to stop the slave trade there and substitute for it what has been described as 'legitimate trade', i.e. trade in palm oil, cotton and other commodities produced by West Africa.

In an attempt to obviate the difficulties posed by the closure of their roads, the British decided, in 1872, to open an eastern route through Yoruba country which would be virtually independent of the Ijebu and the Egba.

The Ibadan under Latosa, an astute politician, and now the Are Onakakanfo, exploited to the full the opportunities thus presented them by the friendship of the Lagos government. The consequent easy flow of ammunition made Ibadan even more powerful. In the 1870s Ibadan carried a series of expeditions into Ekiti country and finally brought under subjection the Ijesha who had been the greatest obstacle to its complete ascendancy to the north-east of Yoruba country.[1]

With these new conquests, Ibadan had come to a position where it could dispense with the patronage of the Alafin, whose earlier support had conferred some kind of sanction on its exploits. Moreover, Are Latosa now started a bid openly for personal leadership in the whole of Yoruba country. He antagonized the new Alafin Adeyemi by harbouring in Ibadan Lawani, a pretender to his throne; he gave this unsuccessful candidate some land between Ade Oyo and Yemetu for building his own compound and settling his own people there.[2] Indeed the roles of Ibadan and Oyo were now effectively reversed not only in the politics of the Oyo community but in that of all Yoruba land; instead of the Alafin taking the initiative in Yoruba politics, and Ibadan and the Oyo people following his lead, Ibadan under Are Latosa became the leading influence in Oyo affairs.

Just as Are Latosa's attitude had led to estrangement from the Alafin, so it strained more the already deteriorating relationship between Ibadan and the Egba and the Ijebu. They felt that only the destruction of Ibadan could bring peace to Yoruba country.[3] Moreover the Ijebu, people of an old established kingdom, resented the fact that this upstart town which could not even boast of a crowned head in its town should supersede well-established kingdoms, and defy all crowned heads. In such a situation war was virtually inevitable. The occasion for the outbreak of hostilities was Ibadan's decision to collect some ammunition, allegedly for the Alafin, from Porto Novo, and its attempt to establish friendly trading relations with Porto Novo, whose inhabitants were not on friendly terms with the Egba. The Egba, and soon after the

---

[1] See Johnson (1957), p. 383, for the importance of the conquest of Ilesha.
[2] His compound situated at Oke Aremo is one of the best surviving examples of Yoruba architecture in Ibadan (see plate 2b).
[3] It was indeed suggested that Ibadan as it existed should be destroyed and the town converted to a neutral state, administered jointly by the Alafin, the Ijebu and the Egba.

Ijebu, declared war against Ibadan in 1877. The latter's Ijesha and Ekiti dependencies, taking advantage of this war, declared their independence in 1878.

In Offa and Ile Ife, Ibadan's allies, the Offa and Modakeke, were also attacked by the Ilorin Fulani and the inhabitants of Ile Ife respectively. Ibadan therefore had to fight on five fronts; first against the Egba, who confined their activities to raids and surprise attacks, secondly against the Ijebu, who pitched a camp against them at Oru under Balogun Onafowokan, thirdly at Kiriji, where their forces fought a long battle against the Ekiti and Ijesha forces, fourthly at Offa, where the Ilorin Fulani pitched their camp against the people of Offa, and finally at Ile Ife.

The need to fight on five fronts taxed Ibadan's strength a great deal. Moreover the Alafin was in secret collusion with the enemies of Ibadan and even though all Oyo forces fought on Ibadan's side, none wished it well, partly because of their sufferings under Ibadan's control, and partly because of the arrogant attitude of Are Latosa. Many Ibadan soldiers lost their lives in these struggles, and Are Latosa who, under normal circumstances, as head of the town, would not have gone to the battlefield, was actually killed at Kiriji.

In spite of Ibadan's disadvantages and set-backs, these five forces could not effect its defeat. A state of stalemate was reached, from which only the intervention of an outside force could redeem the whole of Yoruba country. The war was significant in the history of Yoruba country as an indication of the difficulty in restoring permanent peace after the collapse of the Oyo empire. The failure of Oyo to provide military defence for the Oyo people from the onslaught of the Fulani at Ilorin, had pushed Ibadan into a position of prominence among the towns that succeeded the Oyo empire; it had in consequence wrested effective power from Oyo, but was unable to secure general acceptance as the dominant force in Yoruba country.

Within the Oyo community, where the Alafin's control had been virtually complete, Ibadan's overbearing attitude and the alienation of the Alafin's support had weakened its control, whilst within Yoruba country the fact that it was an upstart town whose real ruler was the Alafin had made it difficult for it to achieve the former prestige of the Oyo empire. Moreover, its inability to reach a *modus vivendi* with the rest of Yoruba country, and its obvious military character, led them to combine against it.

The intervention of the British government of Lagos in the interest of trade in the period of the 'Scramble' saved the day. From 1886 this intervention led to a round of treaty-making with the contestants, culminating, in the case of Ibadan, in the Agreement of 1893. These treaties and the Agreement brought peace to Yoruba country, but they also introduced a new master in the form of the British government. By these treaties the British government of Lagos committed itself as an interested party in Yoruba affairs and allocated to itself the decisive role as the final arbiter in interior affairs. Indeed, within three years of signing the treaties, Governor Carter, an agent of the British government, could claim that much of the power of the traditional rulers was being seriously undermined by the activities of his government.

The Agreement, and the gradual infiltration of British influence, was to start a new phase in Ibadan's history and in a large measure to alter its status and character. From being a community taking pride primarily in warfare, it was to settle down to peaceful pursuits. Its actual position *vis-à-vis* Oyo and the Alafin, which had once been uncertain, was now clarified; Ibadan had now become not only *de facto* but *de jure* independent of Oyo for all practical purposes, whilst, of course, still accepting the Alafin as its spiritual head and ruler. Indeed the treaty of 1886 also gave Ibadan effective overlordship over most of the Oyo towns. Under the new administration, Ibadan was therefore to be superior to Oyo not only in power but also in actual prestige. Hence it was only natural that the first headquarters of the British administration were at Ibadan, a primacy which the city has retained in spite of the subsequent attempts of colonial administrators to revive the authority of the Alafin.

3
THE AGRICULTURAL ENVIRONMENT

by H. A. OLUWASANMI

The Physical Environment

Ibadan Division (comprising Ibadan Urban and Rural areas, together with the independent Ibarapa District) is approximately 2,221 square miles in size and lies wholly within the high forest zone. Structurally, the vegetation of the forest zone consists of an upper stratum of trees (emergents) with isolated crowns, rising to 120 feet and above in height; a middle stratum varying in height from 50 to 120 feet with crowns in lateral contact with each other; a lower stratum or understorey of trees up to 50 feet high with spreading crowns bound together with woody climbers. Beneath the understorey there is still another stratum consisting of small single-stemmed shrubs. Timber comes from the forest zone and is drawn wholly from the emergents. Little, if any, virgin forest remains in Ibadan Division. Everywhere in the high forest zone the prevailing system of farming, aided by bush fires, has resulted in a regrowth of secondary bush, and, in some areas, in the degradation of the forest to derived savannah.[1]

The high forest zone is also a region of high rainfall and humidity. There are two distinct seasons in the year: the wet season (April to October inclusive) when rainfall averages between 40 and 60 inches annually, and the dry season (November to March inclusive) during which rainfall does not usually exceed 20 inches per annum. There is a short dry spell in the rainy season in August with a mean of monthly rainfall figures below 4 inches. From 1905 to 1952 the mean annual rainfall in Ibadan was 48·4 inches. In the 15 years 1937 to 1951 the mean annual rainfall varied between 30·01 inches and 54·80 inches.[2] The warmest months in Ibadan are from February to April, and the coolest from July to August. The harmattan, a dry, cool, north-easterly wind, occurs between November and February when temperature drops to 60°F at night. The average minimum temperature for 10 years (1955–1964) was approximately 70°F, while the mean annual maximum temperature for the same period was about 88°F. The average relative humidity in Ibadan is about 80 per cent. In the early morning hours

[1] For fuller details on the forest zone, see Keay (1959), pp. 14–19.
[2] See British West African Meteorological Services, Nigeria, no. 2 (1955); and also Adejuwon (1962), p. 29.

(7 a.m.) when there is ground mist and dew, relative humidity is as high as 96 per cent. At 10 a.m. the average is about 81 per cent, while in the afternoon (4 p.m.) it falls to about 62 per cent. During the harmattan season the relative humidity may fall as low as 35 per cent.

Apart from narrow valley bottoms, the land in Ibadan is undulating, and soils ranging from sands to sandy clays are freely drained. Under forest, or under a crown of natural regrowth of forest species, there is a dark fine-grained top layer of soil about 2 inches thick, formed from broken-up worm casts, and containing about 4 to 5 per cent of humus. The humus and the clay fraction of the soil firmly retain important plant-nutrient elements, and leaching is not normally intense in this area of moderate rainfall, so that the topsoil is normally neutral to only slightly acid. These conditions are favourable for steady microbial decomposition of humus to take place when land is cleared from forest or young forest regrowth, and there is then an abundant supply of nitrate; it has been found that nitrate will continue to be produced in fair quantities for some years by decomposition of the stored-up humus, if cultivation is continued in this area. In the past a fairly good level of crop yields has been maintained under the system of shifting cultivation, in which the chief functions of fallow growth are, firstly to build up the humus and nitrogen contents of the topsoil, and, secondly to accumulate in readily available form nutrient elements other than nitrogen.

In the past 30 years the land within a radius of about 5 miles from the centre of Ibadan has deteriorated seriously, through the elimination of forest species and the spread of tall savannah grass. The chief causes have been the prolonging of the period of cultivation, the cutting of firewood, and the fact that the spread of fires through any fallow land in which there is already sufficient grass to give a good burn has been permitted or even encouraged. Near to the city attempts to cultivate some of this land have continued, but worthwhile yields have become impossible to obtain without manure, and much of the area is infested with spear-grass, and some sheet erosion occurs on the exposed surface. None of the vast quantity of plant-nutrient elements contained in the city's refuse and waste materials is returned to the farm land.[1]

The prevailing system of farming in Ibadan, as indeed in most parts of Nigeria, is shifting cultivation, which has been defined as ' an economy of which the major features are rotation of fields rather than crops; clearing by fire; absence in most cases of draught animals and larger

---

[1] I acknowledge the assistance of Professor Vine of the Department of Agricultural Chemistry and Soils, University of Ibadan, in preparing the section on the soils of Ibadan Division.

types of stock; employment of the hoe, with the plough only occasionally important; short periods of land and long periods of fallow'.[1] The system of shifting cultivation is sometimes termed 'bush fallowing'. In this system the farmer cultivates a plot of land for about 3 or 4 years, after which he allows it to revert to bush fallow while he clears and cultivates another plot. The duration of the fallow period depends on the pressure of population and on soil conditions. Except in the immediate vicinity of towns the fallow period in Western Nigeria varies from 5 to 15 years. Land itself is the joint property of a group. In Ibadan Division, as in Western Nigeria generally, the land-owning group is the lineage. Individual members of the group have rights of cultivation only, and are precluded from alienating group land by sale or mortgage. The cultivation of permanent crops, particularly cocoa, has, however, modified this aspect of traditional system of tenure. In the immediate vicinity of Ibadan land is now freely bought and sold, and throughout Ibadan Division cocoa farmers can mortgage their cocoa trees, though, theoretically, not the land on which the trees stand.

The climatic and soil conditions described above are important factors determining the types and varieties of crops grown. The dominant food crops in Ibadan Division are maize, cassava, and yams; a variety of vegetables and pulses are also grown. Because of the long duration of the rainy season farmers are able to grow two crops of maize in a year. Cocoa is the major export crop of the Division, although little cocoa cultivation goes on within a radius of about 10 miles from the centre of Ibadan city. Approximately 25 per cent of the land area of the Division is used for cocoa cultivation and 21 per cent for food crop cultivation; 14 per cent is in fallow, 6·6 per cent in forest, and 33 per cent in thicket, that is, uncultivated bush and waste.[2]

Agriculture in the Economy of Ibadan

To determine the element of rurality in the city proper we will take into consideration patterns of land use, the relative strength of the occupational groups, and the proportion of women in farming as distinct from other occupations.

Patterns of land use in Ibadan bear the imprint of both Western and traditional Yoruba practices. Traditionally, very little farming went on within the limits of a Yoruba town. The belt immediately surrounding a town was used for cultivation of crops. Farmers went from their

---

[1] Buchanan and Pugh (1955), p. 103.
[2] Adejuwon (1963). The data on land use in this paragraph are quoted with the permission of the author.

residences in the city to their farm plots. Town land was used primarily for residential and public buildings, for markets, shrines and paths. The changed economic life of the town has only accentuated the traditional forms of land use in Yoruba towns. Hardly any farming goes on now in the city of Ibadan. Only a very small part of the city lands is used for the production of exotic vegetables—lettuce, tomatoes, carrots, and cucumbers, in response to the demand of Europeans and upper-income Nigerians. These are grown on the flooded plains of Ogunpa and Kudeti rivers. Land in the city continues to be used for residential purposes and for the building of commercial houses, markets, factories, roads, railways, schools and recreational facilities. The area within an approximately 5-mile radius of Ibadan, which was once used for farming by city dwellers, has become impoverished land, suitable only for the cultivation of cassava and cocoyams. The city is fast engulfing these overfarmed zones in its rampaging expansion. The result is that city-farmers have to go farther away from the city to carry out their farming operations.

One should mention too that the Forestry Department has close to 2,000 acres of city land in teak and cassia plantations. These consist of the Ibadan Fuel plantation (771 acres), the Eleiyele plantation (813 acres) and the Ogunpa Dam and Oke Aremo plantations (337 acres). They are exploited primarily for fuel and for poles. Twenty years ago these plantations were outside the city boundaries; today they are squarely in the expanding city.[1]

(Land use in Ibadan contrasts with the situation in Tokyo where 22·3 thousand acres, or 32·8 per cent of the city proper, is devoted to farming. It should be noted that in Tokyo, with a population of 7 million in the city proper and 8·9 million in the metropolitan district, farming remains a significant economic factor.)[2]

The figures in the table below, drawn from the 1952 Census, give the proportions of occupied men and women engaged in agriculture, crafts, trade and the professions. One may note that a third of the men counted within the urban area are described as farmers; far more than these hold rights in farmland but rather fewer are perhaps accurately described as full-time farmers. The figures demonstrate too the relative absence of 'urban' occupations—crafts and trade—in the rural area, save that nearly a quarter of the rural dwelling women are traders. With the population enumerated in the urban area being nearly double

---

[1] I am indebted to Mr. J. Wyatt-Smith of the Forestry Department, University of Ibadan, for the data quoted in this paragraph.
[2] See Wilkinson (1961), p. 50.

that in the rural area, we find that over half the male population of Ibadan is engaged in farming and that the proportions engaged in the 'urban' occupations—crafts, trade and the professions—are from 30 per cent to 50 per cent higher than the Regional average.

As we have seen, no serious farming goes on within the city proper. The one-third of the occupied male and two-fifths of the employed female population of Ibadan city classified as farmers in the 1952 census carried out their farming in the rural district. A survey of 66 farmers in five wards of the city showed that 10 of these have their farms within a distance of less than five miles from the city, 47 in places varying between five and thirty miles, and 6 villages ranging from thirty-one to eighty miles. Only 2 of the farmers said their farms were situated more than one hundred miles away from the city. One farmer did not know how distant his farm is from Ibadan.

Table 3.1 : *Percentage Distribution of the Occupied Population in the Main Occupations.*[1]

Occupation	Ibadan Urban Area		Ibadan Rural Area		Western Nigeria	
	M %	F %	M %	F %	M %	F %
Agriculture and Fishing	34·8	41·6	86·0	76·2	66·8	68·5
Craftsmen	19·4	—	4·0	—	8·9	—
Trading and Clerical	21·5	58·4	6·3	23·8	10·8	31·5
Administrative, Professional and Technical	8·7	—	0·9	—	4·4	—
Other Occupations	15·6	—	2·8	—	9·1	—
	100·0	100·0	100·0	100·0	100·0	100·0

When the farmers were asked about the duration of their stay on their farms, 7 answered that they stay there for less than one week at a time, 31 for one week or more, 23 for more than two weeks, and 5 for one month or more. There is a correlation between the length of stay on the farms and distance from the city. The farther away the farm the less frequent are visits to Ibadan. Among the reasons given by farmers for returning to Ibadan rather than staying in the village permanently, weekend stay occurred 22 times, urgent family matters 18, festivals and religious ceremonies 22, attending to business or other occupations 7, slack season on farms 8, and relaxation and rest 4. A majority of the

[1] Nigeria *Population Census*, 1952/53. In this Census occupied women were classed under two occupations only; craft workers such as potters and weavers, the makers of cooked food, etc., were ascribed to whichever category seemed most appropriate.

farmers gave as their reasons for not building permanent homes in their villages, family considerations, and lack of schools and other amenities in the villages. Four of the farmers said they did not wish to live in the bush; they wanted to know what was going on in the world.

Residence in the city does not appear to have made a significant impact on the structure of farming in Ibadan. The typical farms of the city farmer vary in size between half an acre and five acres. The hoe and the cutlass are the major implements of cultivation and rotational cultivation the main technique of farming. The crops grown include cocoa, yams, maize, cassava, rice, oranges, plantains, bananas, peppers and vegetables. Fifty of the 66 farmers interviewed sprayed their cocoa against diseases, and, as we have seen, a lucrative trade has developed in exotic vegetables.

Nearly all the farmers interviewed sold one or more of the major foodcrops for cash in Ibadan markets. Eight of the farmers sold all foodcrops, 35 sold yams, 28 maize, 24 cassava and 16 oranges. Only 3 sold rice. Most of the farmers could not tell how much they realized from the sale of foodcrops but remembered their incomes from cocoa, the main export crop in Ibadan. Of the 66 interviewed farmers, 46 had no other occupations beside farming; the rest were engaged on part-time basis either as carpenters, bricklayers, traders, taxi drivers, tailors, weavers or contractors. Incomes from these other occupations vary between £5 and £20 per farmer per annum as compared with incomes from cocoa which ranged from £10 to £400 per farmer. The composition of the incomes of the city farmers is not reliably known. From a study of cocoa farmers Galletti found that receipts from farming constituted 46·6 per cent of the gross earnings of cocoa farmers in Ibadan area, home industry 0·6 per cent, trade 38·1 per cent, services 7 per cent, miscellaneous occupations 2·8 per cent, and earnings on capital account 4·9 per cent.[1]

Conclusion

Despite the size of Ibadan and the rapidity with which the commercial and industrial sectors of its economy have expanded in recent years, agriculture remains a significant element in its economic life. One-third of its occupied males and more than two-thirds of the occupied female population earn their living either wholly or in part from farming and related occupations.

Very little farming goes on in the city boundaries; the urban farmers carry out their farming operations in the rural districts which are extensions of the city proper. These farmers stay on their farms for periods

---

[1] Galletti, Baldwin and Dina (1956), p. 441.

ranging from a few days to one month or more at a time. They return home to attend to family and other matters.

The structure of farming of the city dwellers has not been affected in any significant way by residence in this large urban centre. The development of market gardening in response to the demand of Europeans and upper-income Nigerians for exotic vegetables is the most notable departure from the traditional pattern of farming. The city farmers continue to grow the traditional crops—yams, cassava, maize and plantains—on a few acres of land without the use of fertilizers or manure. A study of the causes of the persistence of traditional farming by farmers living in close proximity to centres generating new agricultural ideas and practices would be a rewarding exercise. It would throw fresh light on the social and economic factors affecting the adoption of new agricultural practices.

The city farmers have, however, made a complete transition from a near subsistence agriculture to production largely for the market. They not only produce cocoa for export, they also sell surplus foodcrops in Ibadan markets.

The persistence of agriculture as an important element in the economy of a city the size of Ibadan shows the incompleteness of the transition from a farming-oriented economy to one based on industrialization. This change is often regarded as the essence of development. Nevertheless, the transition to urban industrialism has been more rapid in Ibadan than in any other area of Western Nigeria. Only a third of the male population is occupied in farming as compared with two-thirds for Western Nigeria as a whole. Even then, a significant proportion as the city farmers derive part of their cash incomes from working of part-time carpenters, bricklayers, traders, tailors, weavers and contractors. The increasing importance of non-agricultural occupations as sources of income for farmers is a measure of the economic transformation taking place in the large Yoruba urban centres.

4

THE MORPHOLOGY OF IBADAN

by A. L. MABOGUNJE

To foreigners, the city of Ibadan represents a complex phenomenon, baffling in its size, unusual in the nature of its economic base and bewildering in its physical lay-out and morphology. Until the late 1950s, Ibadan was easily the largest city in Nigeria and attracted various epithets such as 'a Black Metropolis','the largest city in Black Africa' and not uncommonly 'a city-village'. Although today the honour of being the most populous city in Black Africa probably belongs to Lagos, Ibadan remains the more intriguing of the two cities. It is still more a traditional African creation in a sense that Lagos is fast ceasing to be, and its morphology continues to exert considerable influence in preserving traditional ideas of urban living and interpersonal relations.

The fundamental point to remember in order to understand the physical structure and morphology of Ibadan is that it represents a convergence of two traditions of urbanism—a non-mechanistic, pre-industrial African tradition more akin to the mediaeval urbanism in Europe, and a technologically-orientated European tradition.

Since the morphology of any city is the physical expression of its society's objectives, as well as the use of the material equipment and capabilities that society has at its disposal to achieve these ends, it is necessary to indicate briefly the contrast between the objectives and capabilities of the two urban traditions which today continue to be reflected in Ibadan.

Gideon Sjoberg has provided the most comprehensive characterization to date of pre-industrial urbanism. In many urbanized pre-industrial societies, the city, he noted, is often

'a mechanism by which a society's rulers can consolidate and maintain their power, and, more important, the essentiality of a well-developed power structure for the formation and perpetuation of urban centres.... Often these are fortified places to protect the upper class against local marauders or invading armies. But invariably they are the focal points of transport and communication, enabling the ruling element not only to maintain surveillance over the countryside but to interact more readily with members of their own group in other cities as well as within a city. The congestion that defines the city increases personal, face-to-face communication therein, essential if the heads of the various bureaucratic structures—governmental, religious, and educational—are to sustain one another. So too, craftsmen and merchants prosper in the urban milieu, whose density and occupational heterogeneity foster economic activity.'[1]

Political power, often buttressed by military power, constitutes the major aspirations of pre-industrial societies, and effective administrative devices for easy mobilization of the populace in case of an external

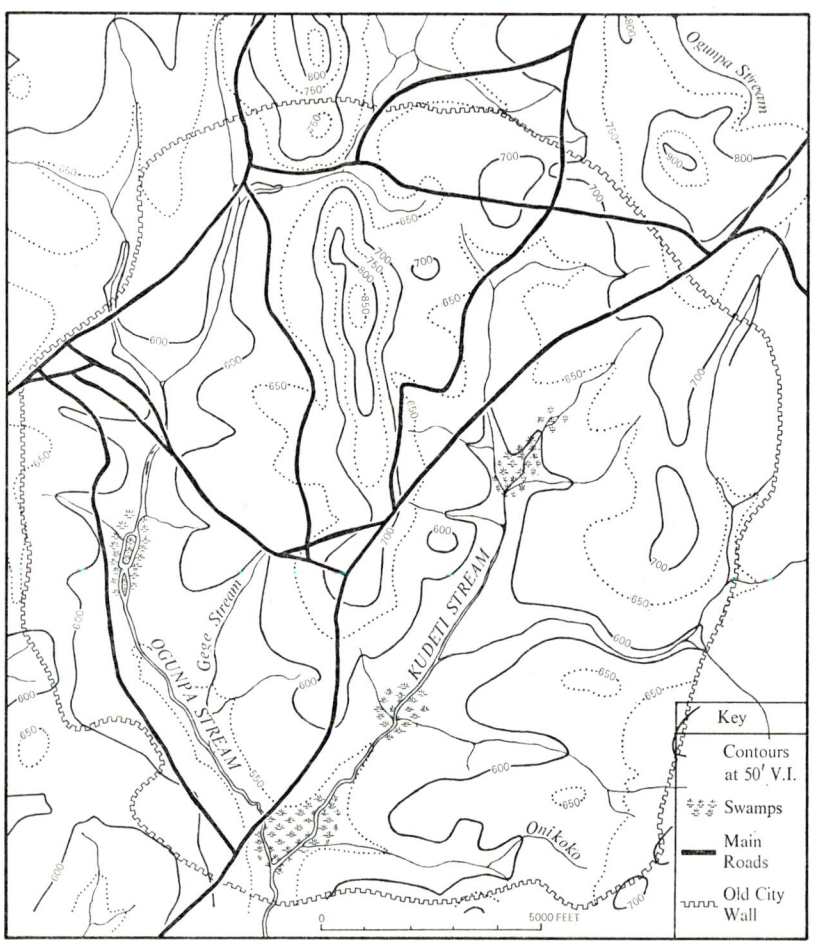

MAP 4. IBADAN, PHYSICAL FEATURES.

threat form a major objective of city life. Whether this fact can be substantiated in medieval Britain or Germany, it remains essential for the Yoruba cities. Trade, of course, was a necessary factor in city life, but even in its organization and direction it was strictly under the control of the power groups in the city.

[1] Sjoberg (1960), pp. 67-8.

THE MORPHOLOGY OF IBADAN

Pre-colonial Ibadan

It is thus no wonder that the basic elements in Yoruba cities are the twin institutions of the ruler's palace and the central market. In nearly all instances their location is central within the city, and they are usually adjacent. In Ibadan, the peculiar historical circumstances of its founding has meant the absence of a palace, although the central market —Oja Iba—still forms the focus of traditional city life.

The history of the founding of Ibadan has been treated at great length in an earlier chapter and need not be repeated here. There are, however, a few salient points which should be stressed because of their relevance to an appreciation of the morphology of the city. By comparison with other Yoruba towns, Ibadan is a city of no great antiquity, founded only in the mid-1820s. There was, however, an older town of Egba people whose central institutions—the palace and the market— probably occupied the same site as those of the present town. As late as 1913 portions of the walls of this former settlement were visible at a point some 200 yards south of Bere Square.

The present new Ibadan arose as a base for military operations against the Egba, following the defeat of the Owu, whom the Egba had supported against the combined forces of the Oyo, the Ijebu and the Ife. Two types of power-struggle thus resulted within the settlement in the early period of its history. The first was a struggle among the allies—the Oyo, Ijebu and Ife—which resulted in the victory of the Oyo, who have continued to dominate the affairs of the city ever since. The Ife moved from the city almost entirely, whilst the Ijebu continued to occupy rather unobtrusively a quarter of the city known as Isale Ijebu. Only once has a member from this group managed to rise to one of the positions of power in the city.

The other type of power struggle was that between the military and the civil authorities about their relative positions in a hierarchy of power. In an age of violence, instability and considerable turbulence, it was inevitable that the military authorities would emerge as the more important group. As a result, one finds that in Ibadan the quarters developed not so much on the basis of ties of kinship, but largely on the basis of dependence on particular chiefs for military adventures. Each chief appropriated a large tract of land to himself, both within the city and in neighbouring rural districts. Thus, whilst his 'warboys' raised their buildings all around him in the town, his slaves stayed on the farms and provided the food necessary to sustain this wide circle of dependants.

The absence of any hereditary rights to titles within the settlement led to the evolution of a peculiar system of succession to the title of Olubadan. At first, this title was limited to chiefs responsible for civil administration. More recently both the military and the civil chiefs are eligible to provide candidates for the office. Because of this situation, no official palace exists in Ibadan, but rather, as the office of Olubadan passes from one family to another, so shifts the residence and the other paraphernalia of office.

None the less, it is important to stress the central position of Oja Iba in the traditional city life. It remains the seat of installation of every new Olubadan, the economic centre for trade both in the morning and particularly at night, and the forum for social contacts and activities. Around it are to be found the compounds of some of the earliest rulers of the city, notably that of Oluyole, as well as the central mosque. In more recent times, its position as a hub of city life has been reinforced by the erection near it of the City Hall (Mapo Hall as it is more popularly known) which also contains many of the offices of the modern, mainly elected, Ibadan City Council.

Modern Development

If the maximization of political and military power defines the objective and aspirations of traditional urbanism, the maximization of income from specialized occupations, especially trade and industry, provides the rationale for modern urban development. According to Lampard, 'the object of specialization is a greater economy of time, effort and resources—the sources of higher productivity and material advance.'[1] In other words, to specialize is to enjoy scarcity value and hence to raise one's level of marginal utility.

For our purpose, this fact gives rise to two consequences which are important for the urban structure of Ibadan. Specialization of functions and of labour has been the basis of industrial development in Europe and it had contributed to their stock of equipment, techniques and skill numerous mechanical devices whose efficient operation has made great demands on the human intellect and his social institutions and organization. Whilst on the one hand increasing specialization helped towards the invention of the steam engine, the locomotive, the motor-car and other technical and mechanical equipment, it also enhanced the rapid expansion of such institutions as joint-stock companies, banks, insurances, post-offices and business offices. For the individual, the needs of both the machines and the new institutions imposed an

[1] Lampard (1955), p. 89.

obligation to acquire at least a minimum of formal education, an ability to read and write.

The second consequence of the modern basis of urbanization is the fact that specialization of functions had tended to make for specialization of areas. Or, to quote Lampard again,

'a real differentiation is, in fact, the spatial corollary of functional specialization and logically serves the same end—economy.... Local concentration of specialized activities is thus an ecological response to certain technical and cost considerations which impel a more selective use of space, a more efficient pattern of land-use.'[1]

The advent of Europeans to Ibadan in 1893 thus introduced alien ideas of urban existence as well as alien institutions to the scene. Since most of these institutions tended to be space-orientated, it was inevitable that they could not be integrated into, or contained within, the old city. They had therefore to find new location beyond the limits of the existing built-up area. First to come were the administrators, with their ideas of specialized roles in a hierarchy of authority. At the bottom were the messengers, the clerks, the chief-clerks and so on; at the top were the Assistant District Officer, the District Officer, the Provincial Officer, the Resident and the Governor. With each of these ranks went not only a residence but an office, often separate from the residence. The latter represented a major departure from traditional pattern. It meant increased space consumption within the city and it began the process of a major separation of place of work from place of residence. Eventually it was to impose on Ibadan the familiar modern city problem of a journey to work. The administration located itself at the north-eastern end of the city and this today has grown to become the centre of government for the whole of the Western Region.

After the administration came the railway in 1901, with its needs for hundreds of acres of land. This, in turn, was located at the western extreme of the city, just outside the city wall. With the railway came the business community—the shops, the banks, the insurance companies, the motor-sales and repair-establishments, produce stores, wholesalers and light industries, such as bakeries. Their need for efficient transport to the coast explains their location close to the railway station to the north west.

These three institutions constitute the important new elements introduced into the traditional urbanism of Ibadan. But each in its own way was to effect significant transformation in the life of the city and help in creating the complexity which is now Ibadan. It remains to

[1] Lampard (1955), p. 92.

analyse how these new institutions helped to increase the range of socio-economic differentiation within the city, how this in turn has made for an increasingly complex city morphology. We should also examine the consequence of the morphology for the efficient functioning of the city, and the implications of this for its future development.

Social Categories

Traditional urban society was made up broadly of four classes—the farmers, the traders, the artisans and the rulers. The farmers were easily the most numerous but they were quite often an undifferentiated mass. So that apart from closely occupying large areas of the city they had very little effect on the city morphology. The traders were also a fairly large group. Because in Ibadan (as in other Yoruba cities), most of them were women, their effect on the city morphology was limited to a number of open spaces, usually in front of the compounds of quarter chiefs which served as markets.

The craftsmen tended to be relatively fewer though their absolute number was larger than is often realized.[1] If one were to consider the number of people required to make and repair the hoes and other implements needed by farmers; to weave the cloth for the older members of the community; to construct the houses and fashion the wood; to make leather and bead articles for the rich; to carve door-posts, decorative calabashes, and the various objects of religious worship; to smelt and make brass and bronze objects: it would be found that artisans formed a considerable proportion of the population of most traditional Yoruba cities. That, by the late nineteenth century, they were no longer so important in the community, is to be ascribed to the gradual undermining of their trade by the penetration of cheaper manufactured equivalents from Europe. As with the traders, their influence on the city morphology was limited, for most craft occupations tended to be carried on within individual compounds. The exceptions included the blacksmiths, the potters and the cloth dyers, all of whom required distinct locations for practising their craft.

The influence of the rulers was the most notable in the morphology of the traditional city. It was to be seen in the unusual size of their compounds, often covering more than an acre of land; in the existence of a wide verandah measuring the length of the house frontage and used frequently for public meetings; in the special gabled gateway to the compound; in the line of well-carved wooden pillars and in the generally more substantial nature of the buildings.

[1] See Callaway, below, p. 153ff.

Of all the classes, however, the only one whose position was based on the acquisition of some objective skill was that of the craftsmen, who had to go through a rigorous period of initiation and subjection to a master. For neither the farmer nor the trader was any formal training necessary. As for members of the ruling group, their position was to a large degree based on the respect given them by other people, and their individual advancement on the favour of their superiors.

This point is worth stressing in order to appreciate the importance of the change wrought by the arrival of the European. Status in the new urban tradition was based on achievement—initially on the degree of skill in reading and writing; advancement within the system was based on standards of efficiency, higher education and higher output of work. As soon as the Residency was opened at Ibadan, it attracted a group of Africans from Lagos who had had, since the 1860s, the benefit of European education. With the arrival of each new institution—the railways, the commercial houses, the banks, the agents of the central government—the numbers of these people continued to increase, and they tended to settle around the new institutions which attracted their service.

This group of literate Africans filled mainly the clerical and executive posts in their various establishments. Above them in the administrative class there was usually a diverse group of Europeans. The English dominated the political administration, as well as transport and a part of commerce. The Germans, French and Italians were restricted almost exclusively to commerce. In all cases, the expatriates tended to claim exclusive rights of residence in certain parts of the city and thus began the tradition of 'residential reservations'.

With the approach of independence, the need arose to increase the number of Nigerians with more modern skills and capabilities, so that they could take over from departing Europeans in different spheres of activity. From the early 1950s, scholarship schemes of various types sent numerous young Nigerians to universities and technical colleges in many of the industrial countries. They went mainly to Great Britain, but substantial numbers went also to the United States, to Germany, France, Poland, the USSR and even to Bulgaria. Locally, the University of Ibadan, founded in 1948 (as University College, Ibadan), also played its part in training the small but growing class of people with a higher level of accomplishment than was generally the case in the period before the Second World War. In this task, it was aided at first by the three Colleges of Arts, Science and Technology and more recently by four other universities. Within a decade the impact of this new class began to be felt not only in the social and economic life of Ibadan, but also in the architectural design of its houses, and in its morphology.

The approach to independence also brought into focus a new class of Nigerians—that of the professional politician. It was not that this class was new in the community; in the pre-colonial days, most chiefs would be described as such, although their functions went much farther than those of the politicians. In the colonial period however, when the chiefs had been silenced or induced to co-operate with the new administration, politically active persons were styled 'agitators'. Where they did not possess some professional qualifications, such as in law or medicine, which could give them employment, they lived precariously.

What was novel about the position of the politicians from 1952 onwards, was the prestige and wealth attached to their office. Later, as the system of government became more clearly identifiable as one based on elected houses of representatives, on political parties, and on cabinet rule, Nigerian ministers of state came to be the pace-setters in many spheres of life, not least of which was the character and design of houses and the quality of interior decoration and furniture. Other politicians and members of the fairly wealthy middle class, notably contractors and business men, took their cue from the standards set by the ministers.

By 1964, therefore, the population of Ibadan had become more diverse and heterogeneous in its socio-economic characteristics. This diversity, however, was not only apparent in terms of occupation or of educational status. As the city offered an increasingly wider range of employment opportunities, it attracted people from other parts of Nigeria and from different ethnic groups. Apart from other Yoruba, notably the Ijebu, Ijesha and Egba, who were some of the earliest to move into Ibadan, there were now substantial numbers of people from nearly every other ethnic group within the country. The Hausa were perhaps the earliest to come, for with them the Yoruba had had a long tradition of trading. The Ibo, Efik and Ibibio came, particularly after 1927, with the connexion of the Eastern line of the railway with the Lagos–Kano line. The number of Edo, Urhobo and others from the Mid-West has tended to increase with the improvement of the road links, but particularly with the rise of Ibadan as the political capital of the Western Region in 1952. By the same token, their number has fallen considerably since 1963 with the creation of the Mid-West State and the transfer of most Mid-Westerners from the service of the Western Region Government.

Such diversities in the population of the city create cross-currents

THE MORPHOLOGY OF IBADAN

of segregation which underlie some of the complexities of the morphology of the city. There is, for instance, a rough type of segregation based on ethnic and racial considerations, which distinguishes the areas occupied by the 'indigenous' Ibadan from those occupied by other Yoruba; the latter from areas occupied by non-Yoruba and Hausa;

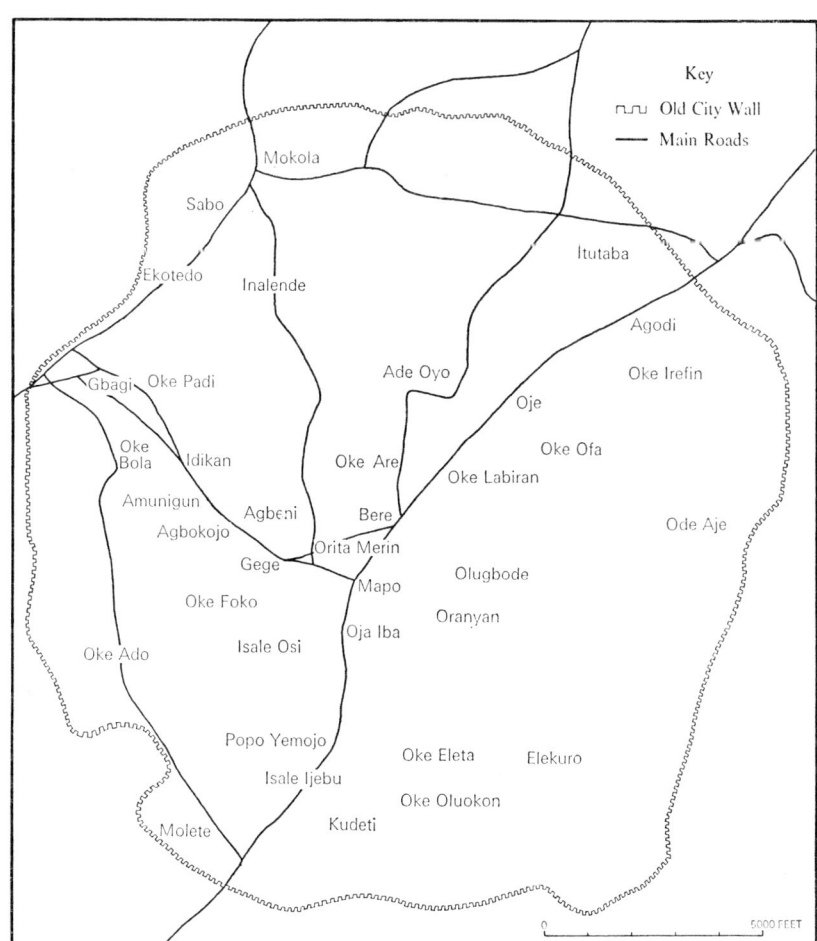

MAP 5. IBADAN, PRINCIPAL LOCALITIES.

and all these from the reservations. Socio-economic factors counter these tendencies. Thus, an indigenous Ibadan man, having attained a certain level of income and social status, will move away from the family house where he pays no rent to live in another part of the city, to be among those of comparable status and income level even though he has there to pay rent.

THE CITY

The Morphology of Ibadan

The basis for the complexity of morphological differentiation in Ibadan had thus been laid. The convergence in this city of traditional and modern economic, social and political institutions, and of the classes of people required to maintain these institutions explains much of the character of the city. Because, in Ibadan, the new has failed to swallow up the old, both continue to exist, strangely juxtaposed, maintaining rather complex relations with each other, and functioning almost despite each other.

Thus, the internal structure of the city shows the existence of two city centres—the older centre around Oja Iba and the new one around the railway station. The character of these centres gives a clue to the type of development to be expected around them. Oja Iba is an area of open ground without any vegetal cover owing to the lateritic nature of the rocks that form it. It serves as a market every day of the week, but it is at its peak in the evenings between 7 p.m. and 8 p.m. Here a large number of small-scale traders converges, peddling a wide diversity of commodities from home-made *ẹkọ*, ready for immediate consumption, to livestock and even textiles and small hardware. In nearly all cases, the capital invested is small and the realizable profit is in consequence insignificant. Largely for this reason, the overhead charges that such traders can bear are limited, so that rents and rates do not feature in the budget of these traders.

But the scale of their trade should not minimize its importance, for these small-scale traders provide an essential link in the distributive chain, selling in units small enough for the poorest to afford. They serve the majority of the low income group and, especially in the older part of the city, where the new economic conditions have undermined the traditional economic base, these traders form a very important class.

Oja Iba, however, has other, and perhaps more compelling attractions for the majority of people in the older part of the city. It is not only a forum of economic transactions, it is also the centre of social intercourse. On an evening, a young man may attend the market in the hope of meeting a young lady who may appeal to him. He may also attend it to hear the latest in the politics of the city or even of the country, to share comradeship with his friends or even just to feel a sense of belonging. Besides, the market is the terminal point for many festivities in the older part of the city and one often notices a number of happy, dancing groups making their way to the market.

The new centre is, in many ways, the converse of the old. Time and space here have acquired scarcity value often measured in pounds sterling. Trading is no longer an activity of the open space. It is properly housed in buildings whose growing height is one measure of the increasing scarcity of land. Most of these are at present only two storeys high, but a number are three storeys high, and in the last few years three buildings have risen, each with at least ten floors. The trade of this new central business district shows all the specialization one associates with modern economic institutions. Retail businesses show a strong preference for locations with clear street frontage. Competition among them has resulted in the gradual concentration of particular trades in distinctive areas of the business district. At the eastern end of the district one finds a concentration of small, African shops selling an assortment of petty wares. To the west are the hardware stores and a few light industries. Westward still, these are replaced by textile stores. Then comes the area of the big department stores—Kingsway, and the stores of the United Trading Company, the Co-operative Society and Leventis. These are followed by the banks and insurance houses, the latter in turn being succeeded by the railway yards and the wholesale stores.

The central business district in Ibadan, as also elsewhere, performs some modest social functions. But in contrast to the old and traditional Oja Iba market centre, these functions are performed at a price. The dance clubs charge a fee for participation, and so do the cinemas. Membership of the libraries—even that of the British Council—demands at least formal registration. The British Council buildings, together with the Obisesan Hall, are, at present, the cultural centre for the modern town-dweller in Ibadan. The former, in particular, encourages participation in modern cultural activities such as lectures, debates, play-readings and drama.

As if to emphasize this dichotomous nature of the city-centre in Ibadan, the natural features of the city tend to keep the two halves of the city almost distinctly apart. The main element is a range of hills over 700 feet high running generally south to north. To the east of the range is the traditional section of the city with, however, a substantial overspill to the west of the range; further west, and especially beyond the Ogunpa Stream, is the newer and modern section of the city. The central axis of the older section is the double-carriageway known as Ogunmola Avenue; that of the newer section is the Oyo Road and the Ijebu bye-pass.

Compounds and Houses

The morphology of the older section is based on traditional social structure, and on the level of traditional technology with regard to building and to changing economic and social conditions. The fundamental unit of traditional social structure is the lineage, comprising the descendants in the male line of a named ancestor. The adult males of the lineage, with their wives and children, live in a compound.

Often the compound has but a single entrance with strong double doors which are barred each night. Inside and against the boundary wall, the rooms of the compound are built. The whole structure used to be covered with a thatched roof which rested on the wall on the outside and on posts on the inside so as to give a covering for a piazza extending all around the enclosed space on the inside. The average compound contains several dwellings occupied by as many separate families. Those of chiefs are very large, sometimes covering several acres of ground. In such cases they are often distinguished, in addition, by the high gabled roof over the entrance to the compound, and by a piazza on the outside, where retainers and others soliciting the attention of the chief can wait.

Because of the level of traditional technology, the main building material used to be sun-dried mud. Brick-making was not introduced into the Yoruba country until the late 1850s and even now the poorer compounds continue to be built of sun-dried mud. This material limited the type of sites which could be used for buildings to well-drained hill-tops and the slopes of hills. Ibadan, fortunately, is notable for its hilliness. This has meant that residential districts tended to begin on hill-tops, spreading down the slope of the hill until they were near the unoccupied flood plains of streams and rivers.

Because of the circumstances of the city's foundation very little attempt seemed to have been made to plan each new district as it was founded on adjoining hills. This was largely because the land was given out as block grants to chiefs who proceeded, with their relations, retainers and followers, to occupy them as they thought fit. Such blocks of buildings came to form a 'quarter' of the town and often bore the name of the chief prefixed by the significant topographic element such as hills (*oke*), roads (*opo* or *popo*) or market-space (*ita*).

Being the oldest settled part of the city, the area around Mapo Hill was the most densely occupied portion of the city. Even in 1856 Hinderer described it as 'the most populous part in contrast to the more widely built and more cleanly parts occupying extensive portions of the places below the hills on every side'.[1]

Today, the congestion in this area of the city, that is, in both the old centre and the suburbs of the 1850s, defies description. The main reason

[1] Hinderer (1872), p. 88.

for this state of affairs derives from significant changes, which also partly explain the fact that this area of the city has hardly grown beyond its 1900 boundary.

To understand the importance of recent changes, it is necessary to stress the nature of the traditional social and economic conditions which sustained compound life in the past. The relation between the compound land in the city and farmland in the rural area was a fundamental factor. Usually, the status of a lineage in a community implied rights over both types of land. In consequence, in a society where the main source of income was from agriculture, much power resided in the hands of the head of a lineage, who decided on issues affecting both town residence and the use of farmlands, and who had powers of dispensing hitherto unused land for the use of the members of the lineage. The concentration of such vital economic powers in the hands of the head of a lineage (apart from other social and political powers attaching to his position within the community) tended to make for great solidarity within the lineage, and to preserve the compound as a single residential unit.

Recent developments have tended to minimize much of the power of the head of a lineage, and to hasten the break-up of the compounds. In the first place, young members of a lineage became aware of a wider range of opportunities to acquire either new skills unconnected with family membership or new employment divorced from the land. Even where an individual remained a farmer, the rise of cocoa production for export, with its unprecedented opportunities for accumulating income and wealth over a relatively short period, meant that the hold of the head of a lineage over his juniors was greatly reduced. As a result, increased differences arose in the range of income within a lineage. These differences in income implied differences in social expectations, and a stronger tendency towards individualism. As soon as chances presented themselves, therefore, members of a lineage separated their portions of the compound and transformed them into single-family houses. This was a much more manageable unit on which to concentrate the improvements they desired for themselves and their immediate family. Compounds then began not only to break-up but to start to show varying standards, which can still be observed: some of the houses have adequate ventilation, others do not; some are plastered with cement, others remain of mud; some are distempered with paint, others retain the reddish-brown colour of local clay; some have electricity, others continue to depend on oil lamps.

Religion also played its part in this transformation. The two dominant religions in the city are Islam and Christianity. In spite of their differences, both religions emphasize that the basic unit of society is the family, a man, his wife or wives, and his children, rather than the lineage. Converts to these two religions thus had little compunction in concentrating their income on the improvement of living conditions for themselves and their immediate dependants, even though the latter group was often extended to include a man's mother, his brothers and sisters.

One other element seems particularly to have encouraged the congestion which today characterizes this part of the city more, probably, than it did in the past. It may be described as the pull of the newer central business districts. Many of the city's indigenous inhabitants sought non-farming work, the location of which was usually on the further side of the older city. Considering the relative poverty of these men, a further expansion of the older city in the direction away from the new business district would mean greater cost of transportation, either in terms of the effort needed to walk the distance, or in hard-won cash. For this reason it was a matter of great convenience not to have to move much further than was essential. As long as there was vacant land within the compound, buildings continued to be crowded onto the available space.

In consequence, the built-up area in this eastern half of the city did not increase for decades. Growth began again only in the 1950s. With the Free Primary Education Programme introduced in 1955, extensive unbuilt areas had to be found to site the numerous new schools. In this part of the city such land existed only at the edge of the city. As the schools grew up in a ring in this area, there was a spate of housing development to provide improved accommodation to lease to the numerous teachers and other workers required to serve these schools.

To sum up, the major features of the morphology of the older section of the city are its amorphous lay-out, its high density of housing and population which only resolves into some order in terms of 'quarters', the indifferent, though highly varied, quality of housing, its sprawl of rusty brown roofs with the towers of churches and mosques providing the only breaks on the sky-line, and its 'green-belt' eastern margin, made up largely of the football fields of the numerous schools, colleges and hospitals, which have grown up here only within the last decade.

Immigrant Areas

The newer half of Ibadan is largely the immigrant section of the city. Its development and differentiation in many ways epitomizes the history of human contact in Nigeria—the mixing of the people, the colonial struggle for internal autonomy and the independence of Nigeria. Each of these events has left its impact on the townscape of Ibadan, and provides clear evidence of the way in which political and economic actions have visible repercussions on the land.

The immigrant areas of Ibadan lie to the west of the central range of hills and especially to the west of the Ogunpa stream. The morphology of this half of Ibadan reflects the ethnic and racial differences among the immigrant groups; the date of arrival of the earliest substantial section of each group; the prevalent idea of housing and architectural design; the incidence of land apportionment and sales; and increasing social and economic differentiation in the city.

The earliest substantial group of immigrants into the city, especially after 1900, were members of neighbouring Yoruba communities—notably the Ijebu, the Egba and the Ijesha. Most of them came as small traders and settled at the western margin of the then built-up area in districts now known as Amunigun, Agbeni, Idikan, Oke Padre and Oke Foko. Their houses retained the rectangular shape of compounds, although few were built as a continuous dwelling. In other words, unit houses with three or four rooms were arranged in a rectangular fashion around an enclosed space which contained common utilities—kitchen, bathroom, latrines, wells—for all the houses. This feature, of course, emphasized that the immigrant came only with his immediate family and although he built his house in the form of a compound, much of it was let out to other immigrants. In contrast to the situation in the older parts, many of the houses were plastered with cement and were generally of higher quality. Where the houses were aligned to the main street, the front rooms were modified to serve as shops. One interesting development has been the spread of a line of small, Nigerian-owned shops from the Agbeni-Amunigun area eastwards to the older part of the city along the Agodi-Railway Station Road. The degree of congestion within this region is approaching that of the older part of the city. This is no doubt related to the continuing influx from Ijebu and Ijesha of people with limited education who wish to join in the extensive small trading which flourishes particularly in this part of the city.

With the arrival of the railway in 1901, a new suburb was established just north of the railway station, called Ekotedo or 'the settlement of the people from Lagos'. As the railway linked diverse parts of Nigeria together, this suburb, largely because the station was nearby, came to attract those coming from other parts of the country, and particularly from the Mid-West and Eastern Nigeria. The arrival of these non-Yoruba elements, with whom there had existed no traditional ties, created a minor problem, both regarding rights to land and to housing. In consequence, a rather indifferent attempt was undertaken to lay the area out and to allow indigenous Ibadan to build houses for renting on the plots. As in the Agbeni and Amunigun areas, the basic design remained that of a compound comprising numerous unit houses. Mud remained the important building material, although the walls were plastered with cement. The major difference in the case of this suburb is the fact that in the attempt to apportion land, the rudiments of a street system were laid out. At the time, little effort was made to maintain this system of streets, but recently some roads have been redefined and tarred.

The settlement of Hausa and Nupe, at Sabo and Mokola respectively, stands in interesting contrast to the position at Ekotedo. Both these groups have had traditional relationships with the Yoruba. Both Hausa and Nupe were granted land for their exclusive occupancy, and were encouraged to appoint a spokesman to represent them in the city administration. These particular non-Yoruba communities live isolated from the rest of the city in small 'northern' enclaves. Although the houses there are not modern in appearance their generally small size and indifferent design attest to the fact that the Hausa community did not think of itself as permanently resident. Even today, this group remains highly mobile, a large proportion of its membership constantly changing as some return to the North whilst fresh arrivals take their place.[1]

It appears, that, up to the 1930s, small trading, especially by the small African shopkeepers, dominated the economic life of the city; for it was not until after that date that Ibadan began to attract young educated Nigerians as clerical staff in business and administration. The result was the rise of the suburb along the Ijebu bye-pass. Most of the houses here were built as lodging houses to provide single-roomed accommodation for these young men. As these two functions became relatively more important in the 1940s, notably with the decision to make Ibadan the headquarters of the Western Provinces, and as the employment opportunities for young school leavers increased in the city, so this suburb continued to expand.

A striking feature of this suburb was the novelty of its architectural design. The style of buildings here belong to that which is generally described as 'Brazilian'. This had been introduced to Lagos in the 1850s and 1860s with the return of a number of freed slaves from Brazil. Its major characteristics were the flamboyant floral designs on doorways

---

[1] See Cohen, below, p. 119ff.

and portals, bas-relief decorations on the lower half of the outer wall, and a verandah in front of the house. Furthermore, the house consisted of an open hallway with a line of rooms opening to it on both sides. Each line consisted of three, four or five rooms, so that on one floor one could have six, eight or ten rooms. The design facilitated the construction of storeyed buildings as multiples of the ground floor. The houses were, on the whole, more solidly built—at first with bricks and later with cement blocks. They were often tastefully distempered, and standard ventilation consisted of two windows a room. Indeed, it was possible to reckon the number of rooms in the house by merely counting the number of windows on one side of it, dividing by two to get the number of rooms in a line, multiplying this again by two for the two lines on both sides of the hallway, and finally multiplying the sum by the number of floors in the house.

Throughout the colonial period this type of house represented the upper limit of local capabilities. But there was a logic in it. The colonial regime reserved all senior positions for Europeans, and the highest to which a Nigerian could aspire was an executive position as chief clerk. With his income he could hardly afford more than two or three rooms in the Brazilian-type house. One notices in the Ibadan of the early 1950s therefore, a sharp jump in the standard and quality of housing from the congested, though modern, African suburbs, to the spacious splendour of the European reservations.

The growing centralization of more and more functions in Ibadan since the 1940s had led to an increase in the number of Europeans in the city. As they came, they were made very welcome by being provided with a type of housing which was the ideal of every expatriate—a detached house with an extensive garden, with a well-laid lawn, flower beds, well-trimmed hedges and other features of landscaping. Even the houses were built to comply with English ideals, to the extent of incorporating even such obviously irrelevant elements as fire-places and chimneys!

With this extensive use of land, it was soon necessary to increase the number of reservations. At first, there were two: the Agodi Reservation to the north, mainly for the administrative corps, and the Commercial Reservation to the west, for the business community. The latter was extended to include the Links Reservation just north of it. Then came the New Reservation to the south-west, which was occupied by a mixed community of business men and administrators.

By 1952 the struggle for internal autonomy came to a head. With victory for the Nigerians came the idea of government by a cabinet of

THE CITY

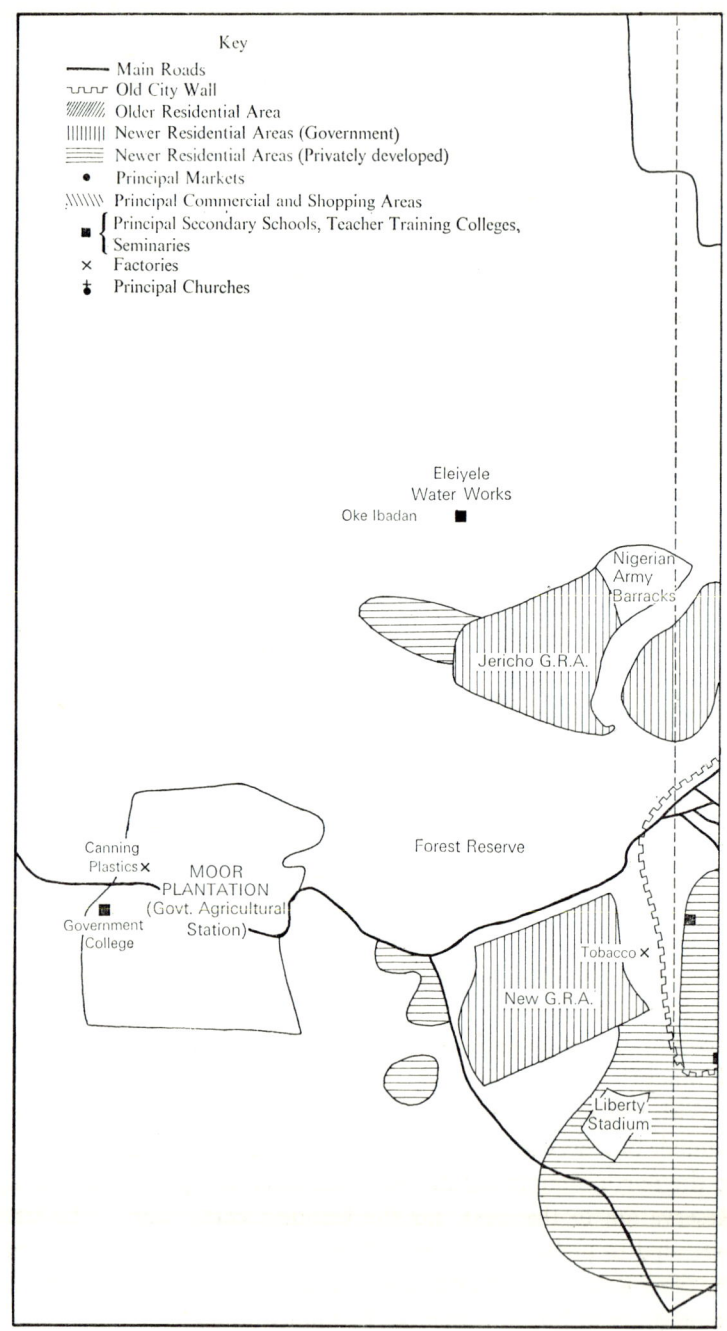

MAP 6. IBADAN, RESIDENTIAL AREAS,

THE MORPHOLOGY OF IBADAN

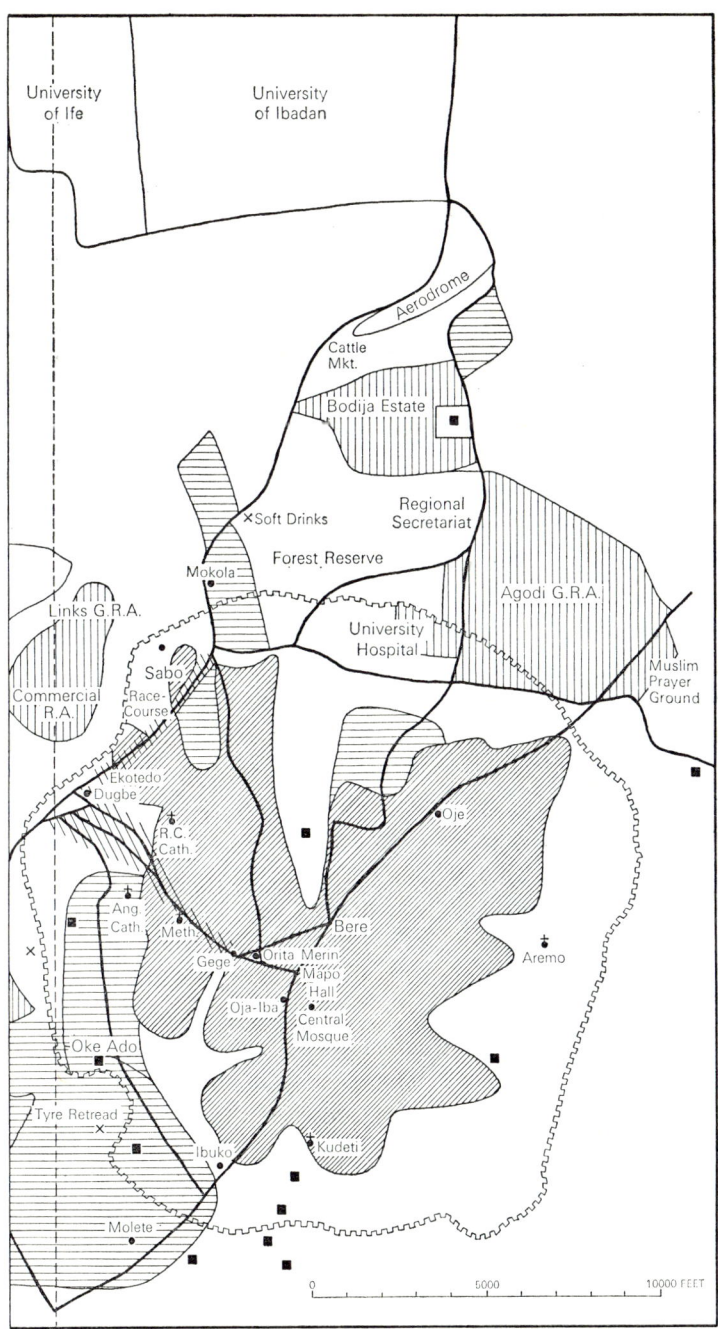

Services and Amenities.

ministers, a representative legislature, and a modified civil service run on the basis of ministries, under a permanent secretary with a team of other officials to aid him. What was significant was that this development went hand-in-hand with the clamour for 'Nigerianizing' the service. Thus, the virtual end of the political struggle created almost overnight a new class of Nigerians—ministers, parliamentary secretaries, members of parliament, senior civil servants—all with an unprecedented level of income, of responsibilities and of social and economic expectations. Soon their ranks came to be swollen by the growing number of professional men—lawyers, doctors, engineers, contractors, teachers—who were trained by various scholarship schemes provided by the new Nigerian Government.

Since this new group succeeded in a sense, the colonial administration, it was to be expected that the reservations would be the first places they would colonize. Thus, in the 1950s all the reservations underwent rapid expansion. But the supply of houses here would not meet the ever-growing demand of the new class. In consequence, other parts of the city which had locational significance began to develop rapidly. Since a large proportion of the new élite were civil servants, the northern part of the city around Ekotedo, Sabo and Mokola, which were near the Secretariat, began to grow fast. Because of the existing concentration of members of the new social class in the vicinity of the Ijebu bye-pass, suburbs here too grew rapidly. In each case, however, the sudden rise in land rent limited attempts to imitate the lay-out of the reservations. The compromise in many cases was a design no longer 'Brazilian' in its external appearance, but which borrowed from that style in its economy of space. The internal division of the new houses was modified to allow for the occupation of each floor by a family; modern household utilities, notably water closets and a bath or shower, became a common feature of these houses.

For some time, private entrepreneurship appeared incapable of meeting this spectacular demand. The shortage of houses, which events have now shown to be only temporary, provoked the Regional Government to create a public housing estate at Bodija. This provided houses ranging in price from £1,500 to over £4,000. In its design and lay-out, it sought to copy conditions on the reservations. Even the smaller houses were detached and had gardens around them. It was remarkable that blocks of flats did not feature at all in this Estate. Being near the centre of administration for the Regional Government, the Estate attracted, in particular, civil servants, especially those of grades lower than the class resident on the reservations. Professionals, notably lawyers, doctors and university teachers, as well as non-Africans in a number of foreign consulates, provide some diversity in the social composition of the Estate.

Conclusion

The morphology of Ibadan exhibits three dominant characteristics, each of which has a significant effect on the functioning of the city. The most obvious is the extensive confused mass of housing which occupies a large proportion of the city. The causes of this have been elaborated earlier in this chapter. Although this situation tends to make for close personal contacts at local level, it creates a fantastic problem of locating people within the city. This results from the virtual impossibility of orderly numbering of houses. Thus, it is difficult to plan mail delivery to houses or to organize the collection of data for purposes of administration, planning or research. More important is the fact that the situation presents an almost intractable problem for organizing proper sewage disposal or refuse collection. Waste household water from the back of one house fouls the frontage of adjoining houses. Apart from creating a nuisance, it represents a serious danger to the population's health. The position is made more serious by the fact that the channel cut by this flow of water is deepened and widened by the torrential rains, and sometimes undermines the foundation of houses.

The second feature of the morphology is the small proportion of land devoted to roads, especially in the older half of the city. Nonetheless, it is this same area which contains the vast majority of the low-income unskilled workers, who provide cheap and low-grade labour for the city's industries and businesses. Since most of the latter are to be found at the western extremities of the city, a common feature in the early mornings in Ibadan is of a formidable troop of workers walking long distances to work. Many of these people have to wake up as early as 4 a.m. to be able to report for duty at 7 a.m. The effect that this long trek has on their work, efficiency and output can easily be imagined. Unfortunately because roads are so few, it has not been possible to organize a cheap and efficient public transport system. The numerous taxis which provide the service at the moment have the advantage of manœuvrability through narrow lanes and alleys, which public transport cannot rival. But their fares are not low enough to be of much use to the workday needs of the lowest income group in the city. Undoubtedly, other factors besides inadequate roads have played their part in preventing the growth of an efficient public transport, but they do not minimize the constraint constituted by the low road density. Furthermore, the low road density means that for a long time no scheme to install major utilities, such as a household water supply, a sewage system and electricity, can be extended to cover more than a limited proportion of the inhabitants of the city.

Finally, a feature of the morphology of the city is the persistence of uncontrolled growth. There is certainly a Town Planning Authority with the responsibility of promoting orderly development. But since it has no overriding powers over land development in the city, its role has been purely permissive. It tries not to impose a lay-out but rather to make sense of the jig-saw of small lay-outs of individual landowners. It is also involved in approving, and thereby ensuring, a certain basic standard of construction and amenities in many of the new houses. But the Authority has tended not to use these powers with respect to the indigenous parts of the city.

Nevertheless, in spite of large-scale immigration into the city, the indigenous population is still in the majority. This is strongly reflected in the election to the City Council; at a time when the city should be attempting to modernize itself, the majority of its rulers represent the declining, older parts of the city, and they fail to see that their home ground constitutes cause for alarm. In consequence, the idea of slum clearance or urban renewal and redevelopment has rarely been given serious consideration by the city council. Even the development of the newer areas where some of them live hardly interests the Council, and there has been no insistence on some orderly development or on providing basic utilities such as good roads. In short, Ibadan remains as perplexing a phenomenon as it is a perplexing problem. Its morphology is only the physical form of a vast array of other problems of a social, economic and political nature. Until these begin to be resolved, the city would continue, in the words of Dr. Mellanby, to look to European eyes as 'a vast, untidy, amorphous aggregation of rusty tin-roofed shacks'.[1]

[1] Mellanby (1958), p. 37.

II. ITS PEOPLE

5

INDIGENOUS IBADAN

by BARBARA LLOYD

Once every sixteen days hundreds of traders, buyers and nowadays tourists, converge in the early hours of morning at Oje market to deal in cloth—narrow handwoven *aṣọ oke*, deep indigo blue patterned *adirẹ*, and varied imported materials. I have chosen Oje market, and in particular fifteen family compounds bordering it, as representative of the original, non-industrialized eastern portion of Ibadan—an area which has its centre at Mapo Hall and stretches south to Kudeti and north, past Oje, to Agodi. Sociological field workers in the past have found the dense and sprawling area of old Ibadan formidable, and turned their attention to other towns of more manageable proportions. Little comprehensive information is, therefore, available about the Western Region's capital. By describing Oje, a small area which I know well, I hope to give a representative though limited picture of the life of the indigenous people of Ibadan.

Oje History

The earliest history of the area around Oje market is linked with the careers of two warriors—Balogun Oderinlo and Dele, the Are Ago, one of the senior chiefs to Oluyole, Bashorun of Ibadan from 1836 to 1850. In Oluyole's lifetime Ibadan evolved from a war camp to become one of the major towns in the empire of new Oyo. Ibadan forces fought the Fulani at Oshogbo, and there put a stop to the Fulani march to the sea. Oluyole is remembered both for his achievements, his many successful military campaigns, his agricultural innovation, the list of chieftancy titles still current in Ibadan, and for his vast ambition, which led him to arbitrary and ruthless rule of the town.

During Oluyole's reign, Oja Iba was the centre of Ibadan and its main market. The town stretched out in all directions for a radius of a mile. What was to become Oje market was a forest area beyond the permanent town settlements, to the north on the road to Iwo. The earliest inhabitants were hunters who were probably camping there when the place became known as Oderinlo's farm. It was the custom for important warriors to claim out-lying lands which in future they might cultivate. In this manner, the area west of Mapo Hall, today called Agbeni, had been the farm of the Otun Kakanfo, Lakale. Lakale had been able thus to give it to a friend, Chief Agbeni, when the Ibadan overran the Chief's town at Apomu.

It seems likely that, by 1840, Oderinlo was farming and perhaps permanently settled in the Oje area. Dele and some other warriors came

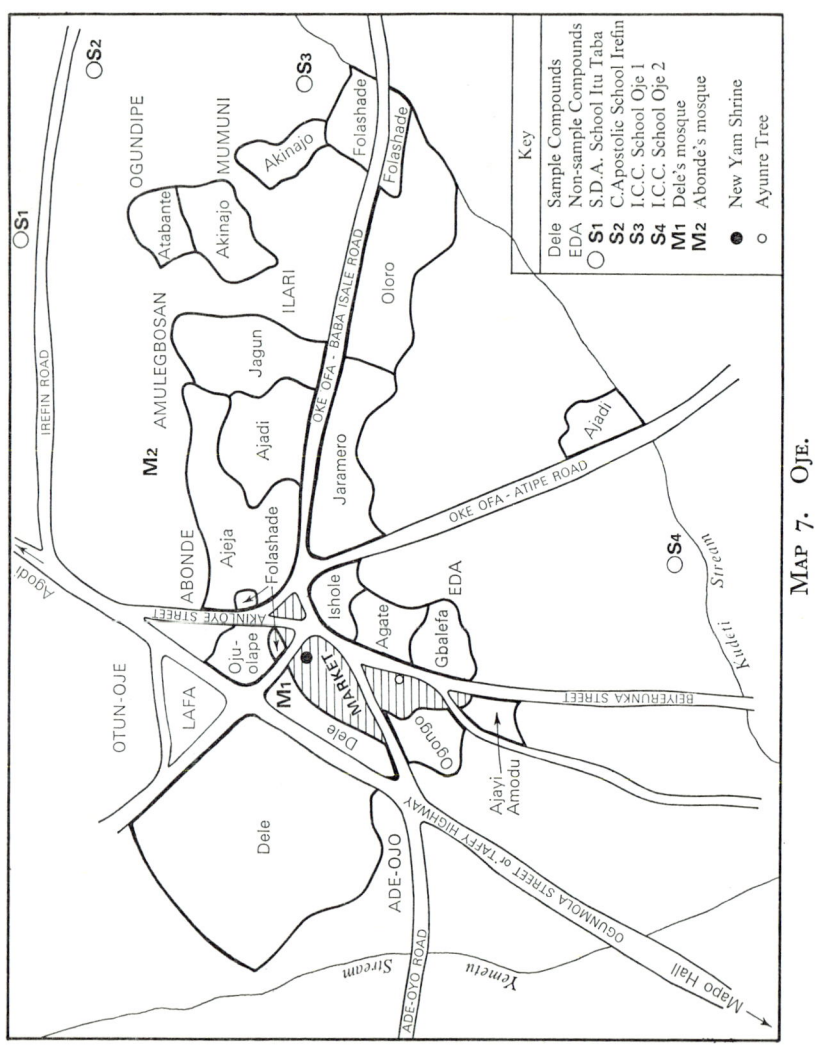

MAP 7. OJE.

from Mapo to settle with him beyond the limits of Ibadan. Oluyole was quarrelling at this time with his senior chiefs; they, fearing Oluyole would suspect the Balogun of trying to establish a rival camp, prevailed upon Oderinlo to return to his old compound in the centre of town. Dele was left to represent Oderinlo, and became the most senior chief in the area. Since that time, Dele's name, as founder of the renowned cloth market at Oje, has been prominent in the history of the neighbourhood.

The official historian in the large, traditional compound of Dele's descendants, which faces Oje market, has preserved many legends of the founder. According to family lore, Dele migrated to Ibadan from the Ijeru quarter of Ogbomosho, in the same wave which brought other famous warriors such as Jurumi, Oluyole and Oderinlo to Ibadan. He first settled with the others at Oja Iba, but when many of his children died, he gained permission, by swearing to support Ibadan in warfare, and paying eleven slaves to the senior chiefs, to make a new settlement outside the gates. Dele, as Are Ago to Oluyole, was also granted the right to appoint worthy local men to serve as junior chiefs under him at Oje, and to have the *egungun* masqueraders dance in his compound on the same day as they danced for Oluyole and subsequent Bales of Ibadan. The *egungun* still dance at Dele's compound on the same day that they dance for the Olubadan, but the right to appoint chiefs was lost about the turn of the century.

Dele's history describes the area as a thick forest, into which the chief sent his slaves to make a clearing. They built a house for Dele and one for his drummer, Agate, who had come from Ogbomosho with Dele. The latter compound of drummers survives today. It is said that, in cutting the bush, lead (Yoruba: *oje*) was found, and that Dele ordered it to be hung from a big tree in the clearing. Hence the place where traders might stop on their way up to Mapo came to be called Oje. Another tale suggests that Oje was named for a foodseller at Dele's market who wore lead bangles.

The actual derivation of the name for Oje market is unknown. One obvious solution lies in the link with Ijeru in Ogbomosho. Present-day Ijeru has its own ruler, the Ompetu, who is one of the *ọba* in the Ogbomosho federation of towns. The Ompetu claims that he is descended from the Oluoje, the rulers of old Oje, a town nine miles from Ogbomosho which was destroyed along with Ikoyi in the Fulani wars. This answer is not necessarily helpful, since it is not at all certain that the site near Ogbomosho is the first Oje. There is probably a link with Owu which was destroyed about 1820 and near which Johnson locates the towns of Ofa and Oje.[1] In tracing the early history of compounds in the Oje area, other than Dele and Agate, the ties with Owu gain importance.

It is certain, however, that Dele established the market at Oje and

[1] Johnson (1957), p. 208; Oyerinde (1935).

tried to encourage trade. In his day this involved seeking magical support for his enterprise. It is said that medicine was buried to make the market flourish, and that Dele, to mark the place, planted an *ayunre* tree which can still be seen standing today at the centre of the thriving sixteen-day cloth market.

Upon Dele's death, Olajifin, his brother, became the next chief of the neighbourhood, and head of the lineage. Olajifin rose to the title of Asaju to Bale Olugbode, but was killed about 1869 while fighting in the Ilesha wars along with the other Ibadan chiefs. Since that time, most of the heads of Dele's lineage, sons and grandsons of Olajifin, have also held chieftaincy titles in Ibadan. Dele's descendants have always controlled the market; the chief receives annual tribute from the traders and arbitrates disputes which the market women cannot settle among themselves. With the rise of modern town government the local political power of the chief has declined, though the family is still recognized as the owner of the market.

The present Chief Dele, a very old man, has risen to the rank of Ekarun Olubadan, and hopes one day to become Olubadan and so bring prestige to Oje quarter.[1] With this end in mind, he is at present improving his compound, plastering the walls, painting, and eventually intending to cover over, his long, arched veranda where elders meet.

The histories of the founding of the other fourteen Oje compounds which I have studied, fall roughly into two groups; those who stress their early connections with Chief Dele, and those who maintain their independence. The three with the earliest and closest ties to Dele are Agate, Ojuolape and Gbalefa. Agate was the drummer who came as a young man with Dele from Ogbomosho. Ojuolape people, from the lineage named in Akinyele's history as one of the noble houses of Oje, trace their origins to Ogbomosho and friendship with Dele.[2] The people of Gbalefa's compound say that they had come from Ikire and were hunting in Oje when Dele arrived. He allowed them to remain and they became his hunters. Less closely tied, but recognizing Dele's seniority is the lineage called Ogongo, in which the Ede warrior and friend of Oderinlo settled, and the compound established by Ibi-agu from Ago Owu. The latter compound is now known as Ishole because the founder was named 'he who keeps the house' (Yoruba: *iṣole*) since he was older, and guarded the settlement when younger Oje men went off to the wars.

The compounds of Akinajo and Atabante were founded later when Bale Figabi (1893-95) sent some Owu men to Dele to be given land.

[1] This Chief has subsequently died before achieving this ambition.
[2] Akinyele (1946a).

About this time too, Folashade, a rich trader and the first woman to deal in European cloth at Oje, was also granted land by Dele.

The people in Ajadi, Oloro and Ajayi-Amadu compounds stress their independence. They say they came from Iwo, the home of Oderinlo. They trace their settlement to the 1850s, but claim rights through Oderinlo, asserting that they are not subordinate to Chief Dele, and that Dele only held the land at Oje in trust for the Balogun.

Today it is difficult to assess how much control the chiefs from Dele's compound have asserted over Oje. It is important to note that Oje grew as a community so that at the time of the civil wars in Ibadan in 1877, when drunken invaders from other parts of the city tried to plunder the neighbourhood, Oje people united to repel them, and felled one of the insurgents.

Oje Today

On a visit to Oje one might first call at the compound of Chief Dele. When the Chief returns from the Customary Court where he serves each morning as an assessor, he often sits within the elaborately carved doorway to his room in the centre of a long veranda, looking out on the open courtyard of his compound. In the courtyard, a few feet from the arched veranda, stands the small, five-foot high walled, rectangular home of the compound crocodile which was brought to the compound on the advice of a diviner after many children of the family had died. Judging by the number of boys and girls under eight years of age, one concludes that the crocodile or its current replacement has done his work well. On the right and left sides of the Chief's low, traditionally styled house stand bungalows and a brick house of modern design with glassed windows. A hole in the earth at the threshold of the tall gateway opposite the Chief's house is the only remaining evidence of the heavy wooden door which once ensured the safety of Dele's people within the walled compound.

Passing through the doorway one stands at the edge of a daily food market. Under the porticos of the compound wall, the women of Dele's family prepare and sell cooked food—ẹkọ, a maize meal pap, or *amala*, a similar porridge made from cassava. In the small stalls, lined at right angles to the compound wall, women sit throughout the day grouped according to commodity, selling their wares. Green vegetables, onions, okra, salt, peppers, fish, snails, beans and prawns are sold here. A man operates a mill for grinding pepper. A few men sit at one edge near the small pan-roofed house of the new-yam shrine selling fresh meat. Near here, too, sits the old woman who today, in the absence of an Iyaloja, a chief woman of the market, will try to settle any disputes which arise among the traders. In the past the Iyaloja would settle quarrels and make certain the market was tidy and in order at the end of each day.

In the evening small oil lamps are lighted, more people come to the market, and it becomes a social centre for young people. About ten p.m. the market women pack up their products and go home to their compounds. Some live nearby and will be with their family in minutes, but others, who still trade in this market around which they grew up, may face a long walk home to husbands in more distant parts of Ibadan.

Beyond the food market bordering Dele's compound, the area of shops and stalls is split up by a number of tarred roads. One road radiating north from the market first passes the place where used clothes are sold, then by the modern storied houses of Chief A. M. A. Akinloye, at one time the Chairman of the Ibadan City Council, and on to join the dual carriageway to Agodi and the Ife Road. The road west to the government hospital at Adeoyo cuts the market in two; one part borders Dele's compound, the other lies alongside Ogongo compound. In this lower section the fortnightly cloth market is centred, but on other days, sellers of native medicine spread out and edge the highways, while women selling live chickens sit close to the compound walls, their chickens in basket cages.

The roads, south and eastwards too, are lined with small shops displaying exercise books, plastic belts, glass chimneys for lamps, handkerchiefs and other small manufactured wares in repetitive profusion. Interspersed are tailors and hairplaiters, petty grocers, palm-oil merchants and palm-wine sellers.

House styles offer almost as much variety as the trade. One can visit small smoke-filled rooms of old women, sit on car-seat settees drinking Fanta and gazing at political heroes' pictures on calendars, or discuss the latest international news with a London-trained barrister in his well-appointed sitting room. Such is the range of income and education in Oje, though it must be emphasized that education and large incomes are rare. The majority of the adult population has had little training— the men some primary schooling, and the women, largely, none. Life is very difficult economically, and many families live on less than £15 a month.

Having described the Oje neighbourhood, let us examine now the fifteen compounds in detail. The selection of the compounds for intensive study was not random; rather were they chosen to include Dele's compound, those near the market, and two others, where initial friendly contacts facilitated research efforts. The data upon which the census material is based were collected between January 1962 and August 1963. Thus, though bias in reporting no doubt occurs, it is most unlikely to be of a seasonal nature reflecting absence due to farm work or an inflation of totals in the town at holiday time.

Before examining the census results it is necessary to consider a few formal features of social structure and define some technical terms. Social anthropologists have written on aspects of Yoruba social organization, hence making a general analysis unnecessary.[1] This discussion is limited to describing roles and relationships useful in understanding topics dealt with in this chapter.

The word compound is used throughout this chapter to describe those divisions which can be seen on a map or actually visited in Ofe. A compound is a physical unit composed of houses, courtyards, and gardens—having definite boundaries. In the past a compound was enclosed within a wall; nowadays the holding may not even be contiguous, i.e. Folashade, Ajeja and Akinajo, each have unconnected sites.

The compound is owned by, and is the home of, a lineage (*idile*), the descent group composed, among the northern Yoruba, of those persons able to trace relationship by recognized genealogical steps through the male line to the founding ancestor, such as the first Chief Dele. Since the lineage is exogamous and marriage is patrilocal, wives of lineage members are from various other lineages. The wives retain certain rights in their natal lineages and may go home for marriages, births and funerals. The children all belong to the lineage of their father. Unrelated men and their families may reside within the compound either by agreement or by paying rent.

Membership in the lineage entitles one to living space in the compound, and the right to use, for individual cultivation, part of the farmland held in common by the entire lineage. Each of the fifteen Oje lineages owns land outside Ibadan. The lineage may claim a whole village near Ibadan, such as one about three miles north on the Oyo Road, called Ajeje Village, share more distant villages with other lineages, as does Dele's family, or lay claim to certain lands as far away as Ago Owu, about twenty miles from Oje, or Ijore-Ekiti, over one hundred miles from Ibadan.

Lineage members also share common religious practices, i.e. particular *egungun* masquerades, praise songs, food taboos, and facial markings. These attributes are often linked to the lineage founder's place of origin. In the neighbourhood around the market, Oje (via Ogbomosho) and Owu are the old towns which predominate. In the

[1] Bascom (1942); Lloyd (1955, 1962); Schwab (1955).

past, a man's occupational choice was largely determined by lineage membership. Examples here are the drummer compounds of Agate and Jagun Akoka. Even modern occupations seem to cluster in particular lineages; and it is noticeable that most men in Ajeje's compound are concerned with transport, while in Ajayi Amuda, the kola nut trade engages one third of the adult residents.

The *bale*, or head of each compound, is usually the eldest male member of the lineage. His authority extends to strangers living in the compound as well as lineage members. In consultation with other compound elders, he arbitrates disputes among members, takes responsibility for their welfare and allocates lineage farming land. Though it is customary for the *bale* to hold formal lineage meetings in Oje today, he usually calls a meeting only when a problem arises. More often, the *bale* calls a few elders, usually representing the several sections of the lineage, to try and settle the matter before calling all the male members together.

The pattern of equating age and authority is carried out in all aspects of compound organization. Brothers defer to each other by order of birth. Among wives seniority is determined by date of marriage which coincides with assumption of membership in the compound. Even children are taught to offer respect to any persons older than themselves and aid to younger children, thereby fulfilling their role as elders.

In a number of Oje compounds a prominent elder member is expected to take an Ibadan chieftancy title. The first appointment is to *mogaji*, a minor title which is not hereditary in a strict sense. Selection is largely determined by lineage members though the actual appointment is made by the Olubadan. Choice within the compound is by membership in the lineage and in particular segments of it, as well as by age and popularity. Therefore, it is unlikely that the present chief Dele's own son would succeed him directly, for the title must first pass to lineage segments deriving from Olajifin's other sons, and cannot return to Oyewole's descendants until it has passed through the other four main lines. Once a man becomes the *mogaji* for his lineage he then begins to manoeuvre his way up one of the two ladders of titles leading either to Olubadan or Balogun of Ibadan. The path is a long one and, as a result, most of the senior chiefs are men of considerable age.

Let us now examine Table 1, which includes everyone in the fifteen compounds who was permanently resident in Oje during the time that the census was undertaken. Compounds are arranged in alphabetical order, for convenience. Adults are divided according to marital status. *Married* here includes any person who has ever been married even though he may now be separated, divorced or widowed. The large difference in total unmarried men and women is probably explained by the respective age of marriage. Women are usually married in their late teens while men are in their middle twenties at the time of their first marriage. The difference is increased too by a drift from village to town among teenage boys who have had some schooling.

Table 5.1: Oje Compound Census

	Adults					Children			
	Men		Women				Parents lived with		
	Married	Un-married	Married	Un-married	Total	Both	Either	Neither	Total
Agatc	18	1	16	—	35	15	1	3	19
Ajadi	19	6	22	—	47	26	2	—	28
Ajayi-Amadu	5	3	10	—	18	10	—	2	12
Ajeja	21	9	35	5	70	38	5	5	48
Akinajo	13	18	24	—	55	22	7	5	34
Atabante	11	6	11	1	29	10	—	3	13
Dele	65	24	117	1	207	113	14	12	139
Folashade	9	2	19	1	31	21	6	7	34
Gbalefa	18	6	25	1	50	27	15	1	43
Ishole	7	1	12	—	20	4	—	2	6
Jagun-Akoka	13	3	13	1	30	11	2	2	15
Jaramero	14	14	26	2	56	20	4	1	25
Ogongo	12	4	22	3	41	11	5	3	19
Ojuolape	21	7	30	1	59	35	8	14	57
Oloro	19	2	28	2	51	35	11	2	48
Totals	265	106	409	19	799	398	80	62	540

Total population: 1,349 persons.
14 years of age and under = 40 per cent.

The presentation of data on children, i.e. persons under fifteen years of age, departs deliberately from usual procedures. The total number of persons under fifteen, 540 or about 40 per cent of the entire population, is in accordance with usual estimates given for Western Nigeria. Division of children according to sex has been omitted from the table as it is in line with expectation. 278 persons, or 44 per cent of the total male population, are under fifteen years, and 262 persons, or 36 per cent of the entire female population. The discrepancy in favour of young males may be partly explained by a generally higher incidence of male to female births. (In the United States 106 male births are recorded for each 100 female births and in Lebanon 111 male to 100 female. Comparable figures are not yet available for Nigeria.) Again, underestimates of pubescent girls are common in Africa. More boys, too, may live in the town to attend school. The division by sex for the total sample, 48 per cent male and 52 per cent female, follows closely Galletti's figures for Ibadan district. Although Galletti's sampling procedures have been questioned, these correspondences tend to substantiate the reliability of the Oje population findings and support the claim that Oje is representative of old Ibadan.[1]

The extreme difficulty encountered in obtaining reliable ages for children has prevented any attempt to breakdown the sample by age. Instead, an analysis of living arrangements of children is presented. It may be noted that only 74 per cent of the children are living with both parents, while 11 per cent live without their natural mother or father. These findings will be commented upon later, in the section dealing with child rearing.

Examination of the total number of adults per compound indicates that great differences in compound size occur. Speaking in round figures, Galletti describes compounds as varying from 40 to 400 persons. After summing the total of adults and children by compound, the three smallest, Ishole, Ajayi-Amadu, and Atabante almost reach 40, while the largest, Dele's, with 346 permanent residents, is under the maximum and Ajeja and Ojuolape, next in size, are well behind.

This difference in size can be explained, in part, by the definition of a permanent resident. A number of people who might be counted as part of the compound live elsewhere most of the year and are excluded. The Yoruba are known for their pattern of town and country dwelling; thus a man who might live most of the year in a village, and only come to town for festivals, still claims membership in a town compound. It is these people, descendants of the compound founder in the male line, and other people tracing through lineage members or long established tenants, who are counted as adult compound members living away. By these definitions, 63 per cent of the adult male population is permanently living in the compound while 37 per cent is away.

Returning for a moment to the three smallest compounds already cited, together with Jagun-Akoka and Folashade, a common feature can be noted. The genealogies for these compounds lack breadth and depth in time. In a typical large compound, such as Dele's, the lineage traces numerous branches, each through about four ascending generations to the founder or his brother. In the small compounds only limited parts of a larger family are represented. Thus Folashade's compound is comprised of her son (the present head), together with his family, a daughter, as well as one son of Folashade's brother. Isole's

[1] Galletti, Baldwin and Dina (1956), p. 196.

half brother settled in Dele's compound rather than with his own kin and his descendants remain there, an unrelated, tenant section. Ajayi-Amadu produced no direct descendants living today and the present residents can all trace descent from a single grandson of the founder's brother. In both Ajayi-Amadu's and Atabante's compound married men tracing descent from the founder are in the minority, forming only 25 per cent of the permanent adult residents. In most Oje compounds, however, descendants in the male line form a majority of both permanent residents and people away.

A majority of the compound members who live away are farming on lineage land and living in a hamlet. Modern occupations and style of life also determine whether a person lives in Oje. Among the vocations which draw people away are those of policeman, soldier, driver and student. A desire for a more sophisticated life than Oje provides prompts people to build houses in other parts of Ibadan, such as Inalende or Oke Ado, or to live in quarters provided by government or commercial employers.

Of the married people living in Oje, 265 are men and 409 are women. The surplus of women, which exists even after the seventeen married daughters who are living in their fathers' compounds following unsuccessful marriages are removed from the total, is explained by polygyny. It is the desire of most men, and often of their first wives also, that they should have at least two wives. Perhaps surprisingly many first wives are often happy to have another woman in the home to share domestic chores. The ideal of plural wives is met, in Oje, by 34 per cent of all married men, and the average number of wives per man is 1·6. The latter figure is considerably below Galletti's of 2·2 wives per man, but may be explained by a bias in his sample towards rich cocoa farmers who can afford many wives.[1] Another limiting factor is the inclusion of current wives only, thus omitting any divorced or dead wives a man had in the past. The distribution of wives among Oje men is presented in Table 2.

Table 5.2: Incidence of polygyny

Married Men	Wives per man					TOTAL
	1	2	3	4	5 or more	
Number	174	54	22	10	5	265
Per cent	66%	20%	8%	4%	2%	100%

[1] Galletti, Baldwin and Dina (1956), p. 73.

In considering polygyny from the wife's point of view a different picture emerges. Though only 91 men have more than one wife, 207 or 58 per cent of the wives presently living in Oje compounds are plural wives. Of the total wives accounted for by Table 2, 416, or 83 per cent, are presently resident in Oje. Numbers of wives per husband does not appear to affect systematically the proportion of wives away from home.

Figures support the casual observation that most Oje women are engaged in trade; in fact, 84 per cent of the women surveyed are so employed. This generalization covers a diverse range of activity. One quarter of the traders might alternatively be described as craftswomen, for they sell cooked foods such as *ẹkọ*, rice, bean cakes or *akara* balls which they first prepare and then market. Most of these commercial cooks have a reputation, and a steady clientèle which comes to them at home in their compound to buy food for breakfast and often supper. A few women sit along the road or in the market offering to passers-by meals and snacks, such as pieces of boiled yam or roast plantain.

One or two have quasi contracts with local primary schools, and on weekdays carry freshly prepared *ẹkọ* or rice to children who can afford twopence for a mid-morning snack.

A majority of the 259 women who function as middlemen, usually buying in bulk and selling in small quantities for immediate consumption, also deal in foodstuffs, either raw produce, live stock, or groceries. Such trade requires little capital, perhaps only enough credit or cash to purchase a gallon of palm oil, or a dozen tins of milk and some packets of biscuits. Only 10 per cent of Oje market women deal in cloth, probably because this line of trade requires at least five pounds initial capital to buy adequate stock. Among the women surveyed there is only one large-scale cloth trader with a Lebanon Street shop, who is prosperous enough to have built her own house, bought a car and made the pilgrimage to Mecca. She had the advantage of having an extremely successful mother who also dealt in cloth.

Of the remaining 68 women, 33 are full-time housewives. Most of the latter are only recently married and will probably begin trade once they are established in their new homes and their husbands are able to give them initial capital. The 26 craftswomen include cloth dyers, hairdressers, seamstresses and the like. Less than 1 per cent of the total female population are girls with some education who no longer wish to follow traditional occupations but cannot find suitable modern employment. This low figure for unemployed school leavers reflects the generally low level of education in the Oje community, for only six Oje women are engaged in modern occupations. Four of these women teach in primary schools, a fifth is employed as a binder in a large Ibadan printing company, and the sixth as a clerk in an expatriate commercial firm.

The 1952 census of Ibadan District describes more than half of all men as being engaged in agriculture; 35 per cent of urban men farm, and 86 per cent of those who live in villages and hamlets. Results of the Oje survey are contrary to this expectation. Only 10 per cent of Oje men are farmers. An explanation lies in the decision to classify people according to their primary occupation. It is most likely that a quarter of the men counted in other categories also farm, though they do not list farming, an occupation lacking status, as their primary vocation. Only permanent residents were surveyed, thus omitting the large number of primarily rural Oje people who are farmers.

Table 5.3 : Distribution of occupations (based on 365 Oje men)

Farming		10%
Trade		18%
Transport	6%	
Building	3%	
General	9%	
Craft		50%
Transport	14%	
Building	19%	
General	17%	
Professional and Technical		17%
Others		5%
School leavers	4%	
Priests (Christian and Moslem)	1%	
		100%

Table 3 shows the distribution of occupations among Oje men. Within the categories of trade and craft there is great variety of employment; thus each has been divided into sub-categories—transport, building and general. The largest craft sub-category—building—includes bricklayers, carpenters, electricians, mudbrick makers and their apprentices. A few of these men work for large firms or the government, but the majority are hired by local building contractors—a type of self-employed labour and materials middleman, who is himself included in the category. Traders in building supplies and construction craftsmen number more than one fifth of all Oje men. The transport sub-category contains taxi, lorry and private car drivers, mechanics and their apprentices. Together with traders in tyres and motor parts, transport embraces another 20 per cent of the population.

The general categories for both trade and craft are residual. Included among the traders are men dealing in cloth, produce and livestock, as well as clerks in large commercial houses and messengers in various offices. A dozen drummers—a semi-hereditary occupation, a few barbers, some tailors, cap makers and mill operators comprise most of the 17 per cent described as general craftsmen.

The professional and technical group ranges from a lawyer to local government policemen, and includes customary court assessors, a commercial artist, teachers, typists and surveyors. The category, *Others*, is formed of unemployed school leavers, four Oje malams and one *babalawo*. It is difficult in interpret the unemployed school-leaver figure, as other men in the same position may be away in Lagos or in other parts of Ibadan. Still others have some marginal employment as taxi-driver apprentices and the like. Again, too, education has not been widespread in Oje, thus school leavers form a smaller proportion of the labour force than in more sophisticated parts of town.

Islam plays a part in the lives of the majority of Oje people. Survey results indicate that 74 per cent of all adults are Muslims. In two compounds, those of Agate and Ajeja, all adults follow Islam, while in Dele's and Jaramero's compounds fewer than 10 per cent profess other faiths. Christianity has attracted a small following; only in the compounds of Akinajo, Folashade and Ajayi-Amadu are Christians in the majority. In every compound, however, people are allowed their individual beliefs, and there appears to be no bitterness because some members of the family are Christians and others Muslims. In fact, about 1 per cent, mostly old people, are still entirely faithful to their traditional Yoruba gods.

Over half the Muslims, about 350 persons, attend prayers at Dele's mosque. Another large group belongs to Abonde's mosque, while others pray in mosques in Munmi's and Kasali's compounds. All of these mosques are located within Oje.

Christians, with few exceptions, must leave Oje to attend religious services. The Anglicans, numbering 144, form the great majority of Christians; they attend services either at St. Peter's, Aremo, or the nearer, though newer, church of St. Paul at Yemetu. The half-dozen Catholics worship at St. Cyprian's in Oke Ofa, the Baptists at Idikan and the Seventh Day Adventists, just north of Oje in Itutaba. Only a few people attend the Apostolic Church, the Aladura or prayer healing church, in Oje. About twenty people belong to the Cherubim and Seraphim Church, founded by an Oje chief, but moved, in 1947, to nearby Ode Aje to gain a large enough building site.

Christians thus disperse about the town, while Muslims, excepting the few who attend the central mosque on Friday, worship within Oje. Often it is said that Islam is more conservative, while Christianity is the religion of educated people. It should be noted that circumstances force the Oje Christians to have a wider view of Ibadan, and perhaps a generally more cosmopolitan outlook. It is beyond the scope of this chapter to analyse this point, but to understand Oje more completely, it is necessary to consider how Islam and Christianity each affect the community.

Both Christian and Muslim influences had been felt in Ibadan by the time Oje was established. Islam began to penetrate Yoruba country in the nineteenth century, along the trade routes to the coast, and Ilorin, under Fulani rule, became an important centre of Islamic learning. The Rev. David Hinderer visited Ibadan in 1851 and opened St. David's, an Anglican school at Kudeti.[1]

It was not Ibadan Muslims, but rather men from Iwo and Ede, who brought Islam to Oje, and settled in Dele's compound. In Ojuolape's compound it is recorded that the first conversion to Islam occurred about 1895. The people of Ogongo, Agate and Gbalefa are said to have followed in this order. In the time of Bale Irefin, 1912–14, Momadu became the first Muslim Chief of Dele's compound. Shortly afterwards the present mosque was built in the compound.

In the early days of Islam in Oje, the *Lemanu* (Yoruba for Imam or spiritual leader of the mosque) was a stranger, often trained at Ilorin. The present *Lemanu* of Abonde's mosque recounts that his grandfather went from his home in Iwo to Ilorin about the time of the Kijiri War, 1879–86, and there learned the Kur'an. Today, a number of *malams* hold classes in Oje. One student for example, reported that in three years he would know the Kur'an and be able to write Arabic.

The mosque in Oje is today a thoroughly Yoruba institution. At its head is the *Olori* (head man) and he supervises the *Lemanu*, the spiritual leader, who is popularly chosen, and unpaid. Male members are divided by age into two societies, the *Majekobaje* (Don't let it spoil), composed of the young men who look after the mosque, and the *Samari Adine* (elders), who settle disputes and perform marriage ceremonies or other special rituals. Islam has no formal clergy in the Christian sense.

Conversion to Christianity seems to be determined more by individual circumstance. One path which a number of middle-aged men followed was to attend a mission school, where they became converted.

[1] See Idowu and El-Masi, below, pp. 235ff.

A few men of middle age report that their own fathers had been converted, but can remember quite clearly that their grandfathers worshipped Ifa, Shango or some other Yoruba deity. Folashade came to Oje about the turn of the century from one of the leading early Christian families of Ibadan.

Though traditional beliefs have lost ground, complete rejection is not imminent. Political conditions allowing, the *egungun* festival is still celebrated annually. The new-yam shrine at the market is swept clean every four days and offerings made. Ancestors are still given a yearly sacrifice at a secret place in Dele's compound, and the Chief claims that, although participation is not compulsory, a good number of Muslims take part because they have difficulty in having children. Physical difficulties, such as infertility or tremors also draw people who regularly attend other churches, to the Aladura, or prayer healing church in Oje.

It is not unusual for Islam and traditional beliefs to co-exist. Two young Muslim men reported that a *babalawo* is still more powerful in combating witches than the Islamic healer or *alufa*. At Oloro's compound the man who pointed out the family shrines for Obatala, Shango and Ibeji, first claimed to worship them; later he said he was a Muslim but worshipped Shango as well.

Daily Life

Old men accustomed to sleeping little, and women who must call at a corn mill or the wholesale food market at Oritamerin before starting the day's trade, begin to rise about 5 a.m. Soon they are joined by men destined for work at the farm or in distant parts of Ibadan, and women who cook the family breakfast or sell cooked foods to others. Before 8 a.m. even the unemployed young men and children not yet of school age are awake, and Oje begins the day.

In most compounds a man is formally greeted by his wives and children. He in turn greets each of them, often using special pet names (*oriki*). Most Muslim men wash quickly, clean their mouths, and hurry to the mosque for prayers; Muslim women and youths pray alone at home. Among Christians, it is common for the whole family to gather in the parlour for a brief service. Often, this is the only opportunity throughout the day for the entire family to be together. The father may work at some distance and buy his breakfast along the way. Even if he stays at home he will probably eat alone, or occasionally, in more educated families, eat with a wife or a few older children.

Women whose trading duties allow, will cook breakfast and eat with their children; those who attend early markets may rush through the household chores, sweeping and drawing water, then buy some breakfast to eat in the stall where mother and small child spend the morning. A woman who sells breakfast food, will have a hurried snack, or often none at all, tie her small child to her back, and set off, tray on head to offer others the convenience of a ready-cooked breakfast.

Men return home for lunch if their business is nearby and trade permits; but on some days a tailor, carpenter or barber, with a shop next door or even in the compound, may be so busy he only buys a snack and has a proper meal in the evening. When farming, a man usually sets off early and is gone all day. If he has another wife in the village he is well fed, otherwise he may eat lightly until he returns to Ibadan. A few wage-earners and government employees return after 2 p.m. from work, in time for a large midday meal and rest; but most men find little time for a long nap, and only relax briefly before returning to work in the afternoon.

A woman's daily activity is determined by her age and status in the compound, as well as by the needs of trade. Commonly a junior wife cooks and cleans up afterwards. When there is some friction in the family, a schedule will be drawn up and carefully followed, to determine which wife is cooking for the husband; each woman cooks for herself and her own children. Only when a junior wife is newly married would an older woman assume domestic responsibilities for her new partner. One young wife with twin baby girls was given much help by a sister, and had little cooking, washing or trading to do, although care of the twins appeared most demanding. Women past their thirties, even without junior wives, can often commandeer a daughter or niece to help them. A woman may also be able to afford help in her weekly or bi-weekly chores. Most women themselves renew the floor periodically, either with a cement-like mixture of mud and dung, or with a starchy, indigo residue from cloth dying, but it is common to employ a professional man or woman to wash the family clothes.

Towards late evening men often bathe, dress in fresh clothes and go out visiting friends. Women too, whose trade allows, may go off to their own compounds, or to visit married sisters. Women who sell food for supper, leave home shortly before 8 p.m., either to sit in the market or to hawk their wares for the next two hours. Many people buy their entire supper or reheat lunchtime soup and buy cassava, yam or maize to eat with it. In some families moral instruction is offered the children through folk-tales and riddles which are carefully explained and discussed. By 10 p.m. the *Disai*, the fifth, and final, prayer of the day has been recited at the mosques, and almost everyone is preparing for bed.

A young couple will often share a sleeping room, the husband occupying an iron bedstead whilst his wife and children sleep nearby on their mats. Women with nursing babies wake two or three times during the night to feed their children. A polygynist tries to provide a room for each of his wives—and if possible a parlour and bedroom for himself. Such a prosperous man usually sleeps alone or with a young son. His parlour could be used by his unmarried sons and apprentices. Girls too old to sleep with their mothers spend the night together on their own mats, lined up along the corridor outside the women's rooms.

This description of daily life has, so far, neglected to discuss children in any detail. Rather than attempt to follow children of varying ages through the hours of the day, let us trace, instead, a child's life from birth to adolescence.

In the past all babies were born in the compound; the woman delivering would be assisted by her mother or mother-in-law, sisters or sisters-in-law. No men were present except the *babalawo* who might have been consulted for medicines during the pregnancy, especially in the third and seventh months, when additional precautions against premature birth are usually taken. If it is his first-born a father may be so nervous that he hides until the delivery is over. Children, too, are kept away and the front gate is shut to discourage visitors.

For delivery, the woman kneels on the floor grasping the thighs of her mother who stands in front, or rests her arms on a chair seat while holding the frame. Another woman may offer comfort by rubbing her back. When the placenta fails to follow the baby quickly, the floor is beaten with a mortar; but once it appears the cord is cut. Owu people use a small knife, but Oje people believe that the use of a knife to cut the cord makes children stubborn in later life; instead, the Oje use the bark of a special palm tree. Once the blood is pressed out and the umbilicus tied, the new-born child is cleaned with palm oil, bathed with a sponge and water, his head rounded by hand shaping, his limbs stretched for exercise, tossed in the air to make him brave, and he is given a few drops of cold water. Heated, herbally treated cloths are applied to the navel each day.

The mother is helped to wash, her stomach is often bound and she is clothed. After taking light food, she receives women visitors who may repeat the baby's first bath as a sign of affection. During the days, seven if the child is a girl, nine if a boy, preceding the naming ceremony, food taboos associated with the lineage prevent the mother from having salt, pepper, palm oil, or, in Dele's compound, more than one measure of pap at a time. On the second day the infant is force-fed with a herbal liquid. In many compounds the baby is fed while it is held between the thighs, with head lowered near the knees. Dele's women are forbidden this method, and the old Oje custom of force-feeding while sitting the child upright is used instead.

Until the naming ceremony, mother and child must remain indoors. Guests arrive early in the morning of the appointed day. The baby is given salt, pepper and palm oil, which the mother tastes and which ends her taboo. Honey to ensure a sweet disposition and similar substances are placed in the baby's mouth. Coins dropped in a special basin filled with water are given to the child. All the names given to the child have meaning; one usually describes the circumstances of the birth, another tells about the family's condition (e.g. Ayodele 'joy comes into the house'), and finally the *oriki* of name or endearment. In the past, new mothers would not leave the compound till three months after delivery, but many women now resume their normal activities after forty days.

Nowadays, increasing numbers of Oje women go to the hospital or maternity centres to deliver. In a sample of 251 children under five years only 23 per cent were delivered in the compound. Scarcity of post-natal facilities, however, demands that most return to the compound within 24 hours of their confinement. Naming is now often performed according to Muslim practice on the eighth day for both boys and girls. Occasionally, Christians as well as Muslims perform both the traditional ceremony and a modern religious one. In every family the naming is an opportunity for merriment and feasting.

Usually within a fortnight of birth, though there is no rigidly prescribed time, face marks may be cut according to lineage tradition. Young mothers have reported that the older women in Oje often trick them, and mark their babies' faces against openly expressed wishes to abandon the practice. Circumcision and clitoridectomy are perhaps performed at the same time, without special rituals. In a family that has lost many infants the event may be postponed a month or more until the baby is thought strong enough. The precaution of employing practitioners beyond the age of sexual activity is taken, to insure that the wound heals quickly. The circumcisers, who also make the face marks, are paid in money and kola nuts.

Once the infant settles down, he is fed regularly at 8 a.m., 1 p.m. and 6 p.m. Major feedings are often preceded by force-feeding of *agbo*, a warm, brownish, herbal liquid which seems to be given the child until a bowel movement occurs. It is also reported to strengthen the bones. Though *agbo* is no longer universally administered to Oje infants, in any compound one can find mothers who use it and are willing to demonstrate how it is given to the baby. At any time of day, if the baby frets or cries, the breast is offered and later on, when the child can hold them, bits of bread or orange are given.

Unless the morning is particularly cold, the child's day starts with a bath, followed in the first year with stretching of the arms and legs, massage and tossing in the air. After bathing, young babies may sleep till lunch and then again till supper. When the infant begins to spend more time awake children and grandmothers play with him. When he cries older women try to comfort him, carrying him about on their backs and singing lullabies or songs of the lineage's glory. If the mother must go any distance from the compound, the baby will be tied to her back, but if her absence is brief and she will be nearby, an eight-year-old child or some older woman is left in charge. At night, the baby sleeps with the mother.

As a child reaches two years, his mother begins to think of having another baby. Before a woman can resume marital relations her nursing child must be weaned. Though still nursed, a two-year-old can eat adult foods. Once a mother decides to wean the baby she tries to do it quickly, refusing the breast day and night, but offering substitutes such as biscuits or pap, whenever the child cries. Mothers often rub lime juice or other bitter substances on the nipples or tie their wrappers very tightly to discourage the child. Even after the child has been weaned he may still share his mother's mat. Once she becomes pregnant again, however, he must walk about on his own, and can no longer be carried on his mother's back.

The two Oje school teachers reported giving powdered milk to their babies almost from birth. Since these children could not be carried to work as traders' children might be, they became accustomed to supplemental feeding at an early age. Both babies were completely weaned well before two years. Even among less educated young women, the pattern of earlier supplemental feeding and weaning is coming into vogue.

By and large, the children under five years of age have a happy carefree life in Oje compounds. Until they can manage adequately, assistance is given in eating, they are usually bathed once a day and chores are not expected until they are quite old enough to understand instructions. Even jealousy of the new baby is recognized, and rather than punishing severely, mothers try to distract the older child's attention. Until a child reaches five he is given pennies to stop crying. Aggressive behaviour towards the newborn would be punished by spanking or beating.

Pre-school children are encouraged to learn polite greetings and gestures of respect, prostration for boys and kneeling for girls, but performance is treated with amused pleasure by parents, rather than sternly demanded, until the child is six or seven.

Children still too young for school usually play in mixed groups of boys and girls from neighbouring compounds. In a large compound the children might only play among themselves. Moulding houses and utensils from mud made with earth and water is a favourite game. Though such play is encouraged to develop co-operation and sociability, mothers often frown upon its messiness.

School-age children begin to separate into groups by sex. Boys enjoy fighting with one another, and leadership changes rapidly in their gangs. Girls seem less physically aggressive and are said to focus instead on gossip. Girls' groups are often larger and more stable. They may organize little dances or practise songs learned in school. In Folashade's compound the girls can be organized within a few moments' notice to enact a folktale about an ọba, or to portray the misadventures of a girl who chooses her own suitor despite parental protest.

Older children are also called upon to help their parents. In the past, boys were expected to work on their father's farms, but school reduces the time available for this. Nevertheless, boys and girls still assist their mothers, often in trade at weekends and during school holidays. Girls will also be called upon to draw water from the public taps, sweep, mind small children, wash clothes, and do some grinding or simple cooking. Many boys are responsible for kindling fire in the morning, sweeping and drawing water. Most household chores are not seen as invariably masculine or feminine, and when no girls are available boys can even be called upon to mind babies or help in cooking.

All Oje schools are included in the Western Region's scheme for universal, free primary education; there are no fee-paying, private primary schools. Although there are no school fees, parents must still buy books and uniforms, and occasionally make donations to school building funds. From a survey of Oje primary school attendance carried out in March 1962 it is clear that many Oje children begin school (approximately equal number of boys and girls), but at present the drop-out rate is high. Attendance falls about 30 per cent by Standard III and boys begin to form the majority. Only half as many Oje children attend Standard VI as begin in Standard I, and among Standard VI pupils there are two boys for every girl. Oje parents seem to value education for their sons more than for their daughters, and will make the sacrifices necessary to meet their sons' school expenses.

Among children attending school the proportion, (77 per cent), of those living at home with both parents is slightly higher than that (74 per cent) given for the overall population of children. Few of the primary school children will continue their education. Beyond primary school, fees must be paid, and to attend grammar schools, entrance is gained by examination. A majority of those continuing their education will enrol in secondary modern schools as day pupils. There is a growing disillusionment with the academic course offered by the Modern Schools as adolescents find increasing difficulty in gaining employment. A few fortunate ones may learn typing or some other skill which might make them more employable.

Children who do not attend school or who drop out of primary school are not granted the freedom they might wish. Girls, who form the majority of those who do not complete primary school, are often put to work. Poor people send their daughters to rich compounds such as Folashade's, to live there and help the successful traders of the house in domestic chores and in their trade. Girls may also be sent to live with married sisters and to help them care for young children. These adolescents also seek employment outside the family. Boys whose families can manage the fees required will apprentice themselves to drivers or other craftsmen and often live in their master's compound. Girls may work as housemaids in the homes of rich Ibadan people.

When girls begin thinking of marriage, however, their attention returns to their own compound. The majority of Oje women say that they met their husbands through relatives, usually older brothers.

Two categories of unusual children deserve comment. The first, twins, is an occasion of happiness. Twins are always given the names of *Taiwo* and *Kẹhinde*; the one who comes first to taste the world, and considered the younger twin, is called *Taiwo*, while the elder, who stays behind, is *Kẹhinde*. The mother of twins buys wooden figures, *ibeji*, to which offerings are made. She should also dance through the town receiving gifts for her twins. Occasionally a mother of twins comes to the large sixteen-day Oje market and is given coins by passers-by.

Following the death of several successive children an *abiku* name such as Malomo, 'do not go away again', is given to the next born. Such children are said to desire return to the spirit world and are described as 'born to die'. This misfortune, at first ignored, will later be treated by marking the baby's corpse to facilitate recognition when it returns. An *abiku* child is appeased and offerings made to keep him on earth. After half a dozen such deaths the mother may be blamed, and it is common for a woman who loses many children to divorce her husband

and try her fortune in another compound. One woman reported that three of her children died before she married an Oje man and bore him four living children.

Oje—a Community?

The remark is frequently heard, that despite its size and vast population, Ibadan is not a city, but rather a collection of villages which have grown together to form an extensive town area. How well does Oje fit this description? Is Oje a self-contained community with clear boundaries and complex internal social interaction, or are its limits vague and its main social focus the life of Ibadan?

Historical evidence, though hardly definitive, supports the view of Oje as a self-sufficient community. Clearly, when it was founded more than a century ago by Balogun Oderinlo and Dele, both warriors of rank worthy enough to command authority, it stood beyond the boundaries of Ibadan in heavy forest. The position was sufficiently removed to suggest Oje as a rival camp to Bashorun Oyewole, who was settled at Oja Iba.

The extent of Dele's authority upon the Balogun's departure is in doubt, but there is no question that Dele's descendants are the owners of the market he founded at Oje. Furthermore, certain compounds claim their rights to land through the authority of Chief Dele, and in the past took disputes which could not be solved within their own compounds, to Dele, for adjudication. Until 1946, when the system of local tax collection was altered, over one hundred compounds, though not every compound in the Oje neighbourhood, paid their tax through the Chief.

In the 1940s, when the neighbourhood was plagued by thieves, all of the compounds contributed to the wages of two nightwatchmen specially employed to guard Oje. Finally, the integrity of Oje was recognized in town government until 1954, when electoral wards, whose boundaries followed tarred roads, were created, and Oje, which had till then been one constituency, represented on the City Council by the head of Folashade's compound, became part of six new wards.

The effect of the dual carriageway which was built in the 1930s on the integrity of the Oje community should not be underestimated. Unlike the older roads in Oje, the new highway completely bye-passed the market. Thus, today, when you ask a taxi driver to take you to Oje, you are deposited on the dual carriageway, and to get to the market you must ask for it specifically. Furthermore, besides destroying the traditional design of Dele's and Ojuolape's compounds, and distributing the graves of the ancestors, the road forms a barrier to the western third of Oje—that area, which, examination of a map indicates, had been naturally delimited on the western side by Yemetu stream and on the southern and eastern edges by Kudeti stream.

Another criterion for determining the cohesiveness of a community is the extent of intermarriage. In examining the origins of Oje wives the most striking feature is that one-sixth of the 80 per cent who come from Ibadan town, come from Oje itself. The proportion exceeds that which might be expected, taking into consideration the area and population of Oje; but this needs to be interpreted cautiously. The positive and negative factors, of increased accessibility countered by rules of exogamy, preclude a simple interpretation. Just as a man is prohibited from marrying one of his father's lineage, so, too, there are restrictions against marrying from the lineages of any grandparent. As there are many ties between the compounds of Ojuolape, Folashade, Agate, Dele, Oloro, Ishole, and Jaramero, among middle-aged and old women, the choice is probably limited for younger Oje men. It seems quite certain, however, that past intermarriage has fashioned family ties which bind the community together along with the impersonal effects of history and geography.

Contemporary social relations also function to produce a sense of community. One organization with this avowed purpose is the Oje Progressive Union, composed of over one hundred Oje traders, civil servants and artisans. The Union lists its aims as: (1) to promote the general development and progress of Oje, (2) to develop the spirit of unity among Oje people, (3) to foster economic and social co-operation by giving financial and moral support to members in need, and (4) to encourage thrift. The Union, whose founding antedates the electoral ward system, tries to maintain close contact with all the councillors for Oje, and by so doing, to ensure that adequate amenities and Council jobs come to Oje. The Union is active, holding weekly meetings and collecting from its members each week, three pence to ten shillings, according to their earning power.

A branch of each national political party exists in Oje and functions to select local and parliamentary candidates for the six electoral wards. The branches are active only during election time, and have no neighbourhood focus, as the wards completely cross cut Oje. The local party branches of the Action Group, United Peoples Party, and National Council of Nigerian Citizens, are not yet strong enough to pose a threat to neighbourhood solidarity, as it is exemplified by the Progressive Union, but they may do so in future.

Young peoples' organizations are not founded as strictly along neighbourhood lines as those of adults. Shared interests appear to determine choice of either the 'Money Makes the Gentleman Society' (Yoruba: Ẹgbẹ Owo Ni Boys) by rather unschooled youths, or the Oje Social Circle by those pursuing a secondary school education. The Circle is only active during school holidays, when boys and girls are home, while the Society has weekly meetings and collects regular dues for self-help and thrift, as in the Oje Union. The most active club in the area is the Oje Boys' and Girls' Club, supported by the Ministry of Economic Planning and Community Development. Though it meets every Sunday in Otun Oje's compound, membership is open to any youth in Ibadan interested and willing to participate. There are about twenty five such clubs scattered through the town; emphasis is primarily on sports, but efforts are made to ensure the sound moral development of the members also. Monthly Ibadan-wide meetings give the local leaders opportunity to meet peers from all over the city.

Evidence is available to support or dispute the claim that Oje is a community in its own right. Certainly in the past the neighbourhood was orientated towards the market, all roads lead to it. Intermarriage and shared religious and recreational activities created social cohesion. Leadership and authority in the community were assumed by Dele's lineage; and the area was able to unite for mutual protection and to obtain amenities. The two City Council-supported primary schools attest to this. However, recent developments in education, government, and transportation, favour the gradual blurring of distinct neighbourhood boundaries in Ibadan. As the ward system, cross-cutting traditional boundaries, becomes firmly established, Oje compounds will probably look to leaders in their own wards rather than to the Union to provide jobs and amenities. With increased education the young are likely to align themselves with people of compatible interests all over the town. Furthermore, new roads and cars make this possible, as all parts of the town become accessible. How far these modern trends will be checked by the local character of Oje, by Islam or by the difficulty in Oje of obtaining higher education, due to poverty, makes prediction uncertain, but change towards a more cosmopolitan outlook seems inevitable.[1]

---

[1] The research upon which this chapter is based was carried out between November 1961 and June 1963 and supported by Grant M-4865 of the National Institute of Mental Health to the University of Chicago (principal investigator, Dr. R. A. LeVine) and by a Ford Foundation grant to the Universities of Chicago and Ibadan.

6
STRANGER COMMUNITIES

A. THE IJEBU

by A. L. MABOGUNJE

Among the non-indigenous or stranger elements in the population of Ibadan, the Ijebu occupy an undeniably unique position. Occupying a territory whose northern limits are less than 30 miles south of Ibadan, the Ijebu have always maintained with the Ibadan rather close relations, occasionally acrimonious but most of the time peaceful, and sometimes friendly. Ijebu Province extends for an area of about 2,400 square miles and has a population of about 350,000 according to the 1952 census. This population, however, provides no indication of the number of Ijebu in the Federal Republic of Nigeria. For, among the Yoruba, the Ijebu are perhaps the most travelled and widely dispersed, being found in considerable numbers in diverse places throughout the length and breadth of Nigeria.

In their homeland, the majority of Ijebu are farmers. The 1952 census, for instance, showed that of a total 97,000 gainfully occupied males in the province, over 70 per cent were engaged in farming. For the females, the percentage was about 75 per cent out of a total of 106,000 gainfully occupied. (For purposes of comparison, Ibadan province returned about 66 per cent of males and 69 per cent of females as engaged in farming.)

These percentages, indicating an emphasis on agriculture in their homeland, belie the more noted characteristics of the Ijebu. As Forde stated, 'The inhabitants of Ijebu-Ode are conspicuous as traders and middlemen and have not a high reputation as farmers'.[1] Although Forde indicated that Ijebu other than those of Ijebu Ode were more often farmers, this must be taken as a purely relative fact. Ijebu, whatever sub-groups they belong to, are distinguished in Nigeria for their irrepressible flair for trading. Indeed, in 1845 D'Avezac remarked that for the Ijebu the retail sale of European articles forms an important part of inland trade, but foreign trade is, above all, the main occupation.[2] Captain John Adams noted much earlier in 1789 that this foreign trade was in locally manufactured cloth, although later it was to be

[1] Forde (1951), p. 50.
[2] D'Avezac (1845), p. 77.

mainly in slaves. Adams wrote: 'These people send so much cloth to Lagos and Ardrah (Porto Novo), which the Portuguese traders from the Brazils purchase from that market, and which is held there in much estimation by the black population.'[1]

This trading characteristic of the Ijebu has had two notable effects, which should be borne in mind when considering their position as strangers in Ibadan. First, being by tradition a trading group, the Ijebu seemed to have achieved a remarkable capacity for assessing the commercial advantages of new situations and seizing the novel opportunities provided by such situations. This is perhaps best illustrated by the avidity with which they took to the new opportunities provided by the British advent into Nigeria, once their initial resistance to the British had been broken at the Magbon War of 1892. Moreover, while putting so much emphasis on the acquisition of material wealth, the Ijebu have become noted for their almost puritanical outlook and their relatively austere way of living.

The second consequence of this strong tradition of trading among the Ijebu is their massive migration from their home area to nearly all parts of the Federation. Once the British had ensured a reasonable degree of law and order in Nigeria and established a relatively cheap, easy and reliable transportation system to link different parts of the country, the Ijebu poured out, as it were, along these route-ways, seeking new commercial opportunities wherever these could be found. Almost without exception, all the large cities of Nigeria boast of a substantial community of Ijebu. But nowhere is their presence felt so much as in Lagos and Ibadan.

The Ijebu in Ibadan

Nevertheless, it was not trade that first brought the Ijebu to Ibadan. For among the very first founders of the present-day Ibadan were a group of Ijebu. Akinyele noted that 'Ibadan town was again repeopled by the conquerers of Owu . . . who comprised the Ife, Ijebu, Oyo and Egba chiefs with their men'.[2] How important a group these Ijebu were in the early history of the city is not clear. What is certain, however, is that one of them, by the name of Sodeinde, rose to become a chief—Balogun Elesin—in Ibadan by 1864. According to Akinyele, Sodeinde was a native of Ijebu Remo, a trader and warrior by profession. During the Kutuje War (1862–4) against the Egba, Ijaye and Ijebu, he had fought with merit on the side of the Ibadan. Partly in consequence,

---

[1] Adams (1823), p. 25.
[2] Akinyele (1946b), p. 4.

three others of his descendants became high-ranking chiefs in Ibadan. This early group of Ijebu in Ibadan occupied part of the older section of the city known as Isale Ijebu.

Almost contemporaneous with this group were the Ijebu who came to Ibadan with the early Christian missionaries. The first Christian missionaries, under the Rev. David Hinderer, had arrived in Ibadan in 1851. In the succeeding years numerous others were to follow. Among these were recent converts among former slaves, who had been freed by the British Anti-Slavery Naval Squadron, transported to Freetown and trained to be literate and Christian. Some of these converts were Ijebu who, from Lagos and Abeokuta, had proselytized among their own people. It was from among the latter that this Christian group of early Ijebu in Ibadan had come. They were housed by their Christian friends in those neighbourhoods of the city, notably Aremo, Opo Labiran and Oke Ofa, where Christianity had won a sizeable group of converts.

Nonetheless, for most of the nineteenth century the number of Ijebu in Ibadan was small. Their large migration into the city came only after Ibadan had emerged as a major trading centre in the new economic environment being created by the British administration. The railway from Lagos reached Ibadan in 1901 and later, around 1911, a road was constructed to link Oyo to Ibadan. As against the hazard of a lagoon trip to Lagos for imported manufactured goods, travelling to Ibadan for much the same goods began to attract many Ijebu, particularly as this route was safer, for all that it was more strenuous. With the arrival of the motor vehicle, late in the 1920s, Ibadan's competitive position with Lagos was assured. In the years that followed the First World War, thousands of young Ijebu adults moved to Ibadan to seek their fortunes in the new economic opportunities that were being presented in this rapidly growing city.

The Economic Role of the Ijebu

Initially, most of those who came engaged in small trading in imported goods. Their small shops lined Agbeni and Amunigun Streets and formed a link between the traditional city and the new commercial centre growing around the railway station to the far west. Among the Ijebu, both sexes participated vigorously in the new commerce. The only distinction lay in the goods traded, with the women preferring to deal in textiles, earthenware, chinaware, and minor household utensils, which were likely to appeal, in particular, to other women.

This emphasis on trade in imported goods has continued among the Ijebu to the present day. Minor developments in the pattern include a wider range in the scale of trading between the small trader and the large, modern joint-stock companies such as the Ikorodu Trading Stores. There is also much diversity in the commodities sold. Ijebu now participate in the internal exchange of agricultural produce. Both male and female Ijebu traders with fairly large capital take part in the commodity trade in beans, onions, groundnut oil and eggs from Northern Nigeria, and are to be found in stalls at Dugbe Market and at various other private stores around the railway station. Smaller traders, mainly women, join in selling foodstuffs at the major foodstuff markets of Gege, Oritamerin and Ayeye.

Apart from commerce, many Ijebu are to be found in crafts and industries. Again, the range of enterprises owned by Ijebu in Ibadan extends from the small, one-man domestic craft to the large modern factory employing hundreds of workers and using machines of modern technological complexity. Most of the crafts and industries are left largely to the men, except for female garment-manufacturing which is organized by Ijebu women among others. Ijebu men, however, tend to show clear preferences for certain crafts and industries. Notable among these are goldsmithing, metal-working, mechanical repair-work, printing and sign-writing. Callaway, in his survey of craft industry in Ibadan, finds a higher percentage of enterprises in this group concentrated in those areas of the city where most of the Ijebu are to be found.[1] Many such enterprises experienced a boom particularly during the Second World War, when there were shortages of imported goods. Of African-owned large industrial establishments some of the most highly capitalized belong to people of Ijebu descent. Among such establishments may be mentioned some half a dozen printing works and two large tyre-retreading factories.

The profits from trade and manufacturing seemed to have been invested by the Ijebu in three major fields of economic activities: transport, education and landed property.

Almost as soon as motor transport was introduced into the country and had made possible fast land travel in areas not touched by the railway, the Ijebu appreciated its value for their constant weekly commuting between their home towns and Ibadan. At first, 'mammy-wagons' carried the passengers, but soon buses, locally built, largely replaced the 'mammy-wagons'. A few wealthy men emerged controlling fleets of lorries and buses travelling mainly between Ibadan and Ijebu Province. But in spite of them, most of the transport business remained a one-lorry or at most a two-lorry/bus affair.

[1] Callaway, below, p. 153ff.

The transport business has attracted many Ijebu entrepreneurs because of the very real demand for easy transportation. For many Ijebu, in spite of years of living in Ibadan, their major social identification remains with their home towns. Every week-end, or at least once a month, most Ijebu return home. The traders do so even more frequently. A regular pattern of movement from the main towns of Ijebu Province is in the early morning (about 5 a.m.), when there is an exodus of lorries and buses, on Mondays especially, bringing back civil servants and teachers in time for their duties in Ibadan. More recently, the Ijebu transporters from Ibadan have been equally interested in the Ibadan-Lagos road, although here their participation is not dominant.

Although resisting the missionaries and the British to the point of open hostilities with the latter in 1892, the Ijebu, once their resistance was broken, were quick to seize the new opportunities being provided by both groups. As missionary work progressed in their home area, many were not only converted to Christianity but were prepared to send their children to schools in distant centres like Lagos. Soon, the economic advantages of education began to be realized in terms of employment opportunities, earning a regular salary in government or business, and widening trade horizon. This situation increased the avidity with which Ijebu turned to the formal European type of education. As new and higher educational institutions were opened in different parts of Yorubaland, Ijebu were always to be found well represented among the early intakes. Thus, among the students of St. Andrew's College at Oyo and of Wesley College, Ibadan, were to be found from early times numerous Ijebu who had trekked to the colleges on foot.

The result of this, as far as Ibadan is concerned, is that for many years Ijebu filled a number of posts in the city for which a relatively high standard of education was required. This was true in particular of teaching in primary and secondary schools. Since 1952, however, the position has somewhat changed, for two reasons. In the first place, the introduction of a democratic system of administration in place of the former colonial system meant that the indigenous Ibadan people now directly supervise the appointments to teaching posts in the city. As was only natural, they have tended to encourage their own sons and daughters to fill many more of the offices. In the second place, the end of the colonial period and the beginning of internal self-rule in the country has made a wider range of careers available to Nigerians as a whole. Novel and more rewarding opportunities in business, in the civil service and in the professions became open to everyone. Traditionally respectable positions like those of teachers lost their former prestige. Again, the

Ijebu rose to the occasion. Many of the younger generation turned away from a career in teaching and concentrated in particular on professional training, especially in law, medicine and engineering. Today, Ijebu form a sizeable group in this class of people in the city of Ibadan.

Investment in landed property, however, has been one of the major direct commercial activities of the Ijebu in Ibadan. In a situation where land immediately adjacent to the city has been overworked and is of little use for agricultural purposes, families of Ibadan descent have been relatively well disposed to sell this land to developers anxious to build urban houses on them. Many Ijebu, with profits accruing from their other activities, have found it highly remunerative not only to buy plots of land but also to build relatively modern houses on them. The architectural design of most of the houses is that usually referred to as the 'Brazilian'. These houses have the advantage of being more or less a series of rooms opening on to a common central corridor. This interior design thus facilitates the letting out of individual rooms to tenants. In the Oke Bola and Oke Ado suburbs of Ibadan, in particular, well over 75 per cent of this type of lodging house are owned by Ijebu. Their tenants are usually young educated immigrants who have come to Ibadan from all parts of Nigeria, particularly those in salaried employment in the civil service and mercantile houses. Even among this group, people of Ijebu descent form a sizeable group, so that these two suburbs in particular have a high proportion of Ijebu people.

The Main Residential Locations

The great interest of Ijebu property investment has already given some indication of the major residential location of the Ijebu. However, Ijebu are to be found in nearly all quarters of Ibadan. Intense concentrations are found in six major areas.

First, there are the Ijebu who are either descendants or relations of some of the earliest Ijebu families in Ibadan living in Isale Ijebu quarter.

Secondly, there are those in Oke Ofa, Aremo and Labiran quarters who belong to the early Christian families of Ijebu descent in these places. Both these groups are now hardly distinguishable from the Ibadan people among whom they live, and their contacts with their Ijebu home towns remain very tenuous.

A third group, perhaps the largest, is to be found in the quarters of Gege, Agbeni, Amunigun, Oke Foko and Idikan. This is predominantly the group of small traders and craftsmen, and contains some of the first Ijebu families who came to Ibadan early in this century for the purpose of trade. They live a rather austere life, in small box-like rooms, with poor ventilation and in overcrowded and relatively insanitary conditions. They are, however, in closer touch with the indigenous Ibadan, and it is members of this group who extended their commercial interest into property estate in the Oke Bola area.

The Oke Bola and Agbokojo quarters contain the fourth group of Ijebu. Here are to be found those who earlier took to the professions or rose to some eminence in the civil service. The suburb was once relatively fashionable, but now has been invaded by traders and craft workers in particular.

The new generation of Ijebu professionals, civil servants and businessmen are thus to be found in the adjoining suburb of Oke Ado and Molete, and more recently in Mokola. Their houses are either owned by them or by some other Ijebu. Because their social and economic status tends on the whole to be higher than those of most other groups in the city, they live in relative comfort, in houses adequately equipped with modern amenities. On the whole, the average age of Ijebu in these suburbs is low, generally below 40 years and their family size is also relatively small.

Finally, Ijebu men and women are to be found in small numbers in the exclusive residential areas scattered across the western margins of the city. Such include the Jericho, the Commercial, the Link, the Agodi and the New Reservations, as well as the Universities of Ibadan and Ife (Ibadan Branch).

Social Life and Organization

In common with all trading communities, a fundamental basis of social life among the Ijebu in Ibadan is the belief that virtue exists only in hard work, and that leisure and leisure activities undermine virtuous living. For this reason, most Ijebu, almost in the seventeenth century European puritanical sense, tend to eschew indolence and opportunities of social relaxation in public places and bars.

The average Ijebu trader of either sex (and the word 'trader' covers most Ijebu except for those in professions and the civil service) wakes up early in the day, around 5 a.m. to see to his personal cleanliness and attend to his various household duties. By 7 a.m. he is on his way to his shop or to the market. There he spends most of the day, returning home only after nightfall. In some instances he lives, in fact, in his shop and therefore keeps it open till late into the night. His is a six-day week and whether he is a Christian or a Muslim he hardly ever opens his shop on Sunday. Sunday, however, is not simply the day he attends church. In many cases, it is the day he is away at his hometown from whence he returns early on Monday morning.

The daily habits of the Ijebu professionals and civil servants are hardly distinguishable from those of their colleagues in similar socio-economic classes. The working day lasts from 8 a.m. to 2 or 4 p.m. The remainder is devoted to leisure, spent in various recreational centres, or in visiting friends, or in pursuing private economic ventures.

The Ijebu in Ibadan show no overwhelming preference for any particular religion or denomination, although there may be slightly more Muslims than Christians amongst them. The Muslims may predominate among the small traders, but the Christians are undoubtedly in the majority among the civil servants and professional men. Of Christian denominations, there are indications that the Anglican, Methodist, and African Churches, in that order, account for most Ijebu of Christian persuasion. There are relatively few Ijebu Catholics and Baptists. A good number, however, belong to other Christian sects such as Jehovah's Witnesses, the Seventh Day Adventists and the Christ Apostolic Church. The share of the revivalist group of sects, such as the Seraphim and Cherubim, is difficult to assess, since they are often treated as ancillary religions by many who belong to one or another of the formal religious denominations.

Some of the more important churches in those parts of Ibadan where Ijebu predominate reflect this distribution in religious preferences. They include the St. James' Pro-Cathedral (Anglican), the Agbeni Methodist Church and the Ebenezer African Church. In all these churches, the Ijebu form a sizeable part of the congregation. Numerous small revivalist churches in shanty structures of various descriptions are also extremely common around these churches.

Social organizations among the Ijebu in Ibadan are more often on the basis of interest, occupation or religion. In each case, there is much contact with people from other ethnic groups. Thus, Ijebu are found in various sports clubs, local labour unions, market women's and traders' associations, and numerous church societies. There is, however, an Egbe Omo Ijebu embracing all Ijebu as well as numerous smaller societies of people, either from districts of the Province or from individual towns. In very few cases are these societies very active. When they do function, their major concern is with development of the home area. There is, too an Ijebu Students' Association, based on the University of Ibadan, whose main function is to find ways and means of raising funds in order to offer scholarships tenable at secondary grammar schools to deserving but indigent young boys and girls of Ijebu descent. As with the Egbe

Omo Ijebu, there are also students' associations for districts or individual towns. Their major aims and objectives are much the same as that of the overall Ijebu Students' Association, except that those likely to benefit from their activities are more narrowly defined.

The Political Role of Ijebu

In spite of their economic importance and the vigour of their social life, the Ijebu in Ibadan participate in the politics of the city to a degree far below what might be expected. This fact reflects both the nature of traditional practice in such matters, and the operation of a strong sense of social and political identification with the home towns, rather than with the city of their sojourn. Traditionally in Yoruba country, every group of immigrants to a town which forms a sizeable community is encouraged by the host town to select from among its members a local head. Such a head is accorded a chieftaincy position, and is expected to serve as spokesman for his community. Until recently, the Ijebu had a local head in Ibadan, one of whom—Pa Odunsi—at Amunigun, like a traditional quarter chief, established a market in front of his house.

To what extent the local head of the Ijebu participates in the normal running of the city is not clear. It is, however, doubtful whether his presence would be solicited when general matters not necessarily affecting his community were discussed. He is required to participate in formal and ceremonial occasions, and is often in direct touch with the Olubadan when any matter of concern to his group arises. On the other hand, any decision of the Council or Native Authority affecting his community is directed through him. For his own people, he also acts as an arbitrator of disputes.

The importance of the local leader was greatest before the Second World War, when the Ijebu community was relatively little differentiated in terms of socio-economic characteristics. Since then, the position has changed. With the increasing sophistication of the people and the modernization of institutions, the position of a local leader carries very little of its traditional importance. Although the President of the Egbe Omo Ijebu and a number of highly placed, relatively wealthy, elderly Ijebu perform between them the function of the former community leader, most of these people hold their position merely because of the esteem in which they are held rather than as a result of any formal recognition by the city authorities.

One reason why the former office of community leader is no longer important is the introduction, in 1954, of the elected local government council to manage the affairs of the city. This situation has had two effects on the level of participation of Ijebu in the local politics and administration of the city. In the first place, the introduction of the modern democratic system of election extended over the whole Region about the same time and came to involve not only local but also Regional and national politics. One of the qualifications for being eligible to stand as candidate, especially at the Regional and national level, was place of birth. As a result, many who sought a career in politics, preferred to cultivate the electorate in their home town or district, and were almost indifferent to politics in Ibadan. This class of people included most of the better educated and professional people whose chances of making worthwhile contributions to the progress of the country seemed brighter in their home town than in Ibadan, where, in any case, their number was bound to be swamped by that of native-born Ibadan.

In the second place, once there was an elected Council which could claim to rule on the basis of representing all interests, the masses of Ijebu came to realize the need to deal with their problems and complaints direct with the Council rather than through a community leader. And although representatives from city wards seldom feel or act as though they are expected to be responsible to the people, the Council's machinery of administration grinds sufficiently relentlessly for the people to be acutely aware of its existence and functioning.

Among the City councillors, who number over 60, there are about half a dozen Ijebu. They have been chosen in all cases because they were acceptable to the majority in their ward, although, in these wards, the Ijebu were not necessarily dominant. Thus these Ijebu councillors can hardly be said to be representing Ijebu interests in the council, except, perhaps, insofar as any amenities they succeed in attracting to the ward from which they come would probably benefit other Ijebu. Indeed, it is difficult today to define an Ijebu interest since Ijebu in Ibadan are now so heterogeneous in terms of their needs and expectations.

Conclusion

The Ijebu represent one of the many non-Ibadan but Yoruba communities resident in Ibadan, and were attracted there initially by the warfare of the nineteenth century, and later by the trading opportunities of the early twentieth century. Other such communities include in particular the Egba and the Ijesha. Each group has its area of relatively high residential segregation within the city, but in broad terms show characteristics not too dissimilar to those of Ijebu. As stranger communities, they would have passed through a period of acceptance as a member of a group to the present situation in which the group idea has formally dissolved in the face of modern democratic administrative processes.

Yet in spite of this, and of the obvious fact that the number of non-Ibadan of various ethnic origins is increasing daily in the city, it is doubtful whether Ibadan will soon emerge as a melting-pot in the same manner as Lagos. In the first place, Ibadan has survived from the nineteenth century as a large city in its own right. And, in spite of constant migrations to it of non-Ibadan, the Ibadan still form a majority in the city, and their representatives still dominate the affairs of the city. As long as this situation continues, it is bound to discourage other people who, though not Ibadan by origin, could have served the city more meritoriously than circumstances at present permit them to do. Meanwhile, unable to serve in the political sphere, a good number concentrate on economic, social and cultural pursuits. Whether in the church or in social clubs, in trade unions or producers' associations, many Ijebu serve their fellow Nigerians. With the native Ibadan they maintain as cordial a relationship as possible—one which matures occasionally into marriages between members of the two groups.

B. THE WESTERN IBO

by C. OKONJO

Onye moto, ilago manya Ubulu-Okiti?
Diraiva, ilago manya Ubulu-Okiti?
Onye moto, ilago manya Ubulu-Okiti?

Lorry owner, have you tasted palm wine from Ubulu-Okiti?
Driver, have you tasted palm wine from Ubulu-Okiti?
Lorry owner, have you tasted palm wine from Ubulu-Okiti?

(Lorry song of traders in Western Iboland).

Although the indigenous home and traditional heart land of the Ibo lies mainly within the forest belt to the east of the Niger valley, the Aboh Division of Delta Province and the Asaba Division of Benin Province on the west bank of the Niger are also inhabited by Ibo; these are generally referred to as the Western Ibo.[1] These two Divisions, in conjunction with other adjoining hinterland areas on the western and eastern banks of the lower Niger, were famous in the nineteenth century as part of the great palm-oil producing area of southern Nigeria.

As Dike has pointed out, the lure of the great commercial highway of the Niger valley stimulated a migration from the Benin hinterland in the seventeenth century.[2] These migrants established themselves at strategic points on the Niger Valley, where they founded city states. Thus Aboh, for example, situated at the head of the three great outlets of the Niger—the Benin, Bonny and Nun rivers—exercised what amounted to a monopoly of trade on the Niger in the first half of the nineteenth century. While the migratory movements of the Ibo from the east can be traced for the greater part to limited land resources and to population pressure on the land at the given level of technology, the annual slave raids of the Fulani cavalry in the north also gave rise to movements of people from the areas which they raided to the inaccessible forest areas in the south. This movement is exemplified by the people of Ukwu Nzu in Asaba Division, who, apart from Ibo, which they speak in common with their neighbours, also speak a form of Yoruba known as Onukwumi, and who are traditionally said to have come from the Ilorin area. The

---

[1] I wish to thank the officials of the Western Ibo Union, the various town and clan unions as well as the many individuals from the Western Ibo area who have aided me greatly in the preparation of this chapter. Special thanks are due to my wife, who helped in the difficult task of interviewing the women and in contacting informants who would otherwise have been inaccessible, and also to my colleagues, Mr. A. Imohiosen and Dr. M. Yamaguchi, who offered very valuable comments.

[2] Dike (1956), p. 25.

total area of the two Divisions which mainly make up Western Iboland is 2,068 square miles. At the 1952–53 population census it had a population of 342,000, with 212,000 in Asaba Division and 130,000 in Aboh Division. Density of population was then 175 per square mile in Asaba and 153 per square mile in Aboh Division. At the time of counting in 1952–53 there were 216 localities in the two divisions, of which 100 were in Asaba, and 116 in Aboh Division. Of the 216 localities, only 54 had a population of more than 2,000 people (34 in Asaba and 20 in Aboh Division), while only three towns, Asaba (17,837), Ogwashi-Uku (16,011) and Ibusa (12,851)—all in Asaba Division—had a population of more than 10,000.

The inhabitants of the area classify themselves into four groups— (1) Ndi Enuani: those who live on the highland adjoining the western bank of the Niger in the Ogwashi-Uku district of Asaba Division; (2) Ndi Ukwuani: those who live on the lower plains as the delta of the Niger is approached; (3) Ndosimili: those who live in the flood plains of the lower Niger commonly called Osimili and (4) Ndi Ika: the Ibo who live in the Agbor District of Asaba Division.

The Western Ibo are predominantly farmers, although fishing and trading activities are also very important as one nears the Niger Delta. Yams, cassava, cocoyams and maize are the basic subsistence crops, while the major sources of cash income, apart from the crops already mentioned, are palm oil, palm kernels, gari and fish.

In certain parts of the area social and political authority is vested in a sacred king, modelled on the pattern of Benin, who is aided in the discharge of his duties by a bureaucracy consisting of the nobles (*ndime*), the titled persons (*olinzele*), and the elders selected from, and representing the interests of, the patrilineal segments, or, in territorial terms, villages, which they head. Politics in such communities as are found in Ogwashi-Uku, resolves itself into a carefully constructed balance of power between the semi-divine head and the patrilineal segments which are theoretically autonomous in their internal affairs. In other communities like Asaba, age is a factor, but not necessarily the major factor, in determining social and political authority. As Jones has pointed out, in such places the ideology of the age organization is used to support what is in fact a federation of politically equivalent segments (villages).[1] Councillors in such a society, whilst leaders and heads of their segments, are also collectively, as elders, representatives of a vertical segmentary system which cuts across the horizontal one of the politically equal and patrilineal segments (the villages), and which divides the men

[1] Jones (1962), pp. 191–211.

of the community into a hierarchy of age, with the elders at the top. To this group of elders men of all other age grades are subordinate.

The Western Ibo also have a tradition of resistance to any encroachment upon their rights and liberties and to imposed authority. Thus, while Aboh was bombarded by the British in 1862 and again in 1883, it was not till 1896 that the king, nobles and people of Aboh signed an agreement with the Royal Niger Company. Ndosimili district itself cannot be considered as pacified until 1911 when the Abbi Rising was put down. In Ukwuani district, wars were still being waged between city states up to 1919, although effective British occupation and administration could have been said to have begun with the appointment of the first District Commissioner in 1904. In Asaba Division, even though missionary work had already started in Asaba in 1875, it was not until 1914 that the series of wars (1898, 1904, 1912–14) carried on by the Ekwumeku confederation was finally put down by the British. In fact it was only shortly before independence in 1960 that the British ban on the sale of liquor and spirits in Asaba Division was lifted. We shall see the adaptation by the Western Ibo of the social and political forms obtaining in their home societies to their new environment in Ibadan.

Habitat and Milieu

The Western Ibo have lived a corporate life in Ibadan since the early 1920s. In fact three of the oldest members of this community have lived in Ibadan continuously since 1925. The majority of the Western Ibo community, which numbers between 2,000–2,800 people, is to be found in the planned stranger settlements near the old walls of indigenous Ibadan. This is a consequence of the acceptance by the British colonial government and the Ibadan local authorities of the principle of ethnic segregation, following the beginning of the construction of the planned stranger settlement Sabon Gari in 1917 and its completion in 1920. The overcrowding of Sabon Gari, originally intended for a predominantly Hausa population, led to the development of Mokola to house Nupe and Igbirra migrants from Northern Nigeria. In the same way Ekotedo and Inalende were developed as planned settlements for Yoruba coming from outside Ibadan.

The settling of Western Ibo in Ekotedo, Mokola and Inalende in conjunction with other Nigerian ethnic groups has meant in effect that, while the migrant population has been isolated from the social life and the politics of the indigenes, the principle of ethnic segregation on which the new stranger settlements were planned has to a great extent broken down.

Ethnic mixing in a compound—defined here as a building plot with its enclosing walls—is the rule, not the exception. The small numbers of the migrants, however, and their physical separation from the indigenous town, has also meant that these 'strangers' have not taken great interest in the affairs of their hosts, and they have not overtly or otherwise attempted to influence its politics. Smaller Western Ibo groups have grown up in the newly developed areas of Ibadan such as the two Universities, and in the area between the junction of the Liberty Stadium road with the Ibadan-Abeokuta road and Moor Plantation. Relatively few members of the community live at Oke Bola and Oke Ado. Those who live there are often the better paid government and company officials and wage-earners. The distribution of members of the community outside the heart of the Ekotedo, Mokola, Inalende area tends to follow the pattern of industrial and commercial development, with people attempting to live as near as conveniently possible to their places of employment.

The appearance of the area where the Western Ibo live is in marked contrast to that of the indigenous town's irregular layout, with its traditional compounds forming nuclei. Here building plots are allocated on an approved site, while buildings are the responsibility of the owner or lease-holder of the land. The limitations of space in the building plots allocated, and the necessity of squeezing in as much built up space as possible in the plots provided, in order to enable the money invested in building to be quickly recovered, has led to most buildings being bungalows or one-storeyed houses, with rooms opening out on both sides of a long narrow central corridor. When the building is a storeyed one, a staircase is generally placed in the centre of the corridor and another at the end of the first floor corridor at the back part of the house, leading to the open space between the house and the enclosing walls of the compound. It is not unusual to find between 27 to 40 rooms being built in a plot 100 feet by 50 feet. The house is in most cases surrounded by an enclosing wall with the walls of the building forming in sections, part of it. Both cooking and toilet facilities are placed in an out-house near the wall furthest from the street. Entry into the compound is either through the main door opening into the house corridor or through a side door at the front, in the wall enclosing the compound.[1]

Bath and toilet facilities consist of one or two cubicles about three feet by nine feet for bathing, with a pit latrine. Better houses provide in their lavatories an earth closet but the problem of keeping it clean is considerable. Water closets are, as a rule, not to be found. Pit latrines are

[1] See Mabogunje above, pp. 50-51, for a further description of this type of dwelling.

easily washed once a day or every two days, with the families taking it in turns to keep the facilities clean. The kitchen is usually long and narrow with two or three small windows. Three stones placed in a triangle serve as a stove. Wood is used as fuel so that smoke fills the kitchen when food is being cooked. Young Western Ibo bachelors tend, however, to cook on spirit stoves using kerosene as fuel; in this case, cooking is either done in the house corridor or in the rooms. Conditions in such houses are necessarily overcrowded. In a house with 28 rooms for example, two of which were unoccupied at the time of the survey, there were 93 adults and children. This gave an average per occupied room of 4·4 persons. This average, however, does not fully represent the situation in some of the rooms, for five rooms were occupied by bachelors, sometimes with one or two of their friends and relatives living with them. For the three Western Ibo families living in this compound, the average density of occupation was 8 persons per room with one family being relatively 'comfortably' housed with 4 persons per room, while the worst off family had 12 persons in one room. Owing to the insufficiency of the accommodation, quite a number of the older boys and the younger men sleep at night on mats in the corridors.

The rooms of the Western Ibo, generally contain an iron or wooden bedstead with a grass-filled mattress. The better off immigrants have cotton mattresses. Boxes are placed under the bed and in one corner of the room are the pots and pans used for cooking. Where possible the pots and pans are placed in a box, usually referred to as the chopbox or cupboard. In this corner also there is a pot where drinking water is stored. The bed and the corner containing the food chest are as a rule curtained off from the rest of the room. At night mother and father retire to the bed, or, where the family is polygynous, the father and the wife favoured for the night. The others, including all the children and relatives, sleep on mats spread on the floor or in the corridor. Pillows are the exception, not the rule. The adolescent and younger men and women in the family suffer most in this type of arrangement. Becoming aware of themselves as men or women they lack the privacy which their age requires.

Rents range from £1 5s 0d per month for rooms of the poorer sort to £3 for a relatively big room in a new building. Rooms can be had, however, on the slopes of the Aremo ridge and outlying parts of Mokola, and in Sango near the railway crossing on the Ibadan-Oyo road for as little as 15s; such houses do not often have electricity. To this must be added, however, the cost of transport from these areas to the social centres of the Western Ibo. It is mainly those people who have poorly paid employment or who are trying to escape from the interference of relatives and community in their affairs who live in such outlying places. In the case of those forced by economic circumstances to live in such areas, an improvement in the economic position of such persons invariably leads to a shift from such housing to better housing in the central area.

Almost every building in the Ekotedo-Inalende heart area has its own quota of small traders, usually the wives of migrants, each selling a wide range of articles from cabin biscuits, tinned foods and all sorts of imported food-stuffs to vegetables, *egusi*, okra, salt, *agbono*, pepper, snails, beans, firewood, etc. Food is prepared all round and one can buy maize pap, *ẹkọ*, *akara*, *moi-moi*, *ẹba*, rice, *dundu*, *dodo* and other cooked foods in the alleys and lanes that criss-cross the area. The shops on the main streets—the Ibadan-Oyo, Salvation Army and Inalende roads—stock articles such as beer, mineral waters and assorted groceries. Here also are the stalls of the seamstresses who, for some ten shillings a month, give instruction in needlework, dress-cutting and sewing. Photographers' shops also abound while shops that sell records blare music continuously from morning till late at night. Two chemists' shops which serve the area are situated at the Ekotedo roundabout.

Most Western Ibo women do their daily shopping at Dugbe and Mokola markets, with the majority preferring Dugbe market. Bulk buying of food-stuffs is sometimes done at Gege market or at Oja Iba, although those who have lived some length of time in Ibadan prefer to go to the periodic markets such as Ilugun, 17 miles away from Ibadan or to Olodo, where the savings in purchases more than compensate for the time spent on the journey. For children, the race-course and the fields of the schools scattered around the area serve as much-needed playgrounds, although where homes are situated at a distance from such fields, the compound, the street or any unbuilt vacant lot serves as a field for football played here with a tennis ball in groups of two to six or seven, and for other games.

Two cinemas, the Scala at the Sabon Gari roundabout and Queens' Cinema on the Ibadan-Oyo road, serve the area, and are centres of entertainment for the younger generation of Western Ibo. Queens' Cinema specializes in Westerns and Indian films. An evening there is an experience. Each hero is greeted with loud shouts and as the film proceeds shouts of 'Giham!' rend the air, and when the hero finally succeeds in rescuing the charming heroine and killing the villain, the shouts of applause are unending. It is needless to say that in such an atmosphere nothing of the conversation of the actors can be heard. For such an audience the sub-titles too are unnecessary.

Occupations

The dominant note in the life of the Western Ibo migrant to Ibadan is the search for employment and the security of its tenure when it is found. Before the creation of the Mid-West Region in 1963, Ibadan, being the administrative centre of the Western Region, was the natural centre of attraction for anyone who desired employment in any Regional government agency. Moreover, the new commercial and industrial establishments and the educational institutions offered opportunities for employment and advancement which were not normally available in the home areas of the migrants. Furthermore, the larger commercial establishments and the workshops of successful Nigerian craftsmen have facilities for training mechanics, drivers, tailors and artisans. Apart from this, the possibilities of learning skills like typing and shorthand, sewing, bread baking and trading are greater in a large growing centre such as Ibadan than in the villages and countryside of the Mid-West.

The newly arrived migrant, either asked to come by his successful relatives, or coming on his own with the few shillings he has scraped together, arrives more often than not unannounced in Ibadan, and is accepted in the room of his relatives, who put him up until such a time as he decides to move away. One of the first things which a newly arrived migrant does is to report his presence at his village meeting and also at a meeting of his town union. Older members of the community, who have information as to where job opportunities exist, offer their advice and also inform the newly arrived as to the niceties to be observed in seeking any appointment which is open.

Employment is not obtained just by asking for it. Even when it is available and one is qualified there are formalities to be gone through—formalities which have nothing to do with registration at the labour exchange or applying for the post wanted. As a Western Ibo proverb puts it, *wa adi agba aka nkiti afu nwata eze* (one does not go empty handed to see the first teeth of a youngster). It costs about £7 to obtain a job in which earnings are £5 to £10 a month. Selection to take a test costs £2. What is important, however, is that the money being paid is passed to the right person. If the wrong persons are approached it is possible to spend £30 on trying to obtain a job without success. It is here that the experience of the members of the community who have lived in Ibadan longest is of importance. They know the proper channels, or at least they are in a position to influence those who influence those that take decisions. If the new migrant is unable, either out of his own resources or those of his relatives, to put up the money required for securing the job, an appeal is made to his town union which loans him the money. This of course must be repaid as soon as the borrower starts working.

With a job secured, the new migrant begins to think in terms of seeing the sights of the city. So far his lack of money has limited his ability to see what is going on. Here difficulties with his older relatives soon arise. It is customary at the end of the first few months of employment to hand the monthly pay packet over to the older relative who in theory has a right to retain it all for himself. Exercise of this right, however, gives rise to difficulties immediately and may lead to a quarrel which can only be settled at the level of patrilineal segment meeting, or when that fails, at the level of the town union. Usually a portion of the first earnings is sent home to the parents of the newly employed, a portion retained by the host as part payment for food, a third portion as payment for money borrowed and what is left is allocated equally between savings and pocket money.

The supervision of the personal expenditure of the newly employed migrant and guidance as to how to save, how to avoid the 'delights' of the city, very often prove irksome to the migrant, and leads to the newly employed seeking rooms of his own as soon as possible. If the new worker is married, he then sends for his wife and children. If not, after a period of enjoying himself as a bachelor, he looks to his hometown for a suitable wife. Before this he visits his home on leave in order to exhibit his newly acquired status as a wage-earner. If possible he ensures before his first leave that he has acquired one or more of the accepted status symbols— a cycle, a radio, a gramophone or record player and nowadays an electric table fan as well as the obligatory iron bedstead.

The range of occupations held by Western Ibo in Ibadan is quite wide. The community includes among its members a professor, a lecturer and an assistant registrar in the university, as well as a laboratory technician and a doctor; before the mass transfer of civil servants to the Mid-West Region, at least seven very senior administrators and professional civil servants belonged to the group. The low-income group predominates, and at this end of the scale are the labourers, stewards, a couple of thieves and 'protection' men. Earnings are quite low: the group 'Services', in Table 1, averaged £6 4s. 0d. In the 'Unclassified' group successful prostitutes made from £10 to £15 per month, less successful ones about £3 to £6. A sample survey of occupations of 128 persons taken at random from the registration lists of various town unions showed the following distribution:

Table 6B.1: Main occupational classification of a group of Western Ibo (according to the National Standard Occupational (Unit Group) Classification System)

Classification	No. in Group	Remarks
Professional, Technical and related workers	5	(Including 2 lecturers, 1 laboratory technician.)
Administrative, Executive and Managerial Workers	2	
Clerical Workers	8	
Sales Workers	4	(Including 1 sales promoter and 3 shopboys.)
Farmers, Fishermen and Forestry Workers	1	Gardener.
Transport and Communication Workers	15	(Including 8 messengers, 1 telephone operator, 1 traffic pointsman and 3 drivers.)
Craftsmen	20	(Including 11 mechanics, 2 linemen.)
Services	31	(Including 5 cooks, 2 washermen, 11 porters and cleaners, 7 gatemen and watchmen, 4 stewards and 2 policemen.)
Housewives trading	3	
Unclassified	49	(Including 17 unemployed, 24 prostitutes, 1 politician, 1 thief and 6 unknown.)
	138	

As can be seen from the table, transport and communication workers, craftsmen, service personnel and persons in the unclassified category predominate, that is to say that most of those interviewed have selected occupations which require either a minimum amount of formal education or minimum outlay in terms of monetary expenditure for training. The number of prostitutes is remarkably high. Although most unmarried or divorced women on arrival at Ibadan set up house and practise this profession, they also, however, do some petty trading to supplement their income. Housewives are not normally included in the attendance registers of town unions although prostitutes are. The three housewives, shown in Table 1 as trading, were former prostitutes who have since remarried after being successful enough to make trading their primary business.

Daily Routine

For men who have a long distance to walk to their place of employment, the day usually begins at 5 a.m. Men who start to work at 8 a.m. can afford to sleep longer as they either ride a bicycle or take a taxi to work. Water is placed in the bathroom by the wife, or if there is more than one wife, by the wife on duty for the week. A quick bath is taken.

In Christian families the children, except the very young ones, are woken up by 6 a.m., and prayers are said. After the prayers the parents are greeted. Where there is no prayer the parents are given traditional greetings as soon as the children wake up. Sometimes the housewife manages to prepare a quick breakfast, usually a plate of *ẹba* which is hurriedly eaten before the man of the house proceeds to work. Alternatively *gari* is stored in a cigarette tin or other receptacle, and some soup taken from the pot, put into a receptacle, and taken to work. Alternatively, the man might decide to buy his breakfast from any of the food sellers at his work place. When the children wake, they clean the house, sweeping the floor with brooms, and wash the plates used for supper the night before. One or two of the older children then go to the standpipes to draw water; but now that most children above the age of six go to school, water drawing is usually done in the evenings, with the many storage pots being filled then.

In the meantime the soup has been warmed; it is generally cooked in such a quantity as to last the family two, three or four days. A meal of *ẹwa* (beans) is bought, and taken either mixed with *gari*, or *gari* is drunk with the *ẹwa*. In a number of families tea is served, but this is generally for adults only. The children take maize pap, which is readily prepared from the *ogi* bought from a nearby foodseller. Beancake (*akara*) might be bought from a foodseller as an additional item for taking with the pap (*akamu*). After breakfast, the children of school age hurry off and the mother prepares to go to market or sets up her wares in front of the house. If it is a day when new soup has to be prepared, she sets off to the market quite early between 9.30 a.m. and 10 a.m. after doing some household chores.

Although prices are relatively well known there is very often tough bargaining by the housewife and the market women on halfpennies. The housewife returns from the market around noon and starts preparing the afternoon meal for the children and her husband. It is not customary to buy prepared food, although this is sometimes done in the mornings. By 3 or 4 p.m. all are back at home, and the father of the family, after having had his lunch served on a small low table, rests in a chair from the exertions of the day's work. The father eats alone, although he might invite one or two of his sons to eat with him. The wife eats separately, or with her daughter. Where there are many children, father, mother and children eat separately. A good father, on finishing his meal of foofoo (yam and *ẹba* pounded together) or boiled yams, gives each child a little portion of meat from that served to him. As soon as the father or mother finishes eating, well-mannered children greet their parents saying either 'Thank Sir' or 'Ma', as the case might be, or offer the greetings traditional in their particular hometown.

The father now takes a short rest before setting out in the evening to see his friends. The wife sits at home, unless she has important business to transact. Meanwhile the children have formed groups for their games. The compound resounds with their shouts. Cards, ludo, marbles, football, hide-and-seek are all played now, and the children fight among themselves. It is a time of strain for fathers and mothers. Commands and instructions are bawled at the children, who more often than not simply ignore their parents. They are, of course, very quick to detect from the tone of the command whether it can be safely ignored. Where it is feared that a beating might follow, they quickly come to heel.

By 6 p.m. it is time to prepare the evening meal. The older children now go to fetch water from the standpipes. From this time until about 8 p.m. is the time when the adolescents meet members of the opposite sex. Since a visit of a young boy of 13 to 18 years to a girl of the same age at their homes would be frowned upon by both the parents of the boy and the girl, they usually devise means of getting around these restrictions. One favourite method used by boys is to send a younger brother or sister who is not easily noticed by the parents of the girl, to the girl wanted, asking her to come to the standpipe. The girl then takes up a pail to fetch water, or says that she wishes to deliver a message to a friend or thinks of some other excuse to slip out of the house. Conversations and innocent flirtations then take place either at the standpipe or at a street corner where the two cannot be easily observed. Sometimes the young man arranges to whistle a particular tune when he is around.

Supper is usually between 7 and 8 p.m. and, after playing hide-and-seek or listening to folk stories, the children are in bed by 9 or 10 p.m. Studious children work at their books in the evenings, although the noise all around does not help concentration, since most neighbours leave their radios or rediffusion boxes turned on at full blast; conversation is carried on all around with people speaking at the top of their voices. Since there is little or no privacy, children, by the time they are aged sixteen, have already acquired some knowledge of sex, although they are careful not to discuss this before their elders, knowing full well that they are likely to be beaten by their parents if they show any signs of precocity.

On days when the Nestlé Company decides to advertise its products at the race-course, the whole neighbourhood is rent with cries of 'Janway' (John Wayne) shortly before 7 p.m. as the Nestlé van moves in, and all the children drop whatever they are doing, the threats of the parents notwithstanding, in order to see their beloved hero in a free open-air film show.

This is also an opportunity for the women to see films, for it is traditional for the women not to go anywhere after dark. Thus although a woman may have lived in Ibadan for over five years, she may only have been to the cinema once, as a special treat from her husband. After this, she is firmly discouraged from going to the pictures. Children who live near neighbours with television sets go to watch; the parents do not stop them, although they deplore these new-fangled devices, which they see as teaching the children to smoke, to lie and to steal. The evening is also the time to visit friends and relatives and the hours are spent drinking the palm wine which is served. By 10 or 11 p.m. on a week-day most people are in bed.

For the prostitutes the routine is of course different. They sleep in the mornings, waking near noon, and work in the evenings and nights. At week-ends, bachelors and young married men troop into the night clubs of the area at about 11 p.m. where, for prices ranging from one shilling to five, they can be accommodated by itinerant prositutes called lodgers, who come on 'tour' to Ibadan and are accommodated in rooms behind the night clubs. Rent for such lodgers is 5*s*. a night. Prostitutes resident in Ibadan generally have a steady boy friend—a bachelor or a married person whose wife has yet to wean her baby—who pays the rent of her room and gives gifts besides. Since, however, this source of income is not enough to maintain the prostitute, she usually adds to her income by receiving other clients. This is often a source of friction between the prostitute and the boy friend, although any client would acknowledge the prior rights of the boy friend. Quite often such relationships ripen, especially where the woman concerned proves to be steady, reliable and knowledgeable in monetary matters or in helping forward the career of her chosen boy friend, first into a relationship where the woman gives up her rooms to go and live with the man and later into formal marriage. For a prostitute the day usually ends at 2 or 3 a.m., when she goes home with whatever client has been secured for the night.

Town, Village and Clan Improvement Associations

Madu agbazi akali ebo?
'Can one grow greater than his clan?'
(Western Ibo saying)

The rhetorical question asked above is indicative of the central position of the town union in the affairs of the Western Ibo migrants in Ibadan.

This type of association has been ably described by Ottenberg for the Ibo from the Afikpo area.[1] As a general rule, all migrants from each locality in Western Ibo have a village, town or clan union. Where the number of migrants from a locality is too small to warrant the formation of such a union, they tend to associate themselves with the town or village union of their mother's home. Where pride or politics in the Western Ibo area do not allow of this, the migrant regards himself as a distant member of the nearest existing union of his town or village. Union rules generally make provision for the inclusion of distant members.

Town and village unions are considered to be branches of an all-Nigeria union whose headquarters is generally situated in the home town or village. Sometimes, however, where good leadership is not available at home, the headquarters of the union might be sited in a centre where vigorous leadership is available. The general aim of such unions is, to quote the rules and regulations of one town union:

(i) to work for the upliftment of the town's society, spiritually, culturally and materially and
(ii) to encourage the evolution of a new spirit of unity and co-operative effort.

The same theme of improving the home town and encouraging co-operative effort among migrants from a particular locality runs through the constitution of all the unions that we have investigated in Ibadan. Membership is mandatory for all migrants from a locality, although registration and attendance at meetings is not compulsory, especially in the larger unions, provided the member concerned pays his dues.

One meeting is held every month, and emergency meetings can be called at very short notice. Meetings usually take place in the compound where the president or the oldest member of the community, the *diokpa* (always referred to in English as the patron), lives.[2] Large unions make use of nearby schools. Meetings are usually held on Sunday afternoons and are conducted in Ibo. However, minutes are often written not in Ibo but in English. As the time for the opening of the meeting approaches,

---

[1] Ottenberg (1955).
[2] Traditionally town, village or clan union meetings have been presided over by the oldest member of the community who was referred to as the president of the union, the other offices being filled by a general consensus of opinion of members, age and achievement being the main criteria for the selection of officers. In the last twenty years there has been a change in union organization, whereby age no longer serves as a criterion for office-holding. As a consequence of this change, officers are now elected and the oldest member of the community no longer holds executive power but has become the patron of the union. Where the physical facilities permit, meetings are held in the compound where he lives.

members arrive, in twos and threes. The officers of the union—usually a president, secretary, financial secretary and treasurer—take up seats around a table facing the rest of the members. There is a provost to maintain order. Older members of the community take up the more comfortable seats, and where no seat is available a younger member rises in traditional respect and offers his seat to the older member. When the president sees that a quorum is formed he declares the meeting open by asking the oldest member of the community to pray. Kola nuts, provided by the person in whose compound the meeting is being held, are broken while wishes and prayers for the well-being of the association, the progress and welfare of the members and the home town are offered.[1] The kola nuts are then served and the meeting can proceed.

First, all new members are introduced and rigorously examined as to whether they have paid up all their dues in their former branch unions. If they have come straight from home they are registered, even though they might not have belonged to the home branch of the union. Each new member has a sponsor who gives a short background of the man being introduced, of his parents, his occupation and, where he has no work, his needs. Minutes are then read and passed as being correct, after any necessary amendment. The business of the day is then dealt with. This usually involves the settling of disputes between members, the giving and recovering of loans, information about events at home and correspondence with other branch unions, petitions for help by indigent members, and any other business which may crop up. After this the secretary reads aloud the names of members, who then pay their dues while the financial secretary records payments. At this stage fines are also paid, as well as loan repayments. After all have paid, the money is counted and the total collected is announced. The meeting is then closed with the traditional blessing, given by the oldest member present.

The union is the centre of activities for migrants from a locality. Where the number of migrants is small, men and women sit together in one meeting. Otherwise, meetings for men and married women are held

[1] The youngest member of the union takes the kola nuts on a plate to the *diokpa* who then announces: *Ibe anyi oji abiakwanu.* The ceremony then proceeds as follows: *Diokpa, wa nu:* '*Anyi ga di o*', '*Ise.*' '*Ife onye chota oga enwea.*' '*Ise.*' '*Ego, umu, ahudimma.*' '*Ise.*' '*Onye ni kwene na nke anyi ga aga, nkea ama ga.*' '*Ise.*' Translated: 'Comrades, kola nuts have been offered us.' Members then ask him to break the kola nuts. He then continues whilst breaking the nuts: 'We will live long. What we have come here to seek we will find—money, children, health. He who does not want us to progress will not himself progress.' To each of these wishes members reply with *Ise*, meaning 'so be it'. After this kola nuts are served according to age.

separately. Unmarried women sit with the men and have an equal say with men in the proceedings of a meeting. Only in a few instances have unmarried women been allowed to sit in on meetings of married women. In the few cases where this has taken place, the women concerned have been relatively highly educated and respected members of the community, holding positions like that of a secondary school teacher. Such persons often act as secretary or in another official capacity, where their knowledge could be of use to the women's wing of the branch union.

The union thus acts both as a meeting place and as a court of appeal for the immediate family circle in the case of quarrels between members. It also gives to the new migrant a sense of belonging to a community.[1] It must be remarked that very few Western Ibo migrants consider themselves in any way as being citizens of Ibadan. They may have lived for nearly forty years in Ibadan and have returned home in this length of time only once; their children may have been born and brought up in Ibadan; still the belief dies hard—they are in no way citizens of Ibadan.[2] It is extremely interesting to follow up the effects of this belief amongst second-generation Western Ibo in Ibadan. Born and bred in Ibadan, they are all bilingual, speaking Yoruba without an accent. Their playmates are Yoruba. The very young ones, in fact, after their first visit to their parents' home town come back to deride it as being backward, with no electricity and no water supplies. It is only later in life that the prejudices begin to take root. Stereotyped ideas of their hosts develop and the majority end up by marrying not one of their Yoruba playmates but rather one either from the Western Ibo group in Ibadan or from elsewhere.

The unions are seen operating most efficiently in cases where there

---

[1] Most unions have rules stipulating that members must first refer any disputes between them, which might be actionable at law, to the union for settlement. Permission is rarely granted for cases between members to go to the law courts. Unions adjudicate, for example, in cases of fighting, disrespect and insult shown to an elder by a younger, infringement of marital rights, rivalry in a place of employment, family disputes, suspected spell-casting, poisoning or witchcraft.

[2] This does not imply a total rejection of a sense of belonging to Ibadan in all social sectors, but rather in a majority of sectors. There are in fact cases of partial rejection in a sector. In the religious sector of Western Ibo society, for example, while Anglican Protestants belong to the Ibo Anglican Church in Ibadan they feel that they also belong to the Diocese of the Niger, not to the Ibadan Diocese; Western Ibo Catholics, on the other hand, feel that they are a part of the Ibadan Catholic community. The same holds true for the other splinter Christian sects—there is an Ibadan community spirit. It is interesting in this connexion to note the behaviour of traditional religionists when questioned as to their religion. Quite a number do not acknowledge their religion on first inquiry but give themselves out as Christians. Closer questioning then elicits the fact that they are not Christians. No Muslim was discovered in the sample of migrants interviewed.

is an emergency—a need to collect money for an approved project or for a funeral or a feast. We will take the case of collection of money for an approved project first, dealing with the case of funerals under the Western Ibo Union. Worthy projects are generally approved in the annual general meetings of all branch unions held in the home town or village, to which the branch union sends one or more delegates. Such projects are usually construction projects—the building of a school or hospital—or a land case. A flat levy for all persons from the town living anywhere in Nigeria is made. The rates for married women are lower than that of men and unmarried women. Groups to collect these levies are formed, and authorized by the union to use whatever force is necessary and sufficient to collect the dues.

Most people on being visited pay up their levy immediately, or borrow money to pay up at once, for the penalties for not paying are great. Any durable goods in the defaulter's rooms can be seized, only to be redeemed later by a payment much higher than the original levy. If the defaulter attempts to resist the removal of his property, he might be beaten up by the collectors. Attempts to report such fights to the police invariably end in the case not being taken up, since the police are loath to take up what they consider are family quarrels. If the police are, however, 'misguided' enough to take up such a case, and members of the union are fined in a court for what has happened, the defaulter will be promply excommunicated from his union. Letters are written about the incident to the traditional authorities at home and to all branch unions, and the defaulter is boycotted by every member of his town. Very few people ever allow matters to reach such a stage. In fact, if the defaulter is prepared to do this, his immediate relatives will pay his levy and fine for him and any other expenses to which the union has been put. For should any disaster befall the individual during the period of his excommunication, no one would come to his aid.

Feasts are another occasion for active participation in union affairs. Everyone enjoys a feast and all strive to be present. Procedure is similar to a normal meeting with the feast being the only business transacted. As the festivities warm up, palm wine is served, and singing and dancing commence. There is a stock of songs for such occasions, although special ones might be composed for the feast. Two songs deserve mention. The first runs:

> *Onye nyem na onu*
> *Onye nyem o*
> *Onye nyem na onu*
> *Onye nyem o*

Refrain: *Nnemu nyem na onu*
           Nnemu nyem o
           Nnemu nyem na onu
           Nnem nyem o.[1]

The other song is used to attack people who are felt to be mean and do not entertain their townsmen in the right manner when visited. It runs as follows:

           Onye na ala manya ma odi enuta.

Refrain: *Ola manya ma onuo*
           Ola manya ma onuo
           Ola manya ma onuo.[2]

In the next stanza the name of the person being attacked is substituted for '*Onye*' in the first line.

The Western Ibo Union

All town unions are members of, and send delegates to, the Western Ibo Union in Ibadan. This Union, which is a member organization of the Ibo State Union, meets once every month. The purpose of the Union, which according to its constitution is a cultural organization, is to cater for the unity and welfare of the Western Ibo in Ibadan. It also expects to co-operate with any other Western Ibo Unions outside Ibadan. However, although there is a Western Ibo Union in every major town in Nigeria, there is no central Western Ibo organization comparable to the Ibo State Union for all Ibo in Nigeria.

Representatives for two categories of members are admitted to the proceedings of the Union—(1) representatives of town unions and (2) representatives of clan unions. Individual membership is not allowed, although the Union is prepared to consider individual membership where the members of a clan or town are few. Representation is on a basis of 1 representative for not more than 10 members, 2 representatives for not more than 25, 3 representatives for not more than 50 and 4 representatives for 51 members or more for town unions. The scale is slightly different for clan unions, the representatives being 2 for 15 and below, 3 for 16–30, 4 for 31–60 and 5 for 61 members or more. Dues are also paid per representative, the fee being one shilling per

---

[1] Who was it who fed me? Who was it? Who was it who fed me? Who was it?
It was my mother who fed me. It was my mother. It was my mother who fed me. It was my mother.
[2] Who is it that drinks palm wine without ever buying?
The drinker who never buys. The drinker who never buys. The drinker who never buys.

delegate per month. There are the usual officers elected from among the delegates, and a patron, who is the oldest Western Ibo in Ibadan. A meeting is held every second Saturday of the month at 4 p.m., at the patron's residence.

The Union has had a long and chequered history, having often become defunct owing to embezzlement of funds or owing to difficulties arising between member unions because of differences between their respective home towns or villages. Often, too, the lack of a general cause for which to fight has consistently weakened the union, since most Western Ibo consider their individual interests best served by their town unions. The Western Ibo Union has lately been very active in the propagation of the idea of a Mid-West State, and it has spent a considerable amount of money sending delegates to accompany Western Ibo politicians touring the Mid-West, in order to explain the necessity of voting solidly for the creation of a Mid-West State. Western Ibo land has been a traditional National Convention of Nigerian Citizens area, and most of the élite feel, justly or unjustly, that as a result of their political alignment, they had not, in the former Western Region, received their fair share of amenities.

The Union organizes, in co-operation with town and clan unions, traditional Western Ibo dance groups as well as plays. It also offers a platform for the organization of receptions for sons and daughters from the area whose service has been of general benefit to the whole area. One of its main activities is, however, a social and emotional one—assisting town and clan unions or individual families at burials. Although the responsibility for burying any individual is that of the town and clan unions, the Western Ibo Union accepts responsibility for burials where the numerical strength of a town or clan union is small. On the death of any Western Ibo, a report is first made to the officers and oldest member of the town or clan union. These in turn report the event to the officers of the Western Ibo Union, who in turn inform the patron of the Western Ibo Union (i.e. the oldest Western Ibo male in Ibadan) and all other unions and acknowledged elders of the Western Ibo community. The town or clan reporting the death of one of its members receives a gift of £1 10s. at once from the Western Ibo Union

Between 5 and 7 p.m. as news of the death spreads, all members of the community congregate in the premises of the deceased to hold a wake. It is the responsibility of the town or clan union to provide preliminary entertainment in the form of a large calabash of palm wine and kola nuts. Meanwhile the town union has also to make arrangements to buy the planks with which the coffin will be made. The Western Ibo

Union has special carpenters, themselves Western Ibo, who are responsible for making coffins for the community. These carpenters are exempted from all dues which all Western Ibo have to pay on such occasions. Everyone who comes to the wake-keeping ceremony must pay at least one shilling. Condolences are offered to the relatives of the deceased. After as much money as it is immediately possible to collect has been obtained, the amount collected is checked. Out of this money the following sums for expenses incurred are deducted and paid to the town or clan union—£4 10s. for the coffin, 15s. for the burial plot, 2s. as a tip for the gateman of the cemetery, 2s. for nails and varnish for the coffin. The town or clan union is expected to provide the cloth with which the deceased will be wrapped when he is placed in the coffin.

After these expenses have been deducted, a sum of £1 10s. to £2 is handed over to the wife of the deceased (where the deceased is a man) to enable her to live before she returns to her home town. Whatever is left is handed over to the town or clan union. From this point the town or clan union takes over. Where the deceased is a man, members of the town union are appointed to check and make an inventory of his property. This can be a harrowing experience for the wife of the deceased, especially when it is suspected that the wife in one way or the other has been responsible for the husband's death.[1] Even pencil stubs are noted down in this inventory. One list is handed over to the wife, one is kept by the Union and a third list forwarded by registered post to the deceased's patrilineal relatives at home. Arrangements are made to transport the wife, her children and the belongings of the family back home. The money given for transport varies from union to union, but generally a sum of ten pounds is allocated for this. Where it is the wish of the family that the deceased should be transported home, the cost of such an arrangement is the responsibility of the family concerned.

Conclusion

The examination of the social life of migrants of Western Ibo origin in Ibadan shows the central role played by relatives, town, village and clan unions and associations in the socialization process of the migrant in his new environment. While the immediate kin provide the new migrant with a home and help him in the all important search for employment, the union acts as a source of security and provides collective insurance against natural and other types of disaster for migrants. The union also helps the migrant, as Ottenberg has pointed out in the case of the Afikpo Ibo, to sustain his identification as a Western Ibo and

[1] For example, in cases where witchcraft or infidelity is suspected.

as a member of his town, village and clan, acting as a channel through which contacts with home are maintained and perpetuating the various dialects, the family, kinship and lineage structure and other aspects of traditional culture.[1]

The security, protection and sense of belonging offered by kin and clan, by the town or village union in the new environment is, however, bought at the price of ingroup conformity, which tends to perpetuate certain aspects of traditional culture such as dances, the use of the vernacular language and adherence to customary ideals of social morality and discipline.[2] Thus ingroup conformity tends to limit social contact and interaction between migrants and indigenes to work-place relations, market transactions and religious activities. Moreover, although further research needs to be done into this, the degree of uniformity as well as of ingroup conformity shown in the pattern of social and other activities of migrants from different parts of Ibadan do not lend support to Park's thesis of ecological determinism in urban areas, which would lead us to expect that the particular characteristics of specific areas of Ibadan would impose themselves on migrants residing in those areas.

Finally, while first-generation Western Ibo have tended to ignore the conventions and social systems of their host town, the bilingual second generation, although still maintaining a consciousness of belonging elsewhere, is more adapted to respond to changes in the social environment in Ibadan.[3] Nevertheless, the Western Ibo have not just remained a passive element in Ibadan society. Their activities, even their very presence, helps and abets the development of new socio-cultural forms in Ibadan society.

[1] Ottenberg (1955), p. 26.
[2] Coleman (1952), p. 2.
[3] Skinner (1963).

C. THE HAUSA

by A. COHEN

Of all the native strangers in Ibadan to-day, the Hausa stand out as the most exclusive, sharply delineated ethnic group, even though they were among the first of the stranger migrants to settle in this city.[1] The Hausa of Ibadan remain distinct in their dress, food and customs, and continue to speak their own language even in their dealings with other ethnic groups. They number about 6,500, of whom nearly 5,000 are concentrated in the Hausa quarter, known as Sabo, short for *Sabon Gari*, which is the centre of their economic, social and cultural life. They pay allegiance to a Hausa chief, the *Sarkin Hausawa*, who mediates between them and the local authorities, acts as arbitrator in disputes within the quarter and appoints men to various titled positions to regulate the general affairs of the community.

The Hausa interact with the Yoruba only in the market place, as they do not intermarry or spend their leisure time with members of the host community. Although Ibadan is predominantly Islamic, the Hausa constitute a separate ritual community, centred around the central mosque of Sabo and led by their own Chief Imam.

One of the most interesting sociological features of Hausa cultural exclusiveness in Ibadan is that it has deepened with time. During the early decades of their migration, the Hausa were in many respects more integrated within the Yoruba city than they are today.

One explanation which is often offered for this ethnic exclusiveness is that it is the product of external pressure from the host society, and of the policy of the British Administration of rule through Native Authorities. It is true that during the first few decades of their migration to Ibadan the Hausa were subject to pressure and to official discrimination. In 1906 the Bale in Council resolved that, in view of recent waves of burglaries which swept Ibadan and for which Hausa strangers were thought to be responsible, all the Hausa had to be under the control of 'an approved Headman of their race' who would be held responsible for his people in different parts of the city. In 1907 the Bale informed the Council that it was the wish of the Yoruba chiefs that the Hausa strangers should be forced to live in a special settlement which would be allotted

---

[1] The field work on which this paper is based was carried out between September 1962 and November 1963. I am grateful to the School of Oriental and African Studies, University of London, for financing it and to the Nigerian Institute of Social and Economic Research and to the University of Ibadan for their great help to me in carrying it out.

to them, and that they should be confined within that settlement from sunset to dawn and that any of them found outside the settlement during the night would be liable to imprisonment or banishment. The Administration tried only to tone down the harshness and excesses of these pronouncements, but fully supported the planning and final establishment of the present Hausa Quarter.

The Development of Sabo

Settlement in the quarter began early in 1916 and in December that year the names of 400 Hausa, who had already settled in it, were listed. The names of 40 other Hausa, said to have been still living with Yoruba in the centre of the city, were also listed and the Bale in Council were urged by the Administration to speed up their removal to Sabo. A few years later the confinement of the Hausa within the quarter was so complete that there was a complaint that one Hausa stranger had still been living outside Sabo.

Thus, the segregation of the Hausa was an official policy which was pursued down to the early 1950s. The Hausa were always regarded as strangers and, in 1941, the city's Yoruba chiefs felt that the Hausa strangers should be made to realize that, however long they might remain in Ibadan, they would always be regarded as outsiders and that under no circumstances would they be allowed to have the same political status as that enjoyed by the indigenous population.

But this policy cannot explain the phenomenon of Hausa ethnic exclusiveness. In practice the city's authorities were not always strict or consistent in enforcing their policy of ethnic segregation. Even in the heyday of Native Authority rule the Hausa could not be forced to live within Sabo, though indirect pressure was often applied to induce them to do so. Since the early 1930s individual Hausa have always managed to live in town when they have chosen to do so, and at no time did the authorities actually impose any kind of curfew on the Hausa. The authorities also failed to prevent Yoruba from living within the Hausa quarter though, in this case again, indirect pressure was exerted in order to discourage them from doing so, and until to-day their number is insignificant.

The high degree of Hausa separatism which has, nevertheless, developed is to a great extent due to the Hausa's own choice and efforts.

There are no records which describe Hausa reaction to the establishment of the quarter in 1916, but in 1963 the unanimously accepted myth in Sabo was that the quarter had been originally established as a result of the Hausa's own desire to live together. 'Our customs are different'—is their usual explanation.

There is a wealth of evidence dating from the early 1920s down to the present day which shows that the Hausa not only agreed willingly to live within Sabo but that they have always been struggling to maintain the quarter's existence and to prevent any tampering with its identity. During the 1930s and the 1940s the Hausa of the quarter wrote numerous petitions asking the city's authorities to force the Hausa 'floating population' who lived in the centre of Ibadan to move to the quarter, even though Sabo had already become very crowded. Today one of the Hausa's deepest anxieties is that, because of congestion, the local authorities may decide to 'scrap' the quarter.

Thus, external pressure alone cannot account for Hausa exclusiveness. An alternative explanation of this exclusiveness which is sometimes offered is that, on the individual level, the Hausa are temporary residents in Ibadan and that therefore it is only natural that they should cling to their native customs and resist any assimilation.

Its People

Of the 5,000 Hausa of Sabo, 4,184 are 'permanent settlers'. Of these permanent settlers, 1,570 are Ibadan born but are mainly young people. Of the remaining 2,614 people, 2,334 (89·3 per cent) came to settle in Ibadan during the past 20 years while only 280 (10·7 per cent) had settled before 1943.

These figures reflect only one aspect of the mobility of the population of Sabo, as it covers the incoming migrants who were still living in the quarter at the time when the census was taken in 1963. The figures do not show how many of the migrants who had lived in Sabo during the past 47 years had eventually returned to their homeland in the north, or drifted to join other Hausa communities in southern Nigeria or in other countries in West Africa, though it is a well-established fact that the total number of Hausa settling in Ibadan has been steadily increasing all the time, which means that more migrants have been settling in the city than those leaving it.

Hausa population mobility is not confined to changing residence between Sabo and the north. Even those migrants ostensibly permanently settled in Ibadan are often on the move. Many men move periodically in the course of carrying on their business. Thus, a kola agent moves very frequently between Ibadan and other areas in the Western Region in search of kola supplies, and he also moves, though less frequently, between Ibadan and the north to contact local dealers. Many Hausa occupations involve similar kinds of mobility.

Men and women also travel to fulfil kinship obligations which in most cases involve an absence of a few weeks in every year. The social milieu of a Hausa man in Sabo is geographically extended over a wide area and in different directions. He often has his paternal relatives in one place, his maternal ones in another and his affines in a third. Some polygynous men have wives and children in both Ibadan and in the north. Others leave their wives and children in their native towns and villages and stay on their own in Ibadan, paying frequent visits to their families.

Closely interconnected with this mobility and scattering of relations are such traditional Hausa cultural features as bilateral kinship organization, where genealogical depth on either side is negligible, a widely applied system of classificatory kinship terminology, a wide-spread practice of child fostering, an unstable marriage pattern, institutionalized prostitution and a general absence of stable corporate political groupings.

Using a number of criteria which tend to overlap in this community the Hausa of Sabo can be sociologically classified into three categories. The first, which can be called 'The Permanent Core' consists of old settlers who have their families with them, regard themselves as permanent settlers, are usually house owners and are mostly engaged in occupations which require long experience in local affairs and wide connections in both the quarter and the city.

The second category, 'The New Migrants', consists of relatively recent migrants who are mostly males, many of whom are either unmarried or have their wives back in their native settlements in the north. They usually lack both the experience and the capital to engage in business on their own, though many of them work as itinerant traders with a very small capital. They are mostly accommodated in rented rooms, with two or more men sharing the same room. In most cases they are uncertain as to whether they will settle all their life in Ibadan, return to the north, or migrate to other parts of the Hausa diaspora.

A third category, 'The Transient Population', consists of people who come to stay in the quarter temporarily, some for a few days, some for a few weeks and others for a few months. Among them are some labourers who come from the north during the dry season for work in the Ibadan area. Some are northern dealers who come to Sabo to have goods sold or bought for them in the city. Others are visitors who come to stay with their kin in the quarter for some time. Many of them are accommodated in the scores of 'houses for strangers' which are run by people from the Permanent Core, and others stay with friends or simply sleep in verandahs and parlours. Their number fluctuates from season to season, but there is hardly a day when they do not number a few hundreds. Although the individuals change all the time, the category as a whole is a permanent part of Sabo social structure.

Thus, Sabo society is characterized by a high degree of population mobility and this is certainly *one* factor behind Hausa separatism in Ibadan. But it is by no means the most important factor. In fact traditional Hausa institutions and the politics of exclusiveness are maintained and kept alive, not by recent migrants or by the more mobile sections of the population, but by the 'Permanent Core', many of whom have been in Ibadan for two or even three generations.

The Economy of Sabo

Hausa separativeness in Ibadan is essentially based on specialized Hausa economic enterprise and not merely on tribal sentiments or traditions. In other words, the Hausa of Sabo are engaged in such occupations that, under the prevailing conditions, only Hausa can perform economically and efficiently.

The economy of Sabo is organized on the basis of what may be called 'The Landlord System of Business'. The word 'landlord' is a literal translation of the Hausa term *mai gida* which refers, among other things, to the head of a business house. The landlord plays several economic roles. He is a hotelier who runs houses for the accommodation of Hausa dealers from the north or from other parts of the Hausa diaspora. He is a chief middleman who brings Hausa dealers into contact with local Yoruba dealers and for this purpose he has under him several brokers to whom he pays part of the commission. He is also an insurer, or risktaker, as he guarantees that credit given or obtained in the transactions concluded through his house will eventually be honoured.

Sabo is dominated by about 30 landlords, each of whom is the head of what may be called 'a house of power'. Between them they control a large proportion of employment in the quarter's economy and, what is even more important, of housing, which is one of the most fundamental capital assets in Sabo. Houses are power in the quarter and men have been quarrelling over them ever since the quarter was founded. A man needs housing *in the quarter* to secure membership of the community, to establish himself in business, to gather clients around him, to enlarge his family by marrying more wives, to foster the sons and daughters of his kin and to accommodate malams (<*Alim*) whose services in the mystical world are indispensable to his success. There is now an acute shortage of space in Sabo, which has become increasingly more congested since the 1920s. When the quarter was founded, the land was distributed in equal plots among the original settlers, but since then many changes in the distribution and ownership of the houses and the plots have taken place. A great proportion of the houses are now concentrated in the hands of the landlords.

Command over housing is in no small measure command over economic and political power. Between them, the landlords run about 50 houses for the accommodation of strangers. Most of the landlords do not take rent from the tenants who live in their houses and who thus automatically become their clients. The basic principle of political grouping within Sabo is the patron-client relationship which is essentially dyadic, holding between the patron and each client separately without leading to the formation of corporate groups. A man's clients are his employees, attendants and tenants, all of whom are described as his 'servants'. Clients sometimes change house, i.e. change their allegiance from one landlord to another, which usually means literally moving from one house to another. Generally speaking, while the landlords and their principal assistants are from the 'Permanent Core', the clients are mostly 'New Migrants'. By virtue of their long residence in Ibadan and of their business as middlemen, the landlords have developed important connections with various sources of power and authority among the Yoruba, and have thus been in a position to serve as mediators between their clients and these sources, and this has added more to their control over their clients. Through their manifold activities, the landlords maintain Sabo institutions and make it possible for other Hausa to be mobile.

The point which I want to stress is that Sabo is organized on economic bases and that we have in this situation a different type of tribalism to that reported in social anthropological literature for Central African towns.[1] The Hausa of Sabo are associated together on the basis of mutual economic interests and not merely on that of cultural affinity. Above all, the quarter is the means of their livelihood. To the landlords, Sabo represents a vast economic establishment in which they have fundamental vested interests. Also, to fulfill their tasks as middlemen between Yoruba and northern Hausa dealers, the landlords and their assistants have to emphasize their Hausa identity. Under the prevailing economic and social conditions in Nigeria, a Hausa dealer from the north will

---

[1] See Epstein (1958), Gluckman (1961) and Mitchell (1960).

entrust his business in Ibadan only to a *Hausa* middleman who is acquainted with local business conditions.[1]

Hausa norms and values in the quarter are kept alive by a relatively large number of malams who teach, preach, give advice, lead in prayers, divinate and officiate in ceremonies of birth, circumcision, marriage and death.[2] In Sabo belief there seems to be no limits to the mystical powers of the malams and there are countless stories current in the quarter to prove their exploits in effecting dramatic changes in individual fortunes and in inter-personal relations.

Because of many subversive factors inherent in their position, the landlords continually try to attract to their service powerful malams, by offering these free housing, gifts, wives, income and facilities for teaching. In this way every landlord has come to patronize at least one important malam to whom he entrusts all of his problems. A landlord will not embark on any economic or political enterprise before hearing the results of the divination of his malams. Malams are powerful in Sabo society.

Thus in Sabo a most intimate association has developed between landlords and the leading malams. But this does not mean that the malams' main function is to provide support to the position of the landlords, even if in fact they are financially supported by the landlords. The malams exist as a group in their own right. They have their own circles, interest, deliberations and discussions. The junior among them learn under the senior. The malams also travel frequently to visit important malams or shaikhs in different centres of the Hausa diaspora or in the north, in order to get new religious instructions and more learning. Through these contacts among themselves, through continuous learning and discussion, through travel and experience of social conditions in different Hausa communities, the malams develop their own opinion and their own stand on the different current issues relating to the general well-being of the community. Such opinion always finds its way to the attention of the landlords in the course of personal consultation, divination sessions and advice.

Politics and Ethnic Exclusiveness

The ethnic identity of Sabo was endangered when the early 1950s ushered in political processes which eventually led to a decline in the importance of native authority rule and the rise of Nigerian federal

[1] For a more detailed account of the role of the Sabo landlords in the cattle and kola trade, see Cohen (1965, 1966).
[2] In a survey which I carried out in the quarter, there were 119 malams, in a working male population of 1,984.

politics. To-day the Hausa refer to those years as 'the time when politics came' (*locacinda siasa ta zo*)—a phrase which recurs in almost every conversation on the economy or politics of the quarter. Federal politics brought into being political parties which were in principle national, not tribal, and the subsequent elections, as well as the reorganization of the administration, effected some shift of power from the traditional chiefs to a new nationalistic, western-oriented, élite.

Each of the three major political parties of the Federation established branches in Sabo and went into full political activity to win support among its inhabitants. According to the 1952 census there were in the Western Region nearly 41,000 Hausa, and even then it was realized that the actual number was far higher. The two southern parties, the National Council of Nigeria and the Cameroons and the Action Group hoped that, through their activities in Sabo, they would also influence the opinion, not only of the rest of the Hausa communities in the Western Region, but also the masses of population of the Northern Region. These parties condemned tribalism and declared on different occasions that Sabo men would no longer be treated as 'strangers' but as equal citizens.

This meant that the territorial and ethnic principles of Hausa autonomy in the city were no longer officially recognized and in 1952 it was declared that the Ibadan local authorities would no longer support 'tribal areas', that therefore those authorities would give no more land to extend Sabo and that any Hausa individual requiring land should make his own arrangements with Ibadan landowners.

By this time the city of Ibadan had grown immensely and its built-up area had crept northwards, outflanking Sabo, which had thus been turned from a well-circumscribed village to an indistinctly defined quarter within the massive city. At the same time Sabo had become more congested than ever before, and some Hausa had to seek space in the peripheral areas of Mokola and Ekotedo. A few hundreds who are engaged in the kola trade moved towards the centre of the city and secured accommodation as tenants in Yoruba-owned houses.

Another source of danger to Hausa identity in Ibadan was the rapid growth of Yoruba Islam. When Sabo was founded, about half a century earlier, the number of Yoruba Muslims in Ibadan was insignificant. In fact the Hausa themselves had played a crucial role in the spread of Islam in the city, and Yoruba Muslims had always looked up to the Hausa as superior and more enlightened Muslims and many of them used to visit the quarter for Hausa ritual help. But soon Yoruba Ibadan became predominantly Islamic and Yoruba Islam became efficiently organized. Islamic learning and education in the city made significant progress. Thus, the Hausa were soon swallowed by the masses of Yoruba Muslims and no longer occupied a distinct religious status.

These developments constituted a direct threat to Sabo exclusiveness, and hence to Sabo economic specialization. The position of the landlords became vulnerable as Yoruba business entrepreneurs began to challenge Hausa monopoly of mediation between northern and local dealers. Another challenge in this respect came also from the competition of some of the Hausa who lived in the centre of the city, far from the moral constraints of Sabo. Plans to remove the quarter had already existed for a very long time, and the landlords became more afraid than ever before that Sabo might be 'liquidated'. The new political developments affected also the internal structure of the quarter itself, by weakening the position of the chieftaincy and the political authority of the landlords. Some of the tasks of mediation between the people of Sabo and the authorities shifted from the hands of the Chief and of the landlords to the hands of the secretaries of the Sabo branches of the parties in power.

Islam in Sabo

It was during this period of increasing threat to the quarter's autonomy and to Hausa exclusiveness in the city that fundamental changes in Sabo religion took place. The overwhelming majority of the quarter joined the Tidjāniyya Order, after an important shaikh of that Order had visited Sabo in 1950 and appointed local ritual masters, known as *mukaddam*. Sabo had known about the Order long before that time through the frequent visits of Tidjāniyya emissaries and continuous contacts with those parts of Northern Nigeria where it was dominant. But it had not gained a foothold in the quarter. It is therefore sociologically significant that a visit of a shaikh should have been followed by the massive affiliation into the Order.

The Tidjāniyya greatly intensified ritual life in Sabo as, apart from the ordinary five daily prayers it added two daily rites, the morning *wird* and the evening *wazifa*, and one long rite, the *dhikr*, on Friday afternoon. To-day, the average Hausa spends about an hour and twenty minutes on ritual every weekday and about three hours every Friday. More important than that, the Order localized ritual within the quarter. Ordinary Islam is universalistic and a man can perform his daily prayers anywhere he chooses, on his own or with others. But a Tidjāni initiate must have at least the evening prayer and the evening ritual duty (the *wazifa*) under his own Tidjāni leader, the *mukaddam*, from whom he gets his instructions, unless of course he happens to be travelling. Thus, one of the most impressive scenes an observer can witness in Sabo is the massive gatherings of all the men at sunset in groups which fill every yard or verandah to perform that ritual. Even the mid-day prayer on weekdays is attended by large gatherings of men, some of whom halt their business in the centre of the city and make a two or three mile journey to the quarter for that purpose.

The Tidjāniyya has also made Sabo ritual collective. Under the guidance of their *mukaddam*, the ritual group induce themselves into an ecstasy of communion with Allah and men behave as if they are unaware of their individual existence. The nature of the ritual itself conduces to such collectivism, as it consists mainly in the loud choral recitation of certain phrases and passages, each of which is repeated a prescribed number of times, the counting being done with the help of a long rosary which is a constant companion of every Hausa man. Some of the phrases and passages are repeated hundreds of times in the usual daily ritual.

In 1952 Sabo achieved a ritual autonomy for the quarter by finally deciding to hold their Friday mid-day prayer in the central mosque of the quarter, under the quarter's Chief and the Chief Imam. This came after a long and very bitter struggle against sustained opposition from the Ibadan Yoruba Chief Imamate.

The Friday mid-day prayer has always been of great political significance in the history of Islamic communities. According to Maliki tradition, to which West African Islam generally subscribes, the prayer should be attended, *in one central mosque*, by all the Muslims living in a town, led by their political ruler and conducted by the Chief Imam. In this prayer, apart from the ordinary ritual, a sermon is given by the Imam, in which a special blessing is said for the ruler, for the ritual community and for the whole community of Islam. Muslims in one town should have only one central mosque and if more than one existed then this is certainly a sign of cleavage within the community. It has been reported for both West and East Africa that tribal cleavages in the towns often expressed themselves in the building of rival secessionist Friday mosques, and Proudfoot writes that in Freetown even the ethnic groups among which Islam is not predominant now aim at having their own mosques.[1]

Another dramatic change occurred in Sabo during this period when in the course of a few years all the landlords, including the Chief of the quarter, went on pilgrimage to Mecca and returned with the title *Hādjdji*

[1] Proudfoot (1959).

attached to their names for life. At the beginning of the 1950s only six Sabo men had performed the pilgrimage, but by the end of the decade the number rose to 45. The movement started in 1955 when the Chief decided to go on the pilgrimage, taking with him, at his own expense, two of the most important malams of Sabo, one of them the Chief Imam of the quarter. During the years 1959–60 alone, 28 went on pilgrimage. During this short period eight of the malams became *Ḥādjdji*, all except one, at the expense of one or another of the landlords. The pilgrimage came to serve as a symbol of the change in the nature of political authority within the quarter. Today Sabo is led by the *Ḥādjdji* and when the Chief wants to confer over a communal affair he simply asks his messengers to 'call the *Ḥādjdji*'.

It is not possible in this short chapter to discuss in detail these changes in Sabo religious life. But it is sufficient to point out that one aspect of these changes is that they tend to re-emphasize Sabo identity and Sabo separateness from the rest of the city and thus to consolidate Hausa exclusiveness and, indirectly, Hausa economic specialization.

7
THE ÉLITE

by P. C. LLOYD

Traditional Ibadan is centred on Mapo hill. Within a mile and a half of the doric columned city hall lie most of the compounds of the Ibadan people—a densely packed agglomeration of small houses. In a large crescent to the west live the strangers. The more humble—the Yoruba of Inalende and Oke Padre, the Ibo of Ekotedo, the Hausa of Sabo—live in quarters adjoining the old town and within its walls. Outside in their numerous suburbia—the government residential areas, the University campuses—live the élite. The focus of their life is Kingsway Stores.

The growth of Kingsway into the modern four-storey, airconditioned emporium, opened on the second anniversary of national Independence, symbolizes the development of the élite. A decade and a half ago, Kingsway—the retail store of the United Africa Company—was housed in a shed-like building; it had one long counter; staples, such as potatoes, sugar, flour, were frequently out of stock; luxury goods were not stocked—one went to the Lagos Kingsway for these. The other expatriate firms had their own retail grocery departments only marginally different from one another; the French stores sold better wines. In the early 1950s many of these shops closed, squeezed between the competition of their more luxurious Lagos branches and the demand that retailing of standard articles should be left to Nigerian businessmen and women. The firms turned more to wholesaling. Then, suddenly, the tide turned. Supermarkets were opened; the Lebanese no longer confined themselves to retailing cloth, but turned to groceries and electrical equipment; even fashionable dress shops appeared in Lebanon Street. Finally Kingsway, which had been quietly expanding throughout the decade, opened its new stores.

The rapid growth of the élite thus dates from the mid-1950s. Although the Nigerianization of the bureaucracies proceeded quickly, the number of non-Africans also increased. As the expatriate administrative officers left, the technicians and advisers arrived. The University staff increased —Ibadan University, with its two hundred and fifty expatriate staff, is the largest single employer of non-Africans in Ibadan. The Americans have sent A.I.D. teams and the Peace Corps. There are probably seven hundred and fifty non-Nigerian families in Ibadan today. They are a cosmopolitan collection of people. The British still predominate, but the University campuses include Indians, Japanese and Sudanese; the American contingents contain a substantial proportion of Negroes. Few of these men envisage a career in Nigeria; most anticipate a stay of five years or less. The turn-over is rapid. Unlike their predecessors of the colonial service, the present expatriates bring their wives and families with them; the English prefer to send their children home for secondary education —the American parents to keep them with them. Schools, set up to cater for these young people, have attracted too the children of the Nigerian élite. Again, the salaries of the non-Nigerians are high, both absolutely, and relatively, when compared with those of the earlier colonial civil servants. Life in Ibadan is conspicuously ostentatious in comparison with the modest, if picturesque, life on a provincial or divisional government station between the wars.

This chapter will deal, however, not with the non-African élite but with the Nigerians who, through their attainment of appropriate educational qualifications have replaced the expatriates and occupied the many new posts, and who have adopted a style of life substantially European in its external appearances.

The Élite Defined

Styles of living, incomes and occupations are not susceptible to division into neat and clearly separate categories. But when a Nigerian describes a man as 'senior service' he implies not only a bureaucratic post, a well-furnished house but also a car. The possession of a car sharply divides those who are able to live in the suburban residential areas from those who must live in the crowded town; it distinguishes those who may visit widely separated friends from those who cannot. In government service one is eligible for a loan to buy a car and a monthly allowance to run it when one reaches a salary of about £600. This is thus the major income divide between the élite and the masses. In the former category fall the administrators, usually with university degrees, and the higher ranks of executive and technical cadres.

The Western Nigeria government is the largest employer of high-income Nigerians. Currently (late 1963) it has working in Ibadan about 120 men and women on superscale posts (£1,900–£3,200 per annum); 250 in the administrative and professional grades (the 'A' scale, £700–£1,600 per annum); about 200 in the higher executive and technical grades (£850–£1,600 per annum); and about 450 in the lower executive and technical grades (£450–£800 per annum). In all, about five hundred persons are earning above £1,000 a year, and a similar number earning between £500 and £1,000.

THE ÉLITE

The salary scales which obtain in the Nigerianized civil service are basically those of the earlier colonial period. Salaries paid to British officials tended to be higher than those men would receive in their own country for their particular qualifications—an obvious and necessary inducement to encourage them to work overseas. As Nigerians have occupied their posts, they have claimed the same salaries. Thus a graduate Nigerian grammar-school teacher often receives more than his counterpart in England.

The Nigerianization of the civil service is a very recent phenomenon. In the early 1950s there was a high proportion of Nigerians in the educational, medical and judicial fields, but almost none in the administrative service. Thus, even in 1956, two thirds of the men in 'A' scale and superscale posts were expatriates; in the senior ranks of the administrative service (Administrative Officer, Classes I and II) was but a single Nigerian—Chief S. O. Adebo. Recruitment of British officers to the administrative service ceased only in 1953, and whilst a few Nigerians were appointed to the junior ranks in 1954 it was not until 1955 that the intake of Nigerian university graduates really began. Today there are over 650 Nigerians in 'A' scale and superscale posts against about 150 expatriates, only a little over a quarter of the latter being on the pensionable establishment. (Over half of these Nigerians and expatriates are stationed in Ibadan.)

Nigerianization has been rapid not only because local men have taken the posts formerly occupied by expatriates but because the civil service has expanded. The numbers in the administrative and professional and superscale posts rose by 25 per cent in the six years 1957–63. But the greatest expansion has been in the executive and technical grades—a three-fold growth. The visible symbol of this growth is the development of the Secretariat area at Agodi: the one building standing in 1949 has been enlarged and a dozen of similar size added to it. The cause of the growth has been the expansion of all social services—free primary education, the quadrupling of the number of grammar schools in a decade, the new hospitals and dispensaries, the increased attention to agricultural extension work. Whereas the colonial administration tended to be decentralized, with but a minimum number of officers stationed in Ibadan, the modern services are all tightly controlled from the new ministerial buildings. A corrollary of this change is the expectation of many Nigerian (and expatriate) civil servants that they will spend the whole of their service in Ibadan—each new tour of duty will not mean transfer from one Divisional headquarters to another.

In enlarging the executive and technical grades the old barriers between 'Senior Service' (British) and 'Junior Service' (Nigerian) have been broken. No longer can a chief clerk never hope to attain even the starting salary of the university graduate. The new salary grades fully bridge the gap and enable the clerk and technician to reach a four-figure salary. Qualifications for direct entry to the bottom ranks of the higher executive grade are broadly identical for those to a University—three 'A' level passes in G.C.E. However, three quarters of the men in these ranks have reached their status not by direct entry but by promotion from the even lower clerical and technical grades. An avenue is now open for the messenger to become a permanent secretary—even though such a rise is most unlikely in fact.

Promotion, within the upper grades of the civil service, has been rapid. When, in 1960, it was decided that all permanent secretaries should be Nigerians, these posts were filled by men with an average age of 44 years, who had spent a mean of twelve years in administrative, professional or superscale posts. Most of them were drawn from outside the Administrative service—from the departments of Education, Posts and Telegraphs, etc. They replaced British officials of a very similar age and seniority. For both groups promotion had been twice as rapid as was usual in the pre-war service; but in both cases there was late entry to the service—the British due to the war, the Nigerian due to delayed university education. Few Nigerians were studying in British universities in the late 1940s. The rush began in the early 1950s with the suddenly high cocoa prices. These graduates began returning in 1954. For those who joined the civil service in the mid-1950s promotion has been very rapid. In six years they have been promoted to the uppermost level of the 'A' scale or to superscale posts—carrying in both cases salaries of £1,500 or more. Yet these too are not young men—they entered the government service when they were already in their early thirties. Promotion has been fastest in the administrative branches as the establishment has increased, expatriates left, and a series of new ranks been created. The professionals have been jealous of this unequal advance. Competition between civil servants was intense in the late 1950s, as each tried to move into the more rapidly advancing streams. Today the position has stabilized; recruitment into the civil service has again been reduced to a trickle as funds for expanding the social services grow scarce. The recent entrants grow disillusioned as they calculate that, with the men in the highest posts still only in their early forties, promotion in the next twenty years is likely to be exceedingly slow. Suggestions that the compulsory retirement age should be raised from 55 to 65 years meet with a howl of complaints that the aspirations of the junior men are being thwarted.

These patterns of rapid expansion, rapid Nigerianization and rapid promotion are repeated in the public corporations whose conditions of employment and salary structures are very similar to those of the Regional civil service.

The University of Ibadan today employs well over four hundred senior staff, one third of whom are Nigerians. Many of the latter are, in fact, Ibadan graduates of the early 1950s who rejoined the University on their return from Britain with higher degrees. Here, too, there has been rapid promotion for the first Nigerian members of a department—an accelerated promotion from the bottom of the lecture grade (salary now £1,200 per annum) to a professorship (£3,000 per annum) within six or seven years has become a common pattern. But again, those who are but one or two years more junior are advancing much more slowly. Ibadan's output of graduates has grown steadily in geometric progression. In the six years 1949–55, only 165 men and women graduated; between 1956 and 1960 an average of 90 a year; at the present time, 300 a year. (Of these approximately half will have been Western Nigerians.) Most of the graduates who joined government service in the mid-1950s were educated overseas—a significant feature in considering their styles of living and their attitudes.

The numbers employed in the bureaucratic structures—the civil service and public corporations, the universities and secondary grammar schools, the expatriate commercial firms—completely overshadow the privately employed traders and professionals. About 200 lawyers reside in Ibadan. But there are less than a dozen private doctors—members of the civil service or university are catered for by government or university medical officers. Politicians form a category apart—they maintain one home in their constituencies and another in Ibadan. A high proportion of the parliamentary members of the U.P.P.—N.C.N.C., the government party, hold ministerial posts. A minister's salary is £3,000 plus allowances—he must earn more than his permanent secretary! An ordinary member of the House of Assembly receives £800 a year.

Ibadan income tax figures suggest that the number of self-employed businessmen earning over £1,000 a year is roughly equivalent to the number of bureaucrats with this salary. In the £500–£1,000 a year range, the traders exceed the bureaucrats by a ratio of 2:1. Many of these traders, however, live in the heart of Ibadan; few are westernized in the sense of being well educated or maintaining a European style of life; most are lorry owners, produce buyers, retail shop-owners with little knowledge of bureaucratic organization or industrial techniques. They are marginal to the élite of our present description.

We must not forget that, with the expansion of social services, the openings for women have vastly increased. Those women who have gained university degrees become lawyers and magistrates, senior civil servants, university lecturers and secondary school teachers. The less well educated teach in primary schools or are nurses. The former have been largely trained in Nigeria, though many who accompanied their husbands to Britain took further courses there. Nursing is the cheapest form of overseas education, for the parents have only to equip and ship their daughter to England; as soon as she joins a hospital she earns her full keep. Thus many women have gained overseas training at little cost to their parents and without detracting much from the education of their brothers. The present earning capacity of these women ranges from £650 to £1,000 a year for a nursing sister or about £300 a year for a grade II teacher.

How large is the élite? At a guess there are between 1,000 and 1,500 men earning about £1,000 a year; if we were to include the income of their wives the number would, however, be much greater. Nevertheless, in a town of 700,000 people this is a minute proportion.

To recapitulate the characteristics of this élite described so far: most are in bureaucratic employment, their status depending largely on educational qualifications; those in the higher ranks have enjoyed extraordinary rapid promotion; they and those below them are still comparatively young men; their salaries are good—the university graduate starting at £700 a year earns ten times the assumed income of the average farmer or craftsman or of the daily paid wage-labourer.

The Background of the Élite

What is the background of this élite? Since the departure of their Mid-West colleagues to staff their new Region, most of the civil servants are Yoruba. So too are most of the self-employed professionals and traders. The University of Ibadan and similar federal institutions have a moderate proportion of Easterners; Northerners are negligible in number.

Of the Yoruba, men and women from all areas are represented, though there seem to be more Ijebu relative to their own total population and a relative scarcity of people from Oyo and Oshun Divisions. This is not surprising, for Ijebu Division had the highest proportion of children of school age attending school in the years immediately before the introduction of free primary education. The Ijebu and Egba have in the past tended to educate their daughters to a higher degree than other Yoruba and there is a more marked preponderance of educated women from these groups.

Very many of the élite have come from humble homes.[1] Two fifths of those men with post-secondary education have fathers who never attended school and who were, in consequence, farmers or poorer craftsmen; only one quarter have fathers who received post-primary education. These latter fathers were, of course, the élite of their own generation—the chief clerks, the primary school headmasters, the clergy, etc. Between two thirds and three quarters of the mothers of these present-day élite men are illiterate; only five per cent received post-primary education. Very few parents have given their sons less education than they themselves received; thus the members of the old élite tended to give all their sons a good education. But among the children of the illiterates education is unevenly distributed. A striking though not a typical example is that of a poor farmer whose first son gained a doctorate; the next two sons did not complete a primary education; the following three are now in a University, their education largely financed by their elder brother.

Educated élite women tend to come from more educated homes; the Yoruba give a priority to the education of their sons. Thus less than a tenth of the women graduates have illiterate fathers, and of women who have received a complete or post-secondary education a half have fathers who themselves had a post-primary education. More striking, however, is the fact that only one third of the mothers of those present élite women having post-primary education of any type were completely unschooled. An educated mother ensures that her daughters are well educated too.

There are, therefore, more men than women in each educational stratum. The number of men with post-secondary education equals approximately the number of women who have at least some secondary education, a grade II teacher's certificate or an overseas nursing qualifi-

---

[1] In an attempt to trace young children of élite parents for a child growth study carried out by Dr. M. Janes of the Institute of Child Health, questionnaires were distributed, in 1962, in a number of Ibadan primary schools. Parents were asked to give the ages of their children, their own occupations and educational standards, together with those of their respective parents and the home towns of the latter. From this material it has been possible to describe the inter-generation differences in educational standards in different parts of Yoruba country, together with the frequency of marriage between Yoruba of different ethnic groups, correlating the latter with education. Over eight hundred questionnaires were satisfactorily completed; in four hundred of these the father had completed his secondary education, and about one-third of this category also achieving a university degree. Although this sample of the élite was not selected at random, we believe that it is sufficiently valid for the correlations attempted here.

cation. Almost no man takes a wife with more education than he has himself; most take wives with lesser qualifications. Even so, above half the men with university degrees find wives with post-secondary education and only a tenth take women with no more than primary schooling.

The search for an educated wife, together with the fact that men meet such women whilst in university, perhaps overseas, increases the degree to which men choose a partner from a Yoruba ethnic group other than their own: the Ijebu, Oyo, Ibadan, Ekiti, Ondo, and Egba being among the dozen groups one might use for this purpose. Among the illiterates almost all marriages are within such defined groups. (These are henceforth described as endogamous marriages.) But among those men with post-primary education about one third take wives from other groups (i.e. marry exogamously) and among those with post-secondary education the proportion rises to one half. An even greater proportion of women graduates marry exogamously. Only among the Ijebu does there seem to be a stronger tendency for the men to marry endogamously—but they have so many educated women from their home area to choose from. Elsewhere there seems to be no marked preference for men of one Yoruba ethnic group to prefer women from one or more other areas in particular. There does seem to be a rather higher rate of exogamy among those whose parents were exogamously married—but there is no indication that men prefer to take wives from the groups from which a maternal or maternally related grandparent has come. Men who marry exogamously have wives of very slightly higher education than the endogamously married.

The effect of the disparity in education between husband and wife, their exogamous marriages and the varying education of their parents will be discussed further in a later section on family relationships. Let us here stress again the very high proportion of the present élite who have come from very humble homes; within twenty years of their own lifetimes, many have moved from the traditional compound of a poor farmer to a modern government or university house furnished in a manner appropriate to a four-figure salary.

The Residential Milieu

The Agodi government residential area, adjacent to the Secretariat, remains the most prestigious. Here, in spacious grounds along roads lined with flame trees, are the mansions built in the late 1930s for the senior British officials; most are now allocated to Nigerian permanent secretaries. These houses were, however, built for men whose children usually lived in England—most have but two large bedrooms and are inconvenient for Nigerian families. The new bungalows built in the late 1950s at the back of Agodi hill have three or four smaller bedrooms—but equally spacious gardens. Throughout the government residential areas is a very limited range of house styles. On the Bodija estate of the Western Nigerian Housing Corporation men can purchase their own houses on a fifteen-year mortgage; with an income of at least £1,200 a year one may take one of the two-storey, three-bedroomed houses which line the roads. Behind these are the cheaper bungalows for the £600 and more a year family. The colours of the buildings vary though the styles are uniform save for the few independently built houses. In all these suburban estates Nigerians and expatriates live together without any attempted segregation. Bodija hill is in fact crowned by the official residence of the British Deputy High Commissioner in Ibadan.

It is in the privately developed areas that one does find variety. A few modern architect-designed houses may be seen at Molete on the Lagos road. In the rapidly growing area of Oke Ado, near the Liberty Stadium, are more conventional homes. But the man who buys a plot in these areas can never be certain of his neighbours. His own home, designed for a single nuclear family may become encircled with buildings of an earlier style able to accommodate a dozen or more families in single rooms.

None of these areas has any community facilities. No shopping centres exist here, though at Oke Ado there are small stores along the main road where one may buy basic commodities—tinned foods, cigarettes, beer or coco-cola. No churches specifically serve these communities. Since schools tend to be located on the periphery of the town, some are within these areas—but again with no intention, in most cases, of serving a local need. The exceptions to these generalizations are the University of Ibadan campus and that of the University Hospital, each of which has its own complex social life.

The uniformity of house styles is perpetuated in their interior decoration. The hard-wearing and utilitarian designs of the Public Works Department dominate the furniture. (In houses built by a public body, hard furnishings are always provided with the house.) A rather narrow range of fabrics, floor coverings and ornaments is dictated by the small choice offered by Ibadan shops. And yet the overall impression created by the residents of these homes can vary widely.

At one end of the scale are those who seem to hold a purely utilitarian concept of furnishing—curtains are hung one third of the way down the window frame; the floor is covered with linoleum, the chairs line the walls. At the other extreme are homes decorated as tastefully as those of a 'contemporary' upper middle class home of the western world. In the former home one finds almanacs (poster-like sheets containing calendars and portraits of notables) on the wall; in the latter a popular print, perhaps of Van Gogh. Between these extremes, family portraits—frequently wedding-day photos or portraits of the husband in full academic dress—dominate the living room of many homes; alternatively, the academic certificates won, or the welcome-home address from one's townsmen, grace the walls. To the Nigerian, the religious significance of traditional wood carvings, often seen in expatriate homes, is still too poignant and he prefers the 'tourist art'—the ebony head or the cow horns carved either as egrets or as a fish with an electric bulb in the mouth. Other items tend to be baroque, rather than having the simple lines advocated in modern design—ornate clocks, expensive radiograms covered often with an embroidered cloth, coloured tumblers, ornaments often Victorian in their profusion. The book-shelves tend to be dominated by the texts used by the husband and wife at school and college.

Usually the élite are not good gardeners—almost none of them has grown up in a house with a garden. However, those who furnish their homes well do seem to take as much interest in the exterior appearances. Oke Ado houses have no gardens and here one's skills are restricted to potted plants on the verandahs.

Family and Friends

Earlier in this paper we saw that substantial proportions of the present Nigerian élite were born both into illiterate homes and to well-educated parents. This difference in family background undoubtedly influences the pattern of family relationships among the present élite.[1] Conventionally we might divide these families into first and second generations of educated people. But to do so would neglect the fact that the attitudes

---

[1] Data on family roles and friendship networks comes from an exploratory study designed by Barbara Lloyd and P. C. Lloyd and carried out in June–September 1963 by Miss. A. Awogu. Twenty élite couples—mostly persons known to at least one of the three persons cited—were interviewed on two or three occasions for a total of about four hours. The couples provided information on their style of life, family relationships, etc. Each person was then asked, usually in the absence of the spouse, to name his or her ten closest friends (relatives being excluded) giving the home town and occupation of each. Informants were then asked to state whether or not the friendship ante-dated their own marriage and in what circumstances the friendship originated. They were next asked to take each of the ten friends in turn and to state whether the remaining nine were well known or not to this person. The sample was constructed to include couples with a wide range of family types. Within the limits of its small size a number of significant correlations did emerge.

and way of life of the educated first generation of today are very different from those of thirty or forty years ago; the former have far higher levels of educational achievement than the latter—the élite of their own day but, nevertheless, predominantly chief clerks and teachers. Again we must not allow the differences in family backgrounds to obscure the fact that the present élite have all passed through a common educational experience in boarding school and university, though with varying degrees of achievement.

We cannot, thus, present the variations in the pattern of family relationship which we find today as lying along a single continuum from a traditional to a modern type. Instead, we shall describe these patterns with reference to three ideal types of family relationship—the traditional, the Victorian and the egalitarian—which are outlined below. These ideal types are largely theoretical constructions, devoid of any evaluative connotation; none is, in any sense, better or more socially approved than the other. The wide difference between them does, however, suggest the adjustments that many spouses have to make to achieve a happy marriage; disharmony results frequently from differing anticipations of the roles expected from either partner. Furthermore, marital instability will become common if one sex generally expects a different relationship from that offered by the other.

In this section we shall examine the marital relationships of élite couples, their links with their own families and home towns, and their networks of friends. In each of these areas we shall find quite a wide range of practices. But we shall also find that associated with each of our three ideal types of family there tends to be a particular pattern of marital relationships, friendship networks, links with family and town. In other words, we are not dealing with phenomena which vary at random, but with ones which are correlated to a high degree; thus a change in one's relationship with one's family of origin will affect one's relationship with one's spouse. The number of factors which influence family patterns is large and it is often difficult to obtain significant correlations in a small sample. At some times we can associate a particular trait with parents approximating to the Victorian type, at other times with one parental characteristic—high education or monogamy, for instance.

Let us now describe the three ideal types of family relationship cited above and their Nigerian manifestations.

The first we call 'traditional' since it exemplifies the indigenous Yoruba pattern. This has already been outlined in some detail in Barbara Lloyd's chapter on Oje. The polygynous household lives in the large compound of the descent group; wives are strangers here, overtly submissive to their husbands and the other members of the group; the wives retain, nevertheless, strong ties with their own descent groups. Women had their own trade or craft and were thus economically independent of their husbands. With the segregation of domestic tasks between the sexes and the long sex taboo after the birth of a child—usually two years—the relationship between husband and wife was not an intimate one.

The second type we call the 'Victorian' family since it was introduced largely through mission education in the early years of this century. The nuclear family is the ideal, and a much greater stress is placed on the individual than on the corporate group. Domestic roles remain segregated and the father tends to be an authoritarian figure. The woman's place is seen to be in the home—she does not work and is thus economically dependent upon her husband. Great emphasis is placed on the achievements of the children, education being seen as the means of ensuring a high status for one's issue; one does not, as in the traditional family, believe that the children's success in life is governed by a predetermined 'fate'.

This Victorian ideal is one which was approached by many of the élite families of a generation ago. However, local Nigerian conditions produced an exaggeration of some features of the ideal, and understressed others. The members of these early élite families were among the first Christians of their towns—a minority, which developed many of the characteristics common to such groups. Their emphasis on their own religious superiority was reinforced by their tendency to use the British as a reference group—adopting European dress, house styles and the like, but copying these from locally resident expatriates; for few of these men and women had visited England. The missionary was thus a powerful influence. Children were encouraged first to find playmates and later spouses from within the group—parental disapproval was strong for those who disobeyed. Some wives were encouraged not to work—in order to care for their children and train them in the new ethic, or to emphasize the financial standing of the husband; others worked in a 'safe' post, such as the local church school, where the suspicious husband would not fear his wife's moral corruption.

Our data suggest, however, that many of the educated fathers of our present élite had more than one wife, though the second and subsequent wives may have been taken late in life, on the death of earlier spouses, or maintained in separate houses. A majority of the educated mothers appear, nevertheless, to have been plural wives. Monogamy seems to have been rather more prevalent among the better-educated men and women, though one also finds such men as catechists monogamously married, yet too poor to give their children the desired education. Inasmuch as polygyny tends to be correlated with wealth, the present élite may come, to a disproportionate degree, from polygynous families. Yet, even though their polygyny is a serious departure from the Victorian ideal, we do still find many of the attributes of this type in the élite families of a generation ago.

We have described this Victorian type of family to illustrate the background of many of our present-day élite. Many of the individuals in this Victorian category are in fact still living; most would not be included within the present élite, but numbers of them are nevertheless still active in the local affairs of their home towns.

In our third ideal type, the 'egalitarian' family, the emphasis is on shared roles—in the domestic life of the house, in leisure activities. Husband and wife take equal responsibility in family matters; romantic love is stressed; children of both sexes tend to be educated to a similar standard. This is an ideal which many of the present élite seem to approach; those who come closest to it seem to be those with 'Victorian' parents.

Today's élite has grown up in a more secular atmosphere in which Christianity is almost taken for granted, being accepted by half the population. To the extent that they adopt a European style of life, it is a contemporary style which they have themselves experienced overseas, rather than the image given to their parents by the missions—archaic even at the time that it was being transmitted. For many reasons women now expect to take paid employment—to put their training to good social use, to repay their family for the cost of their training, to augment the household income, to safeguard themselves and their children should their marriage be suddenly terminated by death or divorce. In calling for the same employment opportunities as men, women often use the term 'emancipation'. This must be clearly distinguished from egalitarianism, for the latter implies a shared role while the former tends to be a re-emphasis of the traditional independence of the wife, devoid of her overt subservience. Sharing of domestic roles is not often called for in the élite household where most of the manual work is done by male servants and housemaids, and where there is little incentive to improve the employer-owned house in which one lives. However the existence of servants who act as baby-sitters removes any obstacle to spouses going out together in the evenings should they so wish.

Let us now examine the family relationship among the élite in rather more detail.

The nuclear family. None of the élite has been propelled into marriages arranged by their parents; most have met their spouses during student days and their parents have ratified their mutual choice. Yet there does seem to be a strong tendency towards intermarriage between children of Victorian-type families. The age of marriage is comparatively late; the modal age for women seems to be about 24–25 years and for men about four or five years later. With marriage, child-bearing begins. Whilst women express a preference for from three to five children, those with unimpaired fertility continue to have babies every two or three years until their forties. Six children is the mean for those whose child-bearing is complete; this seems to apply equally to both the more and the less egalitarian families.

Few households consist of the nuclear family alone. In half, one finds a junior relative of either spouse who is attending school. Relatives older than the spouses are fairly unusual. Servants are usually not related—they may include two or three domestic servants, house or nursemaids, a gardener, a driver and a night watchman. (There seems to be no correlation between the nuclear family households and the more egalitarian families; older relatives are, however, more often found in the less egalitarian families.) All marriages are, of course, monogamous and the husband's extra marital affairs are conducted outside his house with supposed secrecy.

A more egalitarian relationship between husband and wife seems to be markedly correlated with educated parents, with a small gap in age between the spouses, with a small educational gap between them if not complete equality (i.e. a graduate man and a wife with some post-secondary education, or a man with the latter qualification and a wife with completed secondary schooling), and with a higher educational level for both spouses. An egalitarian relationship does not seem to be more frequent among the exogamously married.

This egalitarian relationship is difficult to measure. One significant trait is the possession of a joint bank or savings account, and a shared control of expenditure. In the great majority of families the wife has her own account, separate from that of her husband. Into it she puts her salary and from it she contributes to domestic expenses, and in particular buys toys and clothes for her children.

In the egalitarian families the wife probably takes more pride in the furnishing of her home; it is, however, a feature of the more traditional

Yoruba family that the wife, from her own earnings, contributes curtains, cushion covers and the like. Egalitarianism thus implies a greater joint choice of furnishing by both spouses instead of the traditional division into two distinct spheres of expenditure.

The Victorian ideals of family unity persist in the modern élite family. Parents and children eat together whenever feasible, although family prayers each morning are becoming less common and in many families church going is perfunctory. But the élite father seems most anxious not to be the authoritarian figure of his own childhood (whether traditional or Victorian). He wants to play with his children and will perform domestic chores associated with them when he does no other— he may be prepared to 'change the baby', when he will never think of offering to sweep the floor. This pervasive interest in all aspects of his children's lives may be connected with his concern for their achievement.

The colonial government bequeathed, and the Nigerian government has developed, an educational system in which entry to schools and colleges is by competitive examination; subsidies result in the fees being similar in good and bad institutions. Thus, if the young are to attain the same status as their parents (and in a world where educational qualifications determine status), they must pass their examinations. The élite child is sent at an early age to nursery school—with the mother away at work he would otherwise be cared for by a barely literate nursemaid. Parents' influence is used to get him into one of the better primary schools, and in his final years he is coached at home in the late afternoon. At home the child is discouraged from playing with neighbouring children from poor houses; he is provided with books and toys; he is encouraged to be inquisitive. His parents are pleased if he sometimes sits on his own and reads instead of playing with others—traditional mothers would fear that such a child was communing with spirits!

The wider group of kin. Great differences in living styles are apt to create social barriers. A mother who has always cooked over a wood fire will inevitably feel awkward in, and even frightened by, her élite daughter's all-electric kitchen. Yet one of the features of the 'African personality' so often stressed by the élite is the solidarity of the wider family group; invidious comparisons are made with the disrupted family life they have witnessed in Britain or America, part-product of welfare state and an achievement-orientated society.

The élite invariably assume financial responsibility for their parents in their old age. In a few cases, one parent will live with the children. In general, educated men and women do not approve of having parents living *en famille*—men in particular are aware of the potential tensions between their own mothers and their wives. The houses, too, are not built to accommodate elderly people who need some privacy. When a parent does live with one of her children the operative factors seem to lie more with the parent's circumstances than with the type of family—traditional, Victorian, or egalitarian—of the host child. It is noticeable, however, that in periods of domestic crisis—sickness or childbirth—it is a mother or aunt who comes to help rather than friends (who are probably too busy working to be of much assistance).

Educated brothers and sisters are in many cases living in Ibadan. All have cars and they can visit one another frequently. It is much more difficult to measure the social distance between the élite and their non-educated siblings working in their home towns as farmers and craftsmen. All the élite visit their homes at least once a year; many go monthly if parents still live there and if the distances are short—not exceeding a hundred miles each way. News from home is also carried by other townsmen. Thus one may have a considerable knowledge of the affairs of one's close kin at home, whatever one's affective relationship with them.

We have already seen that most élite households contain a junior relative at school in Ibadan. Many men are in fact spending a fifth of their incomes on school fees for relatives. A woman's responsibility seems limited to her own siblings—a man's extends to nephews and nieces or even more distant kin. The structure of the family facilitates this inter-kin assistance. The educated man earns a high salary as soon as he leaves the university; but with free state primary schools it will be ten or more years before he has to pay secondary school fees for his own first child. In the intervening period he can repay his debt to his family by educating, in particular, his own junior siblings or the children of his elder siblings. This same pattern is likely to continue for a long period. The present élite will perhaps find it difficult to finance the education of all their children; their youngest will reach university age when they are well into their retirement; but the eldest will already be earning and able to assist him.

With the increase in the number and popularity of private primary and secondary schools, charging high fees for education of a presumed better quality than the state-subsidized schools, the tendency may well develop for the élite to save what they now give to relatives for the future education of their own children. Such a move will inevitably weaken family bonds.

The home town. In the past the literate clerk or teacher in government or

1. Chief Dele of Oje

2*a*. Ibadan in the mid-nineteenth century
An artist's impression

2*b*. Aremo Compound, Ade Oyo

3*a*. Central Ibadan and Mapo Hall

3*b*. A shop in Agbeni

4. Hairdressing

5. The blacksmith's compound, Oke Are

6a. A modern craft: sandal-making

6b. Gbagi motor park

7. The University of Ibadan

8*a*. The Bodija housing estate

8*b*. Élite wedding

mission employment was subject to frequent transfer; nowhere could he put down his roots. Understandably his links with his home town remained strong. What relationships do the modern élite couple retain with their home towns?

Half the men have built a house in their home town—these tend to be older men. This house not only indicates an intention to retire to the home town, but also symbolizes the concern of the owner for the place of his birth. Those who have so built also tend to view with approval the activities of town 'improvement unions' and such associations. They tend too to draw more of their close friends from their own ethnic group.

Men whose marriage relationships are more egalitarian in type tend to have significantly less attachment to their home town; but these tend, too, to be the younger men. It is difficult to disentangle the effects of age and family type. It may well be that these younger men will become drawn further into their home town affairs as they become older, and thus assume seniority in their own descent groups. Again, as the days of retirement draw nearer they may think more of a small business at home, participation in local politics and perhaps the honour of a chieftaincy title. (Title taking is growing in popularity among the more prominent members of the Ibadan élite—the senior civil servants, better-known lawyers, etc.)

Other factors, however, may modify these generalizations. The young man from a small or remote town, who is its first citizen to gain a high educational qualification, finds that pressure is put upon him to assume a relatively dominant leadership role. Conversely a town which has already produced many university graduates will take little notice of the new recruit to the élite. Thus, although Ijebu seem to have a relatively high rate of interaction with other Ijebu, they do not seem to be more strongly associated with their home towns than are other Yoruba.

Educated women do not have such close ties with their own home towns. Only a minority of them marry men from their own ethnic group and, even for these, the chances of marriage to a man of their own particular town are not great. Thus, from the date of their marriage it is unlikely that they will ever live for long periods in their home town, for it is not expected that a man should settle at his wife's home. Their involvement with the political affairs and the local associations of their towns is very slight.

Friendship networks. The educated man or woman who comes to Ibadan to assume a new post finds himself surrounded by countless friends and acquaintances—near and distant kin, townsmen, school and college friends; not for him the loneliness so often attributed to suburban life.

The close friends of the élite are, almost without exception, persons of similar age, occupation, education and income—in other words—co-members of our defined élite. Even the women choose very few friends who are neither teachers nor nurses but traders. Only in the more egalitarian families do we find men and women naming friends of the opposite sex. Three-quarters of the friends cited live in Ibadan, and over half of them are from ethnic groups other than their own. In general, about two-thirds of the closest friendships of both men and women were made before marriage. One-third of the total are school or college friends, and lesser but not dissimilar proportions are friends made at work, through a social club or by co-residence.

To these generalizations a number of modifications may be made. The more egalitarian couples tend to have more friends from ethnic groups other than their own—and in extreme cases, have non-Yoruba or non-Nigerian friends. Similarly there seems to be a tendency for couples exogamously married to have fewer friends from their own ethnic group. On the other hand, Ijebu seem to number a relatively high proportion of their own countrymen among their close friends. Men who are closely involved with the affairs of their home towns tend to have more friends from that area. There is little evidence that the proportion of school friends declines with age.

One's network of close friends may be open—few of one's friends know one another well, or closed—most are friends of one another. In general, about half of the best friends of élite men and women are well known to one another. Among the more egalitarian couples we tend to find a more open network; among the elderly, a more closed network. The factors affecting the type of network seem too varied, however, for other apparently significant correlations to be confidently stated.

Since women retain so many of the friendships made before their marriage, it is not unexpected that they share few close friendships with their husbands. (Shared friends are individuals named by both spouses or cases where a husband names Mr. 'A' and his wife cites Mrs. 'A'.) Among almost half the élite couples no shared friendships existed. In the remainder the mean number was three and a half. A high number of shared friends was found not only among the more egalitarian couples but also in Victorian families. A clergyman's wife cited as nine of her ten best friends the wives of her husband's closest friends, all men associated with him in his work, but nevertheless known to him before his marriage. Shared friendships are also more common where husband

and wife work in the same place—as university lecturers for instance, or a nurse working in her doctor-husband's clinic. Children of monogamous marriages seem to develop a relatively higher proportion of shared friends, irrespective of the education or wealth of the parents.

The paucity of shared friendships is illustrated too by the small number of friends that either spouse has gained through the other. A third of the men claimed between one and three friends gained through their wives, sometimes citing a relative of the wife; these men tended to come from the more egalitarian families. Half the women had between one and four friends gained through their husbands; a tenth had a greater number. Such women come from both egalitarian and Victorian families.

Such patterns of friendship indicate a fairly low degree of sharing of leisure time between husband and wife. At home they may watch television together; they will go together to cocktail parties and to the more formal parties and ceremonies of the friends of either of them. But much of the non-working day is spent by each spouse visiting or entertaining his or her own friends, in exclusively male or female gatherings.

Summary. Among the younger members of the élite, among the better-educated and in particular among those born to literate parents, one finds a tendency towards a more egalitarian marital relationship. Age and educational differences between the spouses are slight, they share more domestic roles, they have more friends in common. Such a tendency is, however, balanced by others which continue to emphasize traditional types of relationship. The husband is closely bound to his kin and to his home town; his wife is equally bound to her kin, but has a much weaker link with her town. The employment opportunities of the modern élite wife enable her to achieve the same degree of economic independence of her husband as held in traditional society. With the small size of the élite, its recent growth and its concentration in Ibadan, both husband and wife find there a large number of friends gained before their marriage; they tend to maintain separate friendship networks which overlap at only a few points.

The Social Life of the Élite

The élite, as we have just seen, are still strongly bound to their families and to their home towns. Are there, on the other hand, associations which provide a spirit of corporate feeling among the élite? To what extent is the élite involved either in the affairs of indigenous Ibadan or in the social life of the non-Nigerians?

One's dominant impression is that the educated Yoruba man is not a good club-member; that is, he does not join associations which expect the regular weekly attendance of most members. (Hence, such associations are rare.) His obligations to visit friends—on the occasion of a birth or death, to discuss affairs in the home town—transcend those to associations of a recreational nature. Economic or political interests seem to be pursued more through individual lobbying of one's acquaintances than through organized pressure groups. Physical recreation has few devotees—and few facilities are available.

Many of the élite are members of the Old Boys' Association of their school—but these groups usually meet but once a year for a formal dinner. Most are nominal members of their professional associations. Some are active in the Ibadan branches of their local town association or 'Progressive Union'. Those with a more egalitarian marital relationship seem to be involved more in associations which are national in character and have a more cosmopolitan membership, than in those which are oriented to one local area. The degree of activity seems unrelated to family type. There do, however, seem to be greater opportunities for the Ibadan-born man to participate in his church-committees, in the educational field, to an extent which absorbs much of his time. The stranger to the town may well spend but one evening a month at a club or committee meeting, though he may informally meet his co-members much more often.

Few associations embrace in their membership both the élite and the people of Ibadan. The Nigerian Women's Association does endeavour to bring together the wealthy but often unschooled market women and the university graduates, to promote schemes of social improvement; but there is no equivalent association for men. As Jenkins's paper shows, Ibadan has its own political groupings, independent of, and often at variance with, the national party organizations. The élite in their suburbs look not to the Ibadan City Council but to the Regional government for the provision of amenities in their area; of the taxes which they pay only a small proportion goes to the City Council. The social life of the heart of the town, illustrated by Barbara Lloyd, has no attractions for the élite. The two cathedrals—the Anglican St. James' at Oke Bola and the Roman Catholic at Oke Padre—do provide a meeting place for the indigenous Ibadan people, the élite and the less educated and less wealthy strangers. But leaderships in these churches seem to reside more with the older men and those who have lived long in the town, rather than with the young and recently arrived élite.

Almost excluded from the life of Ibadan, the élite could perhaps forge links with the non-Nigerian community. The days are now past when the expatriates were a small homogeneous group of British colonial civil servants, their life centred on the 'European' Recreation Club. Past too are the battles for Nigerian admission to this Club. But although segregation no longer exists, those associations which sought to bring together Nigerians and expatriates—the masonic lodges or the Ibadan Club—have either vanished or declined in significance. Nigerians and expatriates do, however, meet, often in mixed parties at Ibadan's intimate night clubs—the 'Gangan' and the 'Osumarena', both airconditioned and furnished entirely in an international style. The expatriate community is now much more cosmopolitan, and its social life seems to consist largely of informal interaction between co-nationals. Thus one has an Israeli community mainly employed in construction, an American community of A.I.D. and consular personnel. The individuals of these groups are transient residents in Ibadan—transient even to Africa, in many cases. They can develop little sense of involvement with the wider local community. These groups can offer little to the Nigerian. Interaction is thus limited to individual friendships, arising in most cases from common employment.

The University of Ibadan, itself a very cosmopolitan community, has become the cultural centre of the town, providing drama, cinema and music. On occasions non-members of the University participate as performers; in most cases they are among the audience. The University's Institute of Education brings together members of the teaching profession; the academic staff of the University social science departments maintain links with civil servants. Many of the élite are in fact Ibadan graduates. Yet the participation of the majority of the élite in the life of the University remains very slight.

Thus there would seem to be few formal associations tending to unite the élite into a single group; no high-prestige social clubs exist to symbolize the élite, no clubs to which the social climber aspires to establish his status—this is already clearly defined by his education and rank in a bureaucratic hierarchy. Yet individual members of the élite are highly active in the affairs of their family and town, of their school or church, in national or regional politics. These affairs are, however, discussed mainly in informal gatherings in the homes of members or over drinks in one of the town's bars. Such meetings constitute the greater part of the social life of the élite. It is supplemented by a visit to the cinema or the occasional dance. Social visits, merely to pass the time of day, are unusual.

The Élite of Tomorrow

The élite of Ibadan is composed of relatively young people, most of whom have come only recently to the town. They live in suburban residential areas with few community facilities. All have cars. It is hardly surprising therefore that individuals retain close ties with their home towns and find their closest friends among those whom they met in their youth. The élite are conscious, of course, of the high prestige of their status. Yet there seems to be, at present, little development of a consciousness of the élite as a corporate group, associated with the area in which most of them will spend the rest of their working lives.

Do the élite still see themselves as transient residents in Ibadan who will, on the day of their retirement, move back to the towns of their birth, to the houses they are currently building? The pull to the home town will be strong. Many provincial towns now have electricity, piped water and an adequate hospital, and permit a style of life little different from that of Ibadan. In his home town the returning son will be assured of high prestige in his own family group, and of opportunities for active participation in local affairs—political, religious, educational. If he is to remain in Ibadan, this town must supply commensurate social rewards. One potent factor may well be the attitude of the wives; younger than their husbands, they may still be gainfully employed when the latter retires, and both spouses may be anxious to retain her income. In the more egalitarian families, where the husband's links with his home town are already slight, the wife may protest against moving to a town where she has neither relatives nor friends.

If the present élite do continue to live in Ibadan after their retirement, if their children grow up almost exclusively in the town and at boarding school or college, and ultimately join the élite of the new generation, we shall see the growth of a Yoruba community owing but the slightest allegiance to the provincial towns and villages of the Region. Such a community would change the face of Ibadan.

III. LIFE AND WORK

8

FROM TRADITIONAL CRAFTS TO MODERN INDUSTRIES

by ARCHIBALD CALLAWAY

In earlier days Ibadan was known as the city of 16 gates and 70 blacksmith shops. These blacksmiths enjoyed a high social standing and a thriving business making weapons and farming tools. Some of their descendants carry on this trade now in the same locations of the city. They may be fashioning hoes and cutlasses with a furnace and bellows similar to that of a hundred years ago, or they may be in a modern workshop welding the patterns of a metal grill to be used for burglary protection in a contemporary house.[1]

The Ibadan scene today is alive with the activities of craftsmen, artisans, and small industrialists. Near Dugbe market, for example, tinsmiths hammer out metal cases and containers in intricate tones and rhythms. A tailor on the veranda of his house sews the seams of an *agbada* (traditional gown) on his treadle machine. At the side of a main road, a carpenter and his apprentices are sawing boards and building the body of a *bolekaja* (a passenger and produce lorry). A mechanic works in an area under the trees between two buildings; his apprentices cluster round the vehicle being repaired.

These self-employed men work long hours. Their creative energies are indispensable in organizing the productive forces of the city's expanding economy. Not only do they supply a wide variety of goods and services, but by means of the apprentice system—its essentials derived almost entirely from traditional culture—they provide vocational training on the job for thousands of young people, so many of whom are now primary and secondary school leavers.

Creating an Industrial Climate

Some of these small entrepreneurs show marked resourcefulness in overcoming the many handicaps of running a business under adverse circumstances. When judged by the standards of more developed countries, their enterprises may seem unimpressive, but their successes point the way to others. Sufficient instances exist of individual Nigerians achieving high incomes as traders and then branching out to invest

[1] I am grateful to Mr. J. A. Ayorinde, noted historian of Ibadan, who first introduced me to blacksmith families.

within the transport and building industries. A few have emerged at the head of promising small industrial enterprises. One has established, on his own initiative, a large modern factory; another a substantial building and contracting business. The examples set by these successful indigenous entrepreneurs have a significant effect in creating an industrial climate.

Some critics believe that the growth of such enterprises in Ibadan is prevented by its framework of traditional culture. They argue that, in the present pre-industrial economy, savings cannot be reinvested in a business because of the demands of the extended family and of traditional ceremonies. They emphasize that local craftsmen have little concern for a long-term relationship with customers and no pride in producing high-quality workmanship. It is true that in many cases these conditions do exist, yet the drive for achievement so characteristic of Ibadan's entrepreneurs suggests that the transition between traditional economic life and the demands of a modern industrial society is already occurring. Keen competition in price-setting and in making higher-quality goods can lead to cumulative progress. The rigours of this competitive system, the effect of education (including advanced technical training), and the high expectations of better standards of living all help economic advance.

Again there are those who believe that a city like Ibadan, with little or no industrial tradition—except the older crafts, can hardly produce innovators capable of substantial improvements. But real innovators in any society are exceptional. First it is necessary to have, and in large numbers, skilled craftsmen with sharpened business sense. They are imitators, adapting known technologies to local conditions—and at this stage in the city's development they are much more important than innovators.

Continuity and Change in Traditional Crafts

The crafts of the city derive from the time when Ibadan had a relatively self-sufficient economy. In those days raw materials were obtained locally. Blacksmiths made fires from palm-kernel shells and local wood. Their bellows were made from the skins of animals, and their furnaces were constructed of local clay. Builders of houses used local mud with thatched leaves for roofing. Potters found the best clay in the vicinity to make drinking vessels, plates, bowls, and cooking pots. Weavers used cotton grown in the area. Dyers used ash mixed with the *elu* plant to effect their indigo colouring. Baskets were fashioned from palm leaves and cane from waterside areas. Mats and hats were woven from grass and plant fibres. Black soap was made from palm kernel mixed with ash, and later from cocoa pods. Calabashes were made from gourds. Belts, mats, bags, and drums were made from the leather from animal skins brought in by hunters. Beer was brewed from plantain and banana; palm wine was tapped from the palm tree in the same way as it is done today.

This economy has, or course, changed markedly over recent decades, particularly in the use of imported machines and tools. Blacksmiths and leather workers make use of some imported tools; tailors own sewing machines; spinners, weavers, dyers, and soap makers use imported needles, cotton, dyes, and soda. At the same time, a whole range of artisans—carpenters, mechanics, masons—has arisen with varying degrees of modern skills.

The crafts and small industries in Ibadan have developed in response to the gradual growth of commerce in Nigeria as a whole. As the interior was opened to trade, the movement of export crops created a cash economy. And to circulate the reverse flow of consumer goods to the farmers in a wide surrounding area, a vast network of trade and transport grew up in the city. The increasing commercial activity in Ibadan thus results from its favourable geographical position as well as from the fortunes of farmers (so many of whom live part of the year in Ibadan) who provide the food and cash crops and depend on the city for goods and services.

Although the decades before showed a steady progress, the period since the Second World War has accelerated the growth of Ibadan as a commercial centre. During the actual war period, because only a few consumer goods trickled in from abroad, local small industries received natural protection. In the post-war period, high prices for export crops with consequent higher incomes for farmers increased the money circulation. Farmers invested in improved houses and in goods. Traders, in turn, put their profits into transport enterprises as well as into houses. The growth in the private sector was also stimulated by heightened government spending, especially since 1955, both from current sources and from accumulated reserves.

Some modern manufacturing industries have been established. The Lafia Cannery, operated by the Western Nigeria Development Corporation, cans fruit for local and export markets. The Nigerian Tobacco Company manufactures various brands of cigarettes; a Nigerian privately-owned factory retreads and remoulds tyres; the Western Nigeria Printing Corporation prints exercise books in large quantities. More recent enterprises include a foam rubber factory, privately owned, and a plastics factory, operated jointly by the Western Nigeria Development Corporation and other interests. Since 1961, however, the drop in the cocoa price coupled with the abrupt fall in government spending has temporarily curtailed this rapid expansion.

The few modern manufacturing units have been set up for the most part with large amounts of government or foreign capital; they make use of the most advanced technologies and are operated by experienced managers; they have a skilled labour force: consequently, they have high productivity. In proportion to their high capital investment, however, they employ only a small number of workers. In contrast, the indigenous crafts and small industries are characterized by low capital investment, relatively low productivity, and low money returns. But their labour-intensity is high. Since in the next few years hundreds of thousands of young people will be coming out of the nation's primary schools, and since the problem of finding a means for training and employing them will be critical, these indigenous small industries should be recognized as a dynamic factor in the economy.

Like other cities in Nigeria and in other developing countries, Ibadan has two rather distinct economies marked by a wide gap in the returns for effort. The high-earnings economy comprises the professions (including government administration), the larger commercial firms, and the few modern industries; while the low-earnings economy includes small trading units, crafts, and small industries. But however vital this distinction may be for purposes of illustrating inequalities of opportunity and income, it should not blind recognition to the considerable changes that have occurred, and are taking place, within these small indigenous enterprises. One way of helping to narrow this gap is to find various means for working with these small units to raise their productivity—and thus to increase their returns.

A further reason for focusing on these indigenous enterprises is as much political as economic. The more advanced their activities become, the lesser need be the role of the state and the foreigner. Healthy small industries in a democracy help to decentralize the industrial structure and to distribute more widely both ownership and economic power.

Industrialization is now an important objective for Nigeria's economic future. Large factories are a common feature of the landscape of an advanced industrial society. But the economies of scale are by no means always on the side of the large units. Why then is so little attention given to helping existing small workshops to modernize? Or to promoting the establishment of more modern labour-absorptive small industries? Part of the reason is that crafts and small industries are usually regarded as backward, that they might be helped for rather sentimental reasons, such as respect for tradition, but not as anything vital to the future. With some encouragement, however, they do have a solid contribution to make towards economic progress.

Craft Enterprises in the City

What are the dimensions of the indigenous industries in Ibadan in the 1960s? What employment and training do they provide for young primary and secondary school leavers? What are the characteristics of their entrepreneurs? Are they Ibadan people only or 'strangers' as well? Are these small units making changes towards modern workshops and small factories? What are the main obstacles to business success? What policies will encourage growth?

Very little has been documented about the indigenous industries in Nigeria although their labour absorption per unit of capital is high, and their apprenticeship system had been training young people long before trade centres or vocational schools were established. To find an answer to these questions, since there was no information about the total number of these enterprises and no way of taking a reliable sample, a complete survey was designed to include all the crafts and small industries with permanent premises in Ibadan. This survey was undertaken during July and August 1961, and checked and brought up to date during the same months of 1963. As a supplement to the survey which showed the general patterns of small industries in Ibadan, 245 selected case studies were made to reveal the problems in greater detail and depth.

The number of blacksmiths' shops now stands at 246, over three times the earlier legendary figure. Since this is a craft passed down through certain prominent families, these shops are still clustered mainly in their original areas—for example, in Agbede-Adodo and Oke Are. The traditional blacksmith is in fact declining; in some cases the old blacksmith's yard has been transformed into a modern foundry producing such items as photographers' stands, barbers' chairs, iron bedsteads, iron chair frames, and a wide variety of farm tools. Here are the beginnings of a light engineering industry.

Weaving, spinning, and dyeing are related crafts which were more vigorous in the past than at present. Passing down their skills from father to son, the weavers still stretch out their yarn in lengths of seventeen yards, weigh it down with a stone or wooden block, and work with great dexterity on their hand-made looms. They weave in strips of four to five inches, and one weaver can produce three yards in a day that lasts from dawn until dusk, with breaks for lunch and rest. It takes four and a half days to complete the fourteen strips for a woman's wrapper and this may sell for as little as fifteen shillings or as much as three pounds, depending on the quality of the weaving and whether it is being made on special order. Like the blacksmiths, the weavers work in compounds in the older parts of the city, close together in Oke, Oluokun and Oke Foko and less closely together in Oja Iba, where there are also dyers.

The *adirẹ* cloth-makers are also found in these areas. These women carry on their craft within their compounds. They paint their designs on imported white cloth with a local starch made of cassava. The designs vary according to the moods of the artist and the fashions of the day; one theme that sometimes appears on Ibadan cloth is Mapo Hall, represented by pillars. The cloth then goes to the dyers, where it is dipped into large clay pots of indigo dye. When the dyeing process is completed, the cloth is a deep blue except for the designs which have not been penetrated by the dye. It is ironical that craft work which has grown out of the Yoruba culture and is so intensely local should now be reproduced by machines abroad and imported into Nigeria.

Goldsmiths are also caught in the competition with imported goods—in this case, with cheap imitation-gold jewellery, although the traditional gold necklaces and earrings are worn with pride by those women who have the wealth to afford them.

Pottery eating utensils have to a large extent been replaced by imported enamelware, but there is still a market in Ibadan for large water jugs, cooking pots, and some plates and bowls. Pottery and basket-making are declining crafts of the urban centre; they are, however, carried on in the immediate surrounding villages where materials are more readily available. The pots and baskets are then carried by women, with enormous loads on their heads, to the main markets of Ibadan. Nor are there any modern pottery workshops in the city. An attempt made by the government in the past has been described: 'One of the most important official attempts was made between 1910 and 1914 at the large Yoruba town of Ibadan, where experiments with a potter's wheel and glazes were made by a British potter. The glazes, however, were not of local materials, their use was not fully taught, and the employees, who were youths and girls, were not members of potters' families. When the master potter finally left the country most of the equipment was taken away and the experiment died.'[1]

The more traditional crafts, if not gradually declining, are not expanding at the same rate as the newer, more mechanized industries. The

[1] Murray (1943), p. 156.

oldest businesses in Ibadan are found among the goldsmiths, weavers, and blacksmiths; in some cases the businesses were inherited and the dates of their establishment not known. Tailors and carpenters form the next wave, with some businesses dating from the 1920s. Enterprises that were not found before 1940 include corn-milling, printing, photography, and, surprisingly, tinsmithing. Ninety per cent of the small businesses have started since 1945; 75 per cent since 1950. Over half of the total of small businesses in Ibadan have been established since 1956. Explanations for this can be found in the business optimism during the late fifties resulting from high government expenditure on construction works, and from high returns to the cocoa farmer. Of the few businesses started in 1961 and after, 10 photographers and 33 dry cleaners predominate. And so the enterprises in Ibadan move in time with the needs and aspirations of its people: from supplying the basic necessities in the older self-sufficient society to catering to the desires of today's public for modern services.

Entrepreneurs and their Apprentices

The present owners have initiated and still run most of these small firms in Ibadan. There are relatively few inherited businesses (with the exceptions already mentioned in some of the traditional crafts). And there are few partnerships. Some craftsmen, however, form loose co-operative groups to buy materials jointly and to share work. And many energetic businessmen organize associations to press for the common good.[1] There are unions of corn-millers, bakers, tailors, mechanics, shoemakers. (Such unions are also familiar in trading and even include an Association of Worn Out Tyre Traders.) They meet to fix prices, often graded in a most elaborate way according to the quality of their products; when there is news of a general wage and salary revision likely to affect their clients, they boost their prices sharply. They discuss problems of materials and marketing and create an element of co-operation within a climate of competition.

Ibadan people are in charge of just over half (53 per cent) of the total number of small businesses in the city. Those from Ijebu Province, 18 per cent; Ondo and Oyo Provinces, each 6 per cent; Benin-Delta Provinces, 2 per cent; Eastern Nigeria, 3 per cent; Northern Nigeria, 2 per cent. The Ibadan owners are rather evenly distributed throughout the 30 areas in the city, with slightly higher proportions for proprietors in corn-milling, weaving, and slightly lower proportions in leather-working, printing, photography firms, and tinsmith shops. People

[1] For an interesting appraisal, see Lloyd (1953).

originating from Ijebu province have high proportions in printing, improved tailoring firms, mechanics; they cluster in the newer parts of the city such as Oke Ado and Oke Bola. Proprietors from Eastern Nigeria show a higher concentration in mechanics' shops and in dry cleaning, particularly in the Mokola-Inalende-Salvation Army Road area. Those from Northern Nigeria are mainly mattress-makers, leather-workers, rope-makers, and tailors in the Mokola-Sabo section of the city.

What are some characteristics of these entrepreneurs? Half of them are between the ages of 30 and 39. Somewhat over half had fathers whose predominant occupation was farming, and almost all had grand-fathers who were mainly farmers. Proprietors in printing have the highest formal education and several have a full secondary grammar schooling. Photographers and signwriters have a relatively high education. Those with the lowest formal education are the entrepreneurs in the traditional crafts of weaving and goldsmithing and in the newer activities of corn-milling, mattress-making, and dry-cleaning. As a group, 64 per cent of the proprietors had no formal schooling; 15 per cent had less than full primary; 16 per cent completed primary school; while 5 per cent went beyond into secondary education. The vast majority of these craftsmen received their training as apprentices to Nigerian masters. Some, for example, printers, tailors, mechanics, have had overseas training, mainly in England; and others had apprentice training with the government public works department and the large commercial firms.

As might be expected from such a variety of enterprises, the amounts of starting capital range from less than £50 (40 per cent of all the units) to several thousand pounds required by the big printing firms. There are some eight modern printing works owned fully by individual Nigerians and capable of printing both in standard form and in colour; in some cases their original capital was saved while proprietors worked in the civil service or with one of the large commercial firms. Other crafts-men accumulated tools during their apprenticeship and journeyman stage; sometimes they were given tools as a gift from the master at the end of a period of service. About one-third of the group raised their capital themselves, sometimes saving through contribution *esusu* clubs, while 60 per cent were helped in various ways by their parents and relatives.

The total employment provided by these small enterprises reaches 14,500, a figure which includes apprentices and journeymen as well as the proprietors.[1] (It should be emphasized that this survey covered only

---

[1] The 1952–3 census gives a figure for craftsmen in Ibadan City of 46,157. This includes such groups as bricklayers, carpenters, and such others who work not in small industries but for the bigger contractors or on odd jobs.

those enterprises with permanent premises and does not include the carpenters and bricklayers who work for contractors; nor does it include the myriad of traders in their shops and market stalls. Service industries such as barber shops, pools agencies, restaurants, transport, or typing institutions have not been included. Nor have the native doctors, who specialize in healing with medicinal plants.) Of those employed by these proprietors, some 14 per cent are in some form of journeyman or employee relationship with the master, 38 per cent are apprentices with no schooling or with less than the full primary course, while 48 per cent are apprentices who have completed at least their primary schooling. The traditional crafts usually have some apprentices who are close relatives of their masters; while the newer industries often have apprentices differing in ethnic group from the master. The duration of most apprenticeships is either three or five years. Fees vary considerably by craft; and when the apprentice relationship extends for five years, there is usually little or no fee paid. In some cases, small payments are made by the master to the apprentices and sometimes contributions in the form of food, clothing, or shelter. Masters in the older crafts often accommodate apprentices in their houses; this is much less true in the new-line artisan workshops. A general rule emerges: the greater the capitalization of a firm, the greater the likelihood that the master-apprentice relationship will approximate to the apprentice contract conditions of government and of the large foreign firms, particularly in money payments from the master to the apprentice. Examples of this are found among the printing establishments, the modern blacksmiths' and mechanics' workshops, and the improved furniture works.

Formal education is becoming more usual in the system of craft industries in Ibadan at both the proprietor and the apprentice-journeyman levels. What is the effect of education on productivity in these small industries? Printers, tailors, furniture-makers, for example, are strong in their preference for school leavers as apprentices—frequently expressed, 'because they understand measurements and plans better'. School leavers can make systematic accounts and are able to grasp rudimentary theory more quickly.

Markets and the Local Economy

How wide are the markets for these Ibadan-made products? Those with the widest markets include tinsmiths, bread bakers, slipper-makers, cloth dyers, and several blacksmiths. Their goods are usually collected by middlemen and sold in stalls in the bigger markets in the city. These middlemen save the craftsmen time and transport costs; they open a wider market; and, when sales are irregular, they hold the goods until prices rise and in this way help to stabilize prices. The middlemen also have an intimate knowledge of the shifting demands of the market, particularly in the face of competition from imported products. They are sometimes allowed credit by the craftsmen until the products are sold.

These small-scale industries constitute a system of interlocking relationships among the various firms and with the men and women traders of the city. Mechanics, for example, are supplied by the spare-parts dealers; blacksmiths get discarded parts from the mechanics; the *jakan* makers help the tailors of national dress; the wood-sellers and charcoal-sellers supply the bakers; plank sellers dispose of timber to furniture-makers and carpenters; pottery-makers supply big earthen pots to the women cloth dyers. To illustrate these sets of relationships fully would require a rudimentary input-output table.

What is the role of women in this scene? In the production processes of industries, women do not play a large part. Some elderly women continue their spinning and dyeing, but these crafts are declining. Women design *adirẹ* cloth. In the more modern activities, women seamstresses sew women's and children's clothes and take on girl apprentices. They are also employed in bakeries, and in a few cases manage and own the bakery firm. Where the women of Ibadan flourish is in trading—and their wares range from a headtray with a few cigarettes, matches, and soap powders to a permanent shop with a yearly turnover of thousands of pounds of textiles. The few magnificently successful women have sent their sons to overseas universities and have invested in houses and in transport. In relation to local crafts and small industries, women take a vital part in extending the markets of their products. Wives of weavers, for example, take the finished woven cloth to sell in the Ibadan markets.

What happens to the level of employment in these craft firms during a period of low business activity such as, for example, that caused by the recent fall in regional government spending? In some few cases, a one-man workshop will close down while the proprietor looks, perhaps fruitlessly, for a temporary job as a labourer. If he is an Ibadan man, he belongs to a family who will help to support him, often with food brought in from the family farm outside the city limits. Almost all who become hard-pressed manage, however tenaciously, to survive the period of business depression. Those with a large plant and expensive machinery, such as the printers, find payments of interest and capital on this equipment difficult and, of course, they are faced with holding excess capacity.

Those who are least affected by business decline are a few part-time tailors, carpenters, shoemakers, who have jobs with the government or commercial firms, and who return in the late afternoons to open their workshops.

Prospects for Raising Productivity

Small industries in Ibadan, owned and managed entirely by Nigerians, have a central place in the industrial future of the city. They have emerged not because of any special government policies encouraging them but rather because they have pursued their best opportunities to win money returns. They provide about seven times as much employment as the larger industries in the city. They also supply goods and services of a wide variety to people in the city and beyond; they draw out latent reserves of scarce resources, especially of entrepreneurship and capital; and they provide a training ground to improve skills of the new and increasing numbers of artisans. Total capital invested, comprising mainly the fixed investment in buildings and equipment, probably reaches to three-quarters of a million pounds. There is thus a low ratio of capital to labour: about £50 per person employed.

The outlook for their continued growth appears to be brightened by the widening market, by the large numbers of low-wage literate applicants in the labour market, and by the array of possibilities for substituting Nigerian-made for imported products. But many impediments make it difficult for the Nigerian businessmen to reach towards these new manufacturing opportunities.

These crafts and smaller industries have certain common characteristics. Most have no specialization in management: the majority, in fact, work on the basis of one-person management. They gain no economic advantage through bulk buying or selling; most use narrow local markets for both the purchase of raw materials and for the disposal of finished products.

These characteristics point to some of the disadvantages encountered by the small industries in attempting self-improvement. They also suggest lines on which a selective programme of aid might be worked out. There are certain advantages: one is the flexibility that comes from intimate personal management where the craftsman-entrepreneur is in everyday association with his raw-material suppliers, his clients, and his workers. This flexibility gives the modern small industry a start in competing with larger manufacturing units.

The entrepreneur often does not have the skills to introduce new products or to compete in quality with the imported products. Happily, there are a few exceptions to this and their numbers will increase. Some have worked as apprentices with masters in backstreet workshops, then spent some years working with a modern firm (a motor works, for example); and after building up a savings fund, they have established their own improved businesses. Some few, at their own expense, have travelled away from Nigeria to gain training and experience. Some have an insatiable interest in whatever they can find in print about the improvement of their particular lines of business; a small number take correspondence courses. But the task of the entrepreneur, in trying to overcome the obstacles to development, is a formidable one. His path as a pioneer is much more difficult than if he were trying to do the same things in a more advanced economy—where the steps are laid out by those who have gone before.

Obstacles: the Firm and its Environment

Through the eyes of the Nigerian entrepreneur, there are two sets of impediments: internal ones, which relate to the organization of his firm; and external ones, which are implicit in the local environment.[1] He is continuously faced with involved questions involved in transforming what is essentially a one-man business into a firm. As a typical entrepreneur, he has to allow for these deficiencies in his business and in the environment: he has to improvise.

The internal problems concern deficiencies in management, in technical ability, and in marketing the products and services. The entrepreneur must possess a wide range of human skills and he cannot easily delegate administrative tasks. This means that every detail must come to his attention: bargaining for raw materials, organizing the work schedule, taking orders from clients, arranging marketing. Since his profits are low, the rate of capital accumulation is meagre. The machinery and the tools, which ideas on progress might suggest to him, are beyond his means. Or if a machine is purchased, he may find that maintenance is difficult: he may not be able to obtain spare parts and there may be no regular service. He may have little confidence that the separate entity of his business will be preserved after his death; there is then less incentive to save in order to achieve growth of the firm. And, although he may appreciate the advantages of combining with fellow craftsmen by pooling capital and technical abilities in a partnership or limited liability company, he may have adequate reasons for distrusting the permanence of such an association.

[1] For a general analysis of the factors in the environment inhibiting the efforts of entrepreneurs in such countries as Nigeria, see United Nations Department of Economic and Social Affairs (1958), pp. 2–4.

Most of these businessmen have family responsibilities. And they have difficult decisions about improving their firms or meeting education costs for their children. Among the case studies, some one-third of the proprietors had more than five children. And the same proportion paid more than half their achieved income from the firm (not counting their wives' earnings, usually in trading) towards their children's education. Again, the higher the level of income the higher the amount spent on education. Children's education is viewed as an investment for the future more compelling than further capital accumulation in the business. A businessman prefers to spend £60 a year to see a son through grammar school than to invest the same amount in improved tools. It is also clear from the evidence that payments for education of relatives' children often turn out to be a type of capital repayment—when, for example, the relative has helped in furnishing initial capital or in providing the entrepreneur himself with his school fees earlier in life. Added to this are the obligations of the extended family and the costs of social and religious ceremonies.

Forces external to the firm—over which he has no control—may operate to his disadvantage. Public utilities may be non-existent or too expensive: he may need supplies of cheap water, of electricity at reasonable rates. Rising raw material prices, rising wage rates, or the weight of taxation may push up his costs of production and make his products less competitive with imported goods. In Ibadan raw materials for many craftsmen contain a high component of tariff duties—for example, leather for shoe-making, cloth for general tailoring and shirt-making, flour for baking—which may reach as high as 15 per cent of the total production costs. Most tariffs in Nigeria are designed for gaining revenue, but this need should be weighed against the urgency for fostering Nigerian businesses.

Individual Proprietors

These profiles of entrepreneurs of small businesses in Ibadan illustrate some of these problems in practice.

Furniture-maker: Mr. J. comes from a large family; most of his brothers are carpenters. Lacking finances, he left school in 1938 after completing standard four. His training began with four years of apprenticeship to his brother, followed by nine years of employment as a carpenter with foreign and Nigerian firms. By 1952 he had married and had saved £50 to start his own business. He now employs two journeymen and trains four apprentices, all of whom have completed their primary schooling.

The apprentices pay him £5 a year each for a period of four years; he provides them with food, shelter, and clothing. Mr. J. shares a plot renting for £1 10s. 0d. a month with another carpenter, though each works separately and displays his products in a separate section. Now 37 years old, and with over ten years in business, Mr. J. has built up his capital equipment to £300 and his bank savings to £150. He has two children too young yet for school. His main problem lies in expanding his market. At least thirty different well-designed pieces of his furniture are displayed on a prominent frontage on a main Ibadan road, but his sales do not encourage the increased production his workshop could achieve.

Mechanic: Mr. O., now 39 years old, did not attend school but served an apprenticeship for five years. In 1951 he started his business with £50 capital provided by relatives. He now has about £150 in tools, including an electric motor. In his workshop are three apprentices, who train under him for a period of four years and pay no fees. Mr. O. has extensive family responsibilities with four wives (all small traders) and six children. He hopes to take another wife soon. He also honours customary celebrations. At the naming-day ceremonies of each of his children, he holds parties, which cost him about £60; last year two children were born. He also holds an annual feast for relatives in remembrance of his father who died eight years ago. Five half-brothers, who have completed secondary modern school but are unemployed, depend on him for food, as well as aged uncles and aunts who come to him for financial aid. During the last religious festival he spent over £50 for new clothes for his wives. In discussing the obstacles to his business growth, Mr. O. says he lacks capital to expand and he lacks customers. He believes his competitors have more successful businesses because they have better equipment.

Mechanic: Mr. A., who is now 40, completed primary school and then secured a place as an apprentice in a foreign firm. After his apprenticeship of five years, he continued with his firm for twelve years. As an apprentice he was paid £5 10s. 0d. a month and as a trained mechanic he began at £180 annually and by the time of his resignation was earning £360. He started his own business in 1951 from his savings and now has capital equipment amounting to some £550. He has 13 apprentices (all have completed primary schooling) who train for a period of five years and pay no fees. The master provides them with food, shelter, and clothing. Mr. A. has a thriving business, but he would like to have more capital to equip a larger workshop. The large proportion of his profits, however, are not reinvested in his business, but spent on children's education. He and his wife have five children. He considers their education of first importance and supports one son studying law in England (at a cost of £800 for the past two years) and two children in grammar school (£130 per year). He also pays some school fees for children of relatives who helped him with his own education. Besides his mechanics' workshop, Mr. A. owns three taxis which provide income and he has built a house in his home town.

Tailor: Mr. O. is now 32 years old. He started his business in 1956 and makes national dresses and shirts for men, and gowns for women. His own training began with four years of primary school and three years of apprenticeship with a tailor. His parents, who farm cash crops, provided him with £25 to buy a machine. It took him six months to find his present site, which is at an intersection in the commercial centre of town and therefore attracts customers. His business has been successful and he now owns six sewing machines, a house in his home town, and a car for his personal use. He employs two journeymen (one is a brother) and eight apprentices, of whom six have completed primary schooling. The apprentices pay no fees, and Mr. O. provides food, shelter, and clothing. His wife is a prosperous trader with an income of about £400 a year; they have four children. Mr. O estimates £250 as the amount spent yearly on school fees for his own and relatives' children.

Blacksmith: Mr. C. has a modern workshop for fashioning iron railings for balconies, iron grills for burglary protection, and metal beds. He also does welding and some repair work. This business was started in 1954 with a commencing capital of £350 from his own savings and gifts from his parents who are traders. Now 35 years old, he completed his primary schooling in 1942 and then served an apprenticeship of seven years at a cost of nine guineas. He now employs two workers at salaries of £12 10s. 0d. and £10 monthly and four apprentices, two of whom are school leavers. His apprentices serve a period of five years and pay no fees; the master provides food and shelter. Although he sells his products in Ibadan and other cities in the Western Region, he finds tough competition from foreign firms who have larger workshops and more up-to-date equipment. He and his wife have three young children; he pays £45 a year to assist a brother in secondary school.

These small businessmen possess an intense capacity to emulate—this is one of the strongest factors for breaking through the many restraints. And Ibadan has several 'standard setters'—modern, medium-size firms—whose high quality of workmanship, punctuality with orders, and ability to out-compete imported goods, have a marked effect on the numerous less-advanced smaller firms. Such 'standard setters' include a modern furniture works with contemporary Scandinavian designs; a factory for the manufacture of food processing machinery (including the small units, such as machine-driven *gari* graters and pepper mills). A Nigerian ex-serviceman has the beginnings of a well-managed, modern shoe-making factory. These examples also help to dispel the tendency among some craftsmen to emphasize too much the commercial aspects of their businesses (perhaps influenced from trading experience) instead of the equally significant production process.

Encouraging Nigerian Industries

The indigenous apprentice system works well. In some few cases the apprentices may be only a source of cheap labour for an entrepreneur who is either not capable of, or does not spend enough effort in, training them in the discipline of his craft. But these are the exceptions, the small negative side of a system which has developed out of the culture of the Nigerian people, and has stood the test of a long tradition. It engenders loyalty to the master and to the craft; it provides low-cost instruction, passing on skills from one generation to the next; and it instils, through years of hard experience, the meaning of business competition.

This system now needs an injection of improved technical skills. Short courses of accelerated training could be arranged for selected masters and apprentices. Since more apprentices are now school leavers, they can understand elementary theory and are capable of more advanced technical work. These apprentices could be admitted into trade schools for short periods. Working with this indigenous system to improve it means that the traditional continuity in the creation of new entrepreneurs is not broken, yet skills are upgraded. And this ready supply of artisans and entrepreneurs is a pre-condition for industrial progress.

Such an education policy might be carried out by an industrial extension service, which might also have a programme of direct help to promising firms. With a staff of trained specialists in various industrial skills and in management, it could assess the interlocking disabilities that retard performance in certain firms. Then a programme of help to an individual firm could be worked out, perhaps including credit provision, specialized technical training, and advice on designing and marketing the product. Certain questions would arise: should technical help be directed towards keeping the low-capital intensity of these small firms by making them more efficient in the use of existing tools and machinery? Or should direction be given to changing backward units into modern small industries using new machinery and production processes, turning out high-quality products? The first procedure would save capital resources, but the latter would press the firm to expand and to become more efficient. In practice, this extension service would no doubt blend both methods according to individual situations. Both would have ready application in Ibadan. Both raise productivity.

What are some of the more immediate prospects for modern small manufacturing units in Ibadan? To mention but a few, factories could be used for making shoes and sandals, men's shirts, agricultural tools in greater quantities; for processing and packaging foods; for crushing palm kernels. (Absurd though it may seem, Nigeria still imports wastebaskets, doormats, house and office furniture, simple engineering tools, tinned fruit and fruit juice, peanut butter.)

Since almost 20 per cent of all purchases of goods and services in the Nigerian economy are by the public sector, by government corporations and ministries, local governments, and centrally controlled schools, here is an excellent means for leading off a scheme for buying locally-made goods. A campaign to buy Nigerian goods is another way of giving the needed push to small industries.

These small industries are necessarily followers rather than leaders. Their growth can also be sparked by the presence of sufficient numbers of larger factories. But Ibadan has only a few large units. When more are established, they will give opportunities to smaller industries as producers of ancillary products; and additional entrepreneurs will arise from among the skilled workers of these large factories.

Encouragement to large industries to set up in Ibadan can only have effect if certain conditions are met locally: in particular suitable external economies need to be created. This is usually the function of an industrial estate which provides factory space with adequate public facilities, such as water and power, in industrial quantities. This lack of external economies in sufficient centres in Nigeria has restricted location of bigger industrial units to a few select areas only. The Ikeja-Mushin estate, for example, is fast becoming but an extension of the industrial complex of greater Lagos. The economies of industrial concentration may soon be thrown off balance by the increasing disadvantages implicit in overcrowding: shortages, traffic jams, leading to interference with continuity of operation, ultimately high production costs, and thus

LIFE AND WORK

Table 8.1: Crafts and small industries in Ibadan, 1963: distribution by area within city

	Black-smiths	Tin-smiths	Gold-smiths	Weavers, dyers	Tailors	Mattress makers	Furniture makers	Leather workers	Corn millers	Bakers	Mech-anics	Printers	Sign-writers	Photo-graphers	Dry cleaners	TOTAL
1. Mokola; Sabo	10	—	9	13	31	5	24	12	4	4	6	1	2	21	32	174
2. Ekotedo; Racecourse; Adamasingba	5	9	11	—	78	10	42	25	2	3	26	9	7	56	17	300
3. Salvation Army Road; Oke Padre; Olorisa Oko; Iyeosa	11	3	11	10	67	—	17	18	8	2	12	8	4	23	18	202
4. Inalende; Oniyanrin	4	8	9	—	49	—	11	11	4	9	13	3	5	11	21	160
5. Idikan	17	11	14	39	39	—	5	9	3	2	9	5	4	10	6	173
6. Gbagi; Amunigun	6	27	11	—	36	—	15	38	4	4	19	4	5	12	—	171
7. Onireke; Dugbe	2	—	5	—	65	30	36	19	2	1	11	—	6	—	—	204
8. Moor Plantation; Ago Taylor; Odo Ona; Apata Ganga	2	—	—	2	21	—	14	9	2	2	7	—	1	7	8	76
9. Oke Bola	7	—	1	—	82	—	44	23	3	3	42	5	7	17	22	272
10. Agbokojo	3	10	8	2	37	—	18	9	2	3	19	2	4	12	10	136
11. Agbeni	3	—	9	—	29	—	10	11	5	1	35	2	4	8	6	121
12. Oke Foko; Gege	9	13	5	2	32	1	13	21	4	2	18	8	7	12	13	204
13. Oke Ado	9	3	25	26	191	—	76	30	5	6	107	15	14	51	56	581
14. Molete; Ibuko	4	—	18	—	27	—	10	5	3	1	21	3	4	7	19	112
15. Isale Osi; Popo Yemoja	10	—	8	—	32	—	22	16	11	1	13	3	3	5	—	148
16. Isale Ijebu; Idi Arere; Agbongbon	13	9	15	9	47	—	20	11	5	1	12	3	4	8	7	177
17. Oja Iba	8	11	24	11	31	—	11	8	6	—	10	4	5	10	6	148
18. Oritamerin; Alekuso	3	—	17	21	48	—	19	8	5	—	8	5	4	12	5	126
19. Bere; Mapo	8	3	9	4	61	—	18	11	16	1	19	2	3	11	8	170
20. Oke Are; Agbede-Adodo; Ayeye	61	10	18	—	32	—	25	7	7	—	5	2	1	6	2	167
21. Ade Oyo; Oke Aremo; Igosun; Yemetu	4	—	16	2	31	—	11	9	6	2	17	7	5	10	11	134
22. Itutaba; Gbenla	10	—	8	18	30	—	25	11	5	—	10	1	2	10	6	107
23. Agodi; Oke Adu; Oke Irefin; Idi Ape	3	—	9	—	21	—	21	14	7	1	8	2	6	21	18	150
24. Oke Ofa; Atipe; Ode Aje; Oje; Agugu	3	—	10	—	39	—	29	8	7	—	13	2	6	13	—	137
25. Labiran; Isale Afe; Beiyerunka; Alafara	7	—	11	25	25	—	31	9	5	—	18	4	2	7	3	142
26. Itabale; Olugbode; Oranyan	6	—	6	12	36	—	17	13	5	1	11	4	4	9	8	134
27. Oja Igbo; Aremo; Aperin	2	—	9	9	32	—	25	8	6	1	18	2	2	11	5	126
28. Elekuro; Labo; Odinjo	2	—	15	11	31	—	10	7	7	—	9	3	1	8	3	105
29. Idiaro; Eleta	9	—	13	4	47	—	19	6	10	1	10	2	1	7	3	131
30. Oke Oluokun; Kudeti	5	—	14	68	22	—	19	5	4	—	4	1	—	3	2	147
	246	126	349	286	1,349	46	641	391	163	50	520	111	123	397	337	5,135

Table 8.2: Activities[1]

Blacksmiths	Makers of farm implements (hoes, cutlasses, axes, files), guns, native fireplaces and ovens, knives, bellows, school band instruments, metal beds, metal grills for burglary protection, photographers' lamp stands; welders.
Tinsmiths	Makers of cooking utensils, buckets, metal boxes for school books, metal trunks, sieves, oil lamps.
Goldsmiths	Makers of jewellery in gold, silver, and copper.
Weavers and dyers	Spinners of thread; weavers; loom-makers; dyers; knitters of sweaters, mufflers, stockings, caps.
Tailors	Tailors of national dress of all kinds, English-style suits, shirts, uniforms; seamstresses of women's and children's clothes; *jakan*-makers (embroiderers of front and back of *agbada*); sewers of cushion covers and curtains; menders.
Mattress-makers	Makers of mattresses, pillows, chair cushions.
Wood workers (Furniture-makers, capenters)	Builders of *ọmọlanke* (pushcarts), lorry bodies, door and window frames for houses; makers of household and office furniture, showcases, coffins.
Leather workers	Manufacturers and repairers of shoes, sandals, slippers; makers of belts and leather bags; tanners; leather dyers.
Corn-millers	Grinders of corn, pepper, beans, yams, melon, cassava.
Bakers	Bakers of bread.
Mechanics	Motor mechanics; battery chargers; repairers of bicycles, motor cycles, sewing machines, typewriters, watches and clocks; repairers of household electrical equipment such as lamps, irons, stoves, record players, radios. Makers of spare parts for these machines.
Printers	Makers of calendars, school progress cards, receipts, posters, job cards, invitation cards; book binders; sellers of printing materials.
Signwriters	Designers and painters of signboards; glass cutters for showcases. Makers of rubber stamps; picture framers.
Photographers	Photographers; darkroom workers.
Dry cleaners	Cleaners; pressers.

inefficient operation. And unpleasant social conditions result from the pressure of rural migration on inadequate housing and sanitary facilities. Ibadan has advantages as an area for siting new industries, for its people not only have a settled cultural life, but are fast developing an appreciation of modern technical skills.

The art of policy is to view the industrial programme on a gradient reaching from one-man craft enterprises to new large factories, and to encourage the transitions by fostering more Nigerian-owned and Nigerian-managed modern industries.

[1] Depending on the size of the business enterprise, all or some of these activities may be performed.

9

THE MARKETS OF IBADAN

by B. W. HODDER

Though Ibadan, as the largest city in tropical Africa and the capital of the Western Region of Nigeria, already contains important shopping and trading areas based on Western models, the bulk of the trading within the city still takes place through the market places, the large number and variety of which constantly surprises and interests the visitor.[1] Ibadan markets, indeed, include examples of most market types, both periodic and daily, to be found within Yorubaland.

Periodic Markets

Surrounding Ibadan are a number of periodic markets and market rings, each of which lies on one of the main roads leading into the town (Fig. 1).[2] The one main road which does not have its own market ring is the Ife road, where there is only one periodic market at Egbeda; but in practice Egbeda is related to the Akanran and Iwo road rings lying immediately to the south and north respectively. Most of these rings, it will be noted, impinge on one another in such a way that a few markets can be considered to be in more than one ring; but there is no regular or complete system of intersecting rings. The size of rings and the density of markets also varies widely, from the large ring containing only five periodic markets to the west of the town, to the smaller northern ring with some eleven periodic markets. These variations are to be explained largely in terms of population density and the history of settlement in the areas concerned.

It must be noted here, however, that the pattern of markets and market rings is always subject to changes; and a number of these have

---

[1] The word 'market' has of course a great number of meanings; and the same can be said of the Yoruba word *ọja*. The sense in which market or *ọja* is used in this chapter, however, is strictly that of an institutionalized activity occurring at a definite place and involving the meeting of people there at a particular time. This definition excludes the innumerable small places of *ad hoc* trading, involving a handful of women meeting at street corners, in front of compounds or on building sites. More important still, this chapter does not include any discussion of 'market' in the wider, more purely economic sense; nor does it include any examination of such phenomena as the various Marketing Boards.

[2] Periodic markets occur at regular intervals which in most parts of Yorubaland are every four days (i.e. 1st, 5th, 9th etc. of a month), or every eight days (i.e. 1st, 9th, 17th etc. of a month). A market ring in this context is composed of a complete and integrated sequence of markets taking place over 4-day or 8-day periods.

occurred and are still occurring in the Ibadan area. Alabata market, for instance, began in April 1962 as an 8-day market fitting into the Akinyele ring system; and the establishment of Alagba market, also in the Akinyele ring, is still under consideration. The application of the local community to start a market there indicates something of the meaning and importance of such markets to the life of the town of Ibadan:

'I have the honour most humbly and respectfully, to speak to your honour on behalf of my people *Alagba Community*, a district in Ibadan Division. There is a new construction branched at Akinyele Market westward by the left which was constructed by themselves to their own village. After finishing the road, walkable by any vehicles, they want to establish a local produce buying station, and new market of every nine days in their village, in order to be increasing produce tonnages in every year, and foodstuffs for the general public in our great city IBADAN. Being that I am their son, they ask me to bring a weighing machine to the place, to be buying Cocoa and Palm Kernels, and they are now busy cutting the bush for the market proposed.

Will your honour kindly put the matter into the project of this year? Awaiting favourable reply and approval. May God crown your efforts. Amen.'[1]

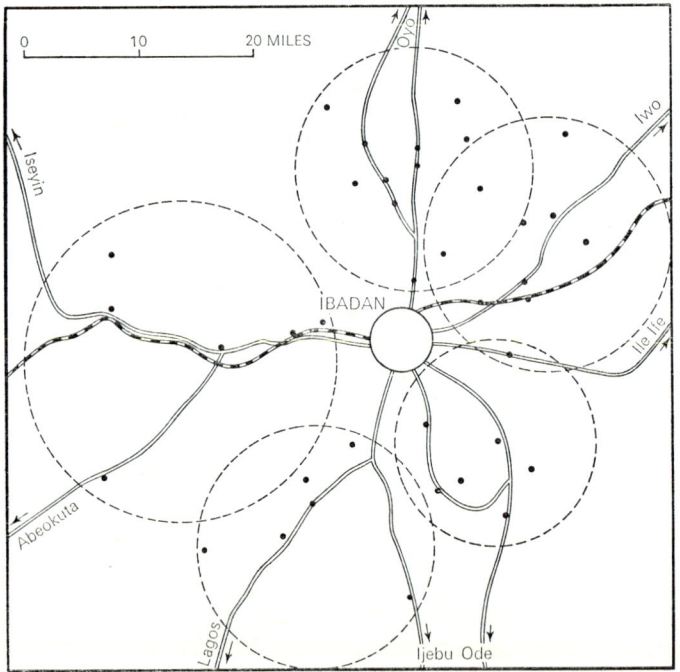

FIG. 1. THE IBADAN RURAL MARKET RINGS.

[1] File T.49/3, 20 January 1954, in the Ministry of Trade and Industry, Western Region of Nigeria. I am indebted to the Minister of Trade and Industry for allowing me to look through all relevant files in Ibadan. The phrase 'nine days' in the letter quoted here refers to the '8-day' period as defined in note 2, p. 173.

All these periodic markets and rings, indeed, must increasingly be thought of as suppliers of farm produce and other locally produced commodities to the large urban population of Ibadan city. And just as within each ring there is some specialization on a commodity basis between markets, so there is a tendency for some commodity specialization between rings around the city: Omi-Adio ring, and its adjacent Ibarapa ring farther to the north-west, for instance, specialize in the production of pepper, cassava flour and yam flour for the city markets.

Within the city of Ibadan there are today only two periodic markets, both of which are held at 8-day intervals: Ibuko (Bode) market at the southern edge of the town on the main Lagos road; and Oje, lying just off the main road leading in from the north-east. These two periodic markets take place on successive days in such a way that Ibuko market immediately follows Oje market day; but in composition and function they now differ radically. Ibuko still retains the characteristics of periodic markets in any rural part of Yorubaland, being primarily a wholesale collecting point for foodstuffs for a source area extending for about thirty miles to the south of Ibadan.

Oje market, however, is nowadays very much a specialized indigenous cloth market.[1] Up to the middle 1930s, Oje was rather like Ibuko in being dominantly a collecting and distributing centre for food crops and the products of craft industries from the surrounding farm districts. In the late 1930s, however, people from Iseyin, Oshogbo and Oyo came to settle nearby and introduced into Oje market the products of their traditional weaving industry; and from this beginning the trade in Yoruba cloth became the dominant aspect of marketing. In the 1940s a wide tarred road leading in from the north-east of the town was constructed and passed within a few yards of Oje market; and this road improved the contact by motor lorry between Oje and the weaving centres of northern and north-eastern Yorubaland. Though part of Oje market still operates in rather the same way as Ibuko (Table 1), this is very much subordinated to the main function of Oje market as a market for Yoruba cloth.

Oje is a specialized market in a unique way, in that the indigenous cloth 'fair', as it is commonly called, takes place every 16 days, that is every other market day, while on the intervening market day Oje operates as a specialized market or 'fair' for black soap. Whilst Oje is strictly an 8-day market, it is a dual-purpose specialized market, each of

[1] I am grateful to Mr. O. Aremu for his help generally on Ibadan markets and Oje market in particular. See also his *Ibadan Markets* (unpublished essay submitted for the B.A. Honours Degree of the University of London, 1963), on which I have drawn freely.

LIFE AND WORK

Table 9.1: Analysis of Periodic Markets in Ibadan (by sellers)

Name of Market	Number of Sellers	% of Foodstuffs	% of Non-foodstuffs	% of European Goods
Ibuko	492	57	43	15
Oje	455	46·5	53·5	6

(excluding cloth and black soap).

two products of local craft industries—cloth and black soap—dominating on alternate market days.

Oje is noted as perhaps the greatest market for indigenous cloth in Yorubaland, some three million yards of cloth being sold there during the course of an average year. The cloth comes from Ilorin, Oyo, Iseyin, Ede and Oshogbo, and the market is attended by up to 1,500 traders from as far away as Ghana to the west, Ilorin to the north, and Enugu to the east. The two main types of cloth are *ofi* (locally woven cloths) from Iseyin, Oyo, Ogbomosho and Ilorin districts, and *adirẹ* (traditional patterned fabrics) from Oshogbo and Ede. From Oje the cloth goes into other Ibadan markets and through a chain of intermediaries to other parts of Yorubaland and beyond. Most of the selling is wholesale, often on a credit basis, and the larger wholesale traders—some 300 of them—are all men.

Table 9.2: Yoruba Cloth: Chain of Distribution

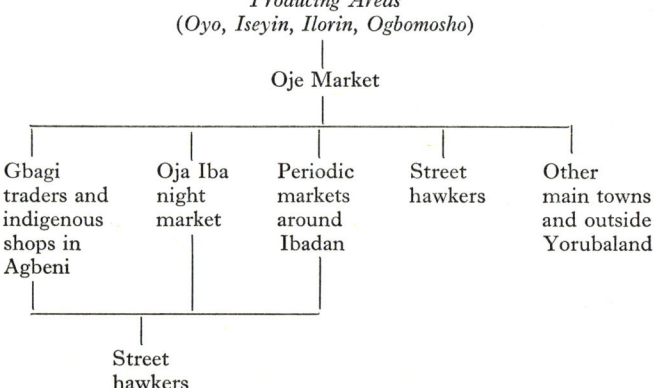

The local weavers in Iseyin, Oyo or Ilorin have their work very much tied to the Oje market cycle. Most of them are full-time weavers who work only to the orders of Oje market traders; so that their incomes from the weaving industry and the extent to which they have time for occasional farming depends on the demands of Oje market. Fluctuations in the volume of trade throughout the year are in fact very considerable.

The supply of cloth is lowest during the July–September period when rain and lack of sunshine make *adire* pattern dyeing very difficult and often interfere with hand-loom weaving. Trading is most vigorous during the November–May period, when weather conditions favour weaving and pattern dyeing and when, moreover, the occurrence of the various festivals raises the demand.

The cloth fair has had a number of effects on the environs of Oje market. A number of local people have taken to weaving; and most compounds in the area now have a cloth merchant (*baba alaṣọ oke*). *Adire* cloth patterning and dyeing units, too, are now commonly seen. Within one mile of Oje market over sixty women work on about forty looms and have been estimated to produce between 3,000–4,000 yards of cloth a month.[1] As people attend the market from so far away, moreover, the cooked foods trade and the provision of overnight lodgings have become important occupations among the local people of Oje. Finally, the piece cloths to be sold in the market are in some cases made up into Yoruba clothes; and this gives some employment to tailors.

The black soap fair is not only much smaller than the cloth fair, but is supplied from a much smaller source area, the main sources of black soap being the oil-palm producing areas around Ibadan—Akanran, Araromi, Lalupon, Lagun, Egbeda and Jago, where surplus palm-oil is to be had. Here, too, however, the fair has had an effect on the activities of those living in or near the market site, for there are today over thirty women engaged in the making of black soap in eight soap-making units within half a mile of Oje market.

These two local craft industries—Yoruba cloth and black soap manufacture—are, on alternate market days, the main items for sale in Oje market. The cloth fair, however, is not only much larger: it is also increasing over the years and is clearly assisting in keeping alive the weaving industry in northern Yorubaland. The black soap fair, on the other hand, is declining in importance, for the industry is finding it impossible to compete with factory manufactured soap.

Daily Markets

Most of the markets of Ibadan are daily markets and, like those of other parts of Yorubaland, are of three types: morning, day and night markets.

Morning markets. The morning markets include Ago Taylor, Eleiyele, Mokola, Idiape, Agugu, Elekuro (Labo), and Ibuko, the last named being sited immediately adjacent to the periodic market. These morning

---

[1] These and other data for Oje market are taken from Aremu, *op. cit.*

markets operate between 7 a.m. and 11 a.m. and are best looked upon as feeder markets. They act primarily as regular daily meeting places for town and country traders. Farm products such as yams and cassava are brought in together with cooking materials such as palm oil, firewood and wrapping leaves. These goods are in most cases bought wholesale by women traders from Ibadan who intend to resell in small lots, in many cases after having prepared them into a variety of cooked foods. The women who have brought in the farm produce, or have simply collected wood and wrapping leaves, sell their goods for cash which they then normally use in buying cooked foods or small daily necessities.

Table 9.3: Analysis of Selected Daily Markets in Ibadan (by sellers)

	Name of market	Number of sellers	% of Foodstuffs	% of Non-foodstuffs	% of European Goods
Morning (Feeder)	Agugu	103	41·5	58·5	7·5
	Ibuko	166	31·0	69·0	7·2
	Idiape	87	47·2	52·8	6·1
Day	Dugbe	5,436	70·8	29·2	13·6
	Mokola	547	83·2	16·8	13·8
	Gege	1,106	93·2	6·8	2·6
	Oja Iba	2,126	70·2	29·8	6·9
Night	Oje	273	92·0	8·0	1·4

The historical associations of many of these morning feeder markets are indicated by their location on or very near the old town wall. Agugu, for instance, lies only a few yards inside the old wall and according to tradition was begun some one hundred years ago during the inter-tribal wars as a collecting point for goods from outside the town walls. These markets still function as important meeting places between town and country, for although individually these markets are quite small, having perhaps only about one hundred sellers and probably no more than 250–300 women in the market place at any one moment, their daily repetition gives them a much greater significance than these figures would suggest. As far as firewood and the perishable wrapping leaves and green vegetables are concerned, moreover, these daily morning feeder markets are essential to the life of the town.

The dominance of certain other commodities in these morning feeder markets reflects the districts from which the farm women come. Elekuru market, for instance, is noted for palm oil and lies at the junction of the Akanran-Olojuoro roads leading from the main palm-oil producing areas to the south-west of the town. These morning feeder markets, however, are rarely supplied from more than eight miles away and are almost invariably attended only by women headloading their goods into market.

The contrast between the Ibuko periodic market, where large numbers of lorries bring goods and traders from as far away as Epe and Oyo, and Ibuko morning feeder market, which is attended only by women who have walked into market with their goods on their heads the same morning, is particularly striking in this respect.

Day markets. The day markets of Ibadan are by far the most impressive markets in the town and with one exception are located in a belt stretching from Dugbe, by the railway station in the west of the town, to Oja Iba in the centre of the old town. Within this belt, or commercial core, lie the main day markets of the city, the central motor lorry park (Ogunpa), the main shopping districts, both Nigerian and European, and the main commercial offices and banks.

The one exception is Mokola market which lies to the north of the town and has a quite separate origin in being associated with the old Hausa Sabo settlement in this area. The way in which this market has developed and changed its location is indicated in Fig. 2. The Hausa market at Sabo was originally the main market for, and served, the Hausa who were interested chiefly in the kola trade and in the importing of cattle from the north through their cattle fair. By 1945, however, this cattle fair had been moved northwards along the Oyo road. This move was designed to prevent congestion at the busy Mokola junction; but the old cattle fair site was quickly taken over by a quite spontaneous and unplanned but vigorous daily market. This new market soon dominated trading in the area and led to the decline of Sabo market into a small night market. By 1960, however, the siting of Mokola market at what was now a very important and busy roundabout was condemned and a new, planned market was built outside the old wall a few hundred yards to the north of the road junction. Today, Mokola is a thriving, well-organized market which is typical of day markets in being interested primarily in retail trading, but has an unusually high percentage of foodstuff sellers, reaching to over 80 per cent of the total.

Dugbe market, like all the day markets, opens daily including Sundays and all holidays, from about 9 a.m. to 6.30 p.m. or so. Dugbe market began in 1919 on the site of a small market and slaughter slab, but in origin Dugbe is believed to have been one of the traditional gate markets around the town wall. The building of the railway station nearby in 1901, however, gave it a much greater importance as the nearest market to what was then the main means of long-distance transport. Finally, in 1919, it was proposed 'to mark out a certain area at Ibadan between the present Government land and the Ogunpa stream, into

LIFE AND WORK

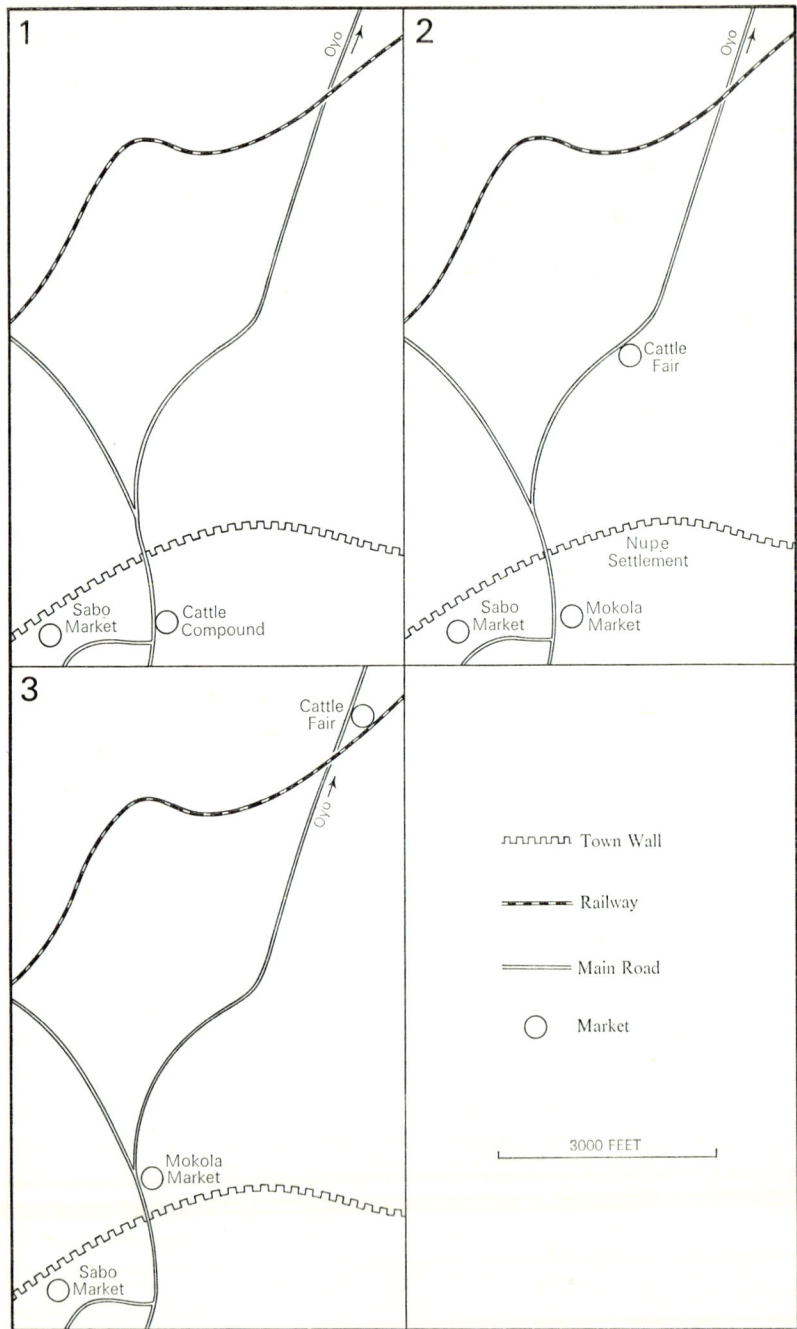

FIG. 2. THE MOVEMENT OF MOKOLA MARKET AND THE CATTLE FAIR.

trading plots with suitable dividing roads to conform with existing sanitary roads and in such a way that Firms can acquire more than a plot if desired'.[1] Revenue from the market rose from £16 6s. 0d. in 1920 to £198 5s. 0d. in 1926.

Today Dugbe is one of the largest daily markets in Ibadan, containing between 5,000 and 6,000 sellers and visited by some 30,000 people on an average day. Dugbe market performs the function of supplying foodstuffs and other items to consumers buying chiefly for family units; and around the market there is already some development of Nigerian stores and shops. Dugbe, however, is not the most popular market for the bulk of the poorer classes in Ibadan. Not only is this market too far away from the oldest, most congested sections of the city, but Dugbe is reputed to cater especially for European and Nigerian middle-class people. In fact, however, even the poorest classes use Dugbe for certain special items, notably imported china, pottery or enamelware.

At the other end of the commercial core lie the daily markets of Oja Iba and Gege-Oritamerin. The main function of this marketing complex, however, is quite different from that of Dugbe in that the bulk of it is devoted to the collection and wholesale buying and selling of foodstuffs from over a very wide area of Yorubaland and beyond. There is a section of Gege market called 'the housewives' market', which is popular in having the highest quality, greatest variety, and lowest cost, of foodstuffs in the town; and part of Oja Iba also acts as a retail market. But the bulk of the marketing complex here is devoted to the wholesale trading of foodstuffs.

This whole marketing complex has developed between the older Gege and Iba markets at the western and eastern ends respectively. Up to the early 1940s the trade in foodstuffs was not at all an important aspect of marketing at Oja Iba market. But by 1950 the foodstuffs trading at Oje and other peripheral markets declined with the great increase in motor-lorry traffic and the construction of tarred roads into the centre of the town. The foodstuffs trade now shifted to Oja Iba market, centrally placed at the junction of major roads near the traditional heart of the town. The motor-lorry parks at Bere, Oritamerin and Ayeye were convenient termini. Goods brought into Ibadan by lorry could in fact now most easily be conveyed to the growing foodstuffs stores in and around Oja Iba market. Gradually the foodstuffs section of the market extended away from Oja Iba downhill towards Gege to create the present maze of paths and stalls in the Oja Iba-Gege-Oritamerin foodstuffs-marketing complex.

[1] Nigerian Record Office, *Oyo Papers*, 1919.

Probably the bulk of the local foodstuffs consumed in Ibadan now comes into the town initially through the Gege-Oritamerin foodstuffs market. This is particularly true of yams, yam flour, cassava flour, beans, corn, peppers, and onions. Travelling merchants, each attached to a group of traders specializing in one or two particular commodities, collect and bulk the foodstuffs from periodic markets or other marketing centres and transport them by lorry or train into Ibadan's Gege-Oritamerin market where the goods are deposited at the stores of individual wholesale traders. The goods are then sold to bulk purchasers in bags and standard measures of one kind or another. Whereas most of the travelling merchants are men, most of those selling in the market itself are women.

Of the three main foodstuffs markets in Ibadan—Dugbe, Mokola, and Gege-Oritamerin—the latter is easily the largest and most important. In fact, many foodstuffs sellers in Dugbe and Mokola get their supplies wholesale from Gege-Oritamerin in the first place. Gege-Oritamerin is not only a major foodstuffs collecting centre for the city of Ibadan, however. It is also an important centre of redistribution of foodstuffs for Yorubaland and beyond: yams from Ilesha and Ekiti, for instance, will be sent to Ibadan, Ijebu and Abeokuta districts through intermediaries in Gege-Oritamerin.

The composition and amount of trading done at Gege-Oritamerin market fluctuates noticeably throughout the year in response to seasonal fluctuations in food-crop production in the various parts of Yorubaland. Though the farming calendar varies slightly from area to area within the country, more goods are certainly brought into the market between November and March, when most food products are harvested. Only yams, harvested chiefly in the August-December period, and cassava, which is harvested throughout the year, are important exceptions to this rule, though the recent widening popularity of crop storage in most parts of the country is tending increasingly to even out the flow of most crops into the market.

Oja Iba market is perhaps best known as a night market, but one part of it is an all-purpose day market, including a large section for goats, sheep and hens. One of the most interesting sections of Oja Iba market, however, is the kola nut centre, which is primarily a collecting and distributing centre for a cash crop which is produced locally but is destined for the markets of Northern Nigeria. The kola nuts are brought by lorry into the market here to be sold wholesale to Hausa traders, who pack the nuts and send them off by rail or lorry to the north, often, however, sending them first to the Sabo kola centre. Ancillary industries—rope-making, the collection of wrapping leaves, the making of baskets—are to be found thriving in and around the kola market site at Oja Iba; but this section of the market only has importance for the Hausa elements in the population of Ibadan, and the surrounding Hausa settlements in Akanran, Araromi, Akinyele, Ikereku, Lalupon, Igbo Elerin, Maun and Iware.

In this respect the Oja Iba market is similar to the Sango cattle market, which is also a specialized daily market monopolized by Hausa elements in the population. Located to the north of Ibadan, near the Veterinary Department's control point along the main Oyo road, Sango receives cattle from the Northern Region; and these cattle have either come down on the hoof or have been conveyed to the railway station at Ibadan before being brought to Sango. From Sango cattle are sent not only to the slaughter slabs of Ibadan but also to many other parts of the Western Region. Whereas the Oja Iba kola market, then, is a point at which the Hausa elements collect local kola nuts for sending to the north, Sango cattle market is the point at which cattle are received from the north for distribution in and around Ibadan.

Night markets. Ibadan night markets are of two types: the central night market of Oja Iba, and the small local night markets. Oja Iba night market is simply one part of the main Oja Iba market site, and is still a striking institution characterized by the same economic and social functions as those of the larger towns of northern Yorubaland—notably Ilorin, Iseyin and Oyo. Yet during the last six years or so, the size and significance of the Oja Iba night market has been steadily declining, and there seems little doubt that the growing sophistication of urban life in Ibadan will eventually, as in Lagos, lead to the disappearance of what was once the main centre of social life for the bulk of the population of the town.

The local night markets draw from about 400 to 800 people each evening. There are about twenty well-known markets of this type in the city, but numerous other smaller marketing centres of the same kind can also be found. These local night markets are fairly evenly distributed throughout the town at intervals of about half a mile. Their function is primarily to distribute ready-made dishes, cooked meals and small items of food to people living in the neighbourhood of the market site. The sources of goods are the morning feeder markets and large day markets from which women purchase foodstuffs like maize, yams, rice, cassava flour or beans; cooking materials such as palm oil and firewood; and leaves for wrapping the food. Many of these women can spend the rest of the day processing the foodstuffs into ready-made dishes (bean bread, *ęko, amala, ęba* or *dundu*) for sale in their local night market; or they may simply break down their purchases into small units for resale at perhaps 1*d*., 3*d*. or 6*d*. a unit.

This kind of night market, in which women connect their local communities with the town's main sources of foodstuffs, can only be understood in the context of the local Yoruba habits of feeding. The bulk of the working-class population eats food that has not been prepared in their own homes. The normal practice is for all members of a family to eat breakfast at a cooked food stall in the morning, to have the midday meal at least partly prepared at home, and to have the evening meal either in the local night market or to bring food from the market into the home to eat. Yoruba food, moreover, takes a long time and much energy to prepare; and it is most economically prepared in larger amounts than any one person or family can usually eat at a time. The explanation of this phenomenon of outside cooking and eating, however, is also bound up with the fact that women put trading first in their interests.

Markets in the Chain of Distribution

It is now possible to illustrate rather more precisely the movement of goods in and out of markets. It is useful to distinguish three main channels of distribution along which goods move into and through the markets of Ibadan to the ultimate consumer. First, there is the movement of goods from farms into the surrounding periodic markets from which the goods are collected and brought into Ibadan, either by headloading to the morning feeder markets, or by lorry to the day markets; in some cases the farmer may bye-pass the periodic market altogether, especially if he lives near to Ibadan. An example of a crop moving in this way is *gari*. Prepared in the farms by the grating, pressing, drying and sieving of cassava, *gari* is probably the most commonly used foodstuff in the township, and cassava is grown widely over most parts of Yorubaland. *Gari* from the farms near Ibadan is brought into the surrounding periodic markets and then into the morning feeder or day markets of Ibadan. If the distance is not great, headloading of small quantities is practised, but if the quantities are large and the distances involved great, lorry transport is always used and the *gari* deposited at Oritamerin market. There some of it is bought retail by housewives, but the bulk of it is sold wholesale to traders—perhaps a whole series of some four or five intermediaries—for eventual retailing in any of the markets of the town. Some of it, moreover, may be bought wholesale by traders for distribution in other parts of Yorubaland, or perhaps to a periodic market in one of the rings surrounding the town. The variations, in fact, are infinite; and a whole series of trading operations may intervene between the moment when *gari* is delivered by lorry at Oritamerin and the moment when it is finally sold in very small lots to individual retail buyers. Even then, the *gari* may be used to prepare cooked foods for selling at a local night market. Any comments on the prices of *gari* are therefore difficult to make with any precision, except for a particular place at a particular time of the year; and this difficulty will be found to apply to most foodstuffs sold in the towns. To give some idea of the way in which prices are made up, however, it can be stated that in July 1962 the wholesale price of a bag of *gari* at Oritamerin was £6 (for *oloyo*) and £4 (for *itoko*). To these prices transport costs of about 4s. a bag, store rents of 2s. a bag and profit margins of 6s. a bag were added to the wholesale price to fix the retail price of the *gari*.[1] This meant that a bag of *oloyo* resold at Dugbe for £6 12s. 0d., and a bag of *itoko* sold for £4 12s. 0d., giving a difference of 10 per cent and 15 per cent respectively between the wholesale and retail prices of the two main types of *gari*.

Table 9.4: *Distribution of Beans from Northern Nigeria to Ibadan*

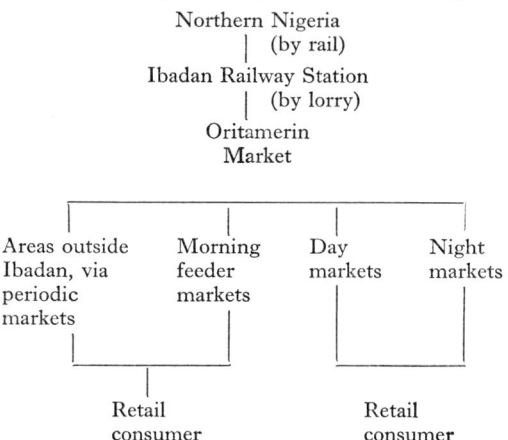

Secondly, there is the long-distance movement of goods into Ibadan from producing areas far distant from the town. Some of the *gari* consumed in Ibadan, for instance, comes from as far away as Ekiti or Oyo from where it is brought by lorry into Oritamerin market. But an

[1] This information supplied by Mr. A. Adediran, of the Ministry of Trade and Industry, in the relevant files, but especially in T.49/3.

even clearer example of this kind of movement is provided by beans. Beans, unlike *gari*, are not produced in the immediate neighbourhood of Ibadan in commercially significant quantities; but the importance of beans in the diet of Ibadan people is indicated by the fact that over 60 per cent of the population of the town take beans at least twice a day. Most of the beans consumed in Ibadan are imported from the far north of Nigeria—notably from Kano, Bornu, Jos, Nguru, and Yola. Only a few black-eyed beans from Ilorin, Ogbomosho, Oyo and Iseyin are imported into Ibadan from within Yorubaland. Most of the supply from further north comes down to Ibadan by train. Traders in Ibadan keep in touch with their personal representatives in the major centres of bean production in the north by telephone or telegram. These personal representatives go to the farms and villages buying in small amounts and gradually accumulating enough bulk in the main centres for bagging and sending down to Ibadan by train. Once in Ibadan, beans are normally taken from the railway station to Oritamerin market stores. From Oritamerin market, beans enter into the same varied channels of distribution as operate in the case of *gari*; but in the case of beans, which are not important in the indigenous cash-crop economy of Yorubaland, there is also a more definite movement out of the town into the surrounding market rings, as well as into the towns of many other parts of the country.

The third type of movement involves those goods imported from overseas. Such goods are normally imported by large expatriate firms through Lagos and sent to their Ibadan depots for distribution. Stockfish, for instance, has over the past ten years become very much a part of the average man's diet in Ibadan; and although imported, it is generally preferred to, cheaper and more plentiful than, fresh meat, fresh fish or locally dried fish. Most of the different types of stockfish consumed in Ibadan are Norwegian in origin. Initially imported through Lagos, stockfish enters the distributive channels in Ibadan through the large wholesale dealers, which are mostly expatriate firms, like the United Africa Company, Inlaks, and Patterson and Zochonis, having their headquarters in Lagos. Most of the stockfish is then purchased by small wholesale traders who are invariably Nigerian traders with sufficient capital or credit standing to purchase several bales of stockfish at a time. These small wholesale traders operate, in many cases, from shops in Agbeni Street; and in front of these shops and elsewhere in the markets of Ibadan sit the vast bulk of the stockfish traders—the small traders, who obtain their supplies from the small wholesale traders, mostly in Agbeni. Some of the more prosperous retail traders are women who have bye-passed the small wholesale dealers and bought direct from the large wholesale dealers, so that their margins of profit are higher than for the majority of women retailers in the markets of Ibadan.

Table 9.5: Distribution of Norwegian Stockfish in Ibadan City

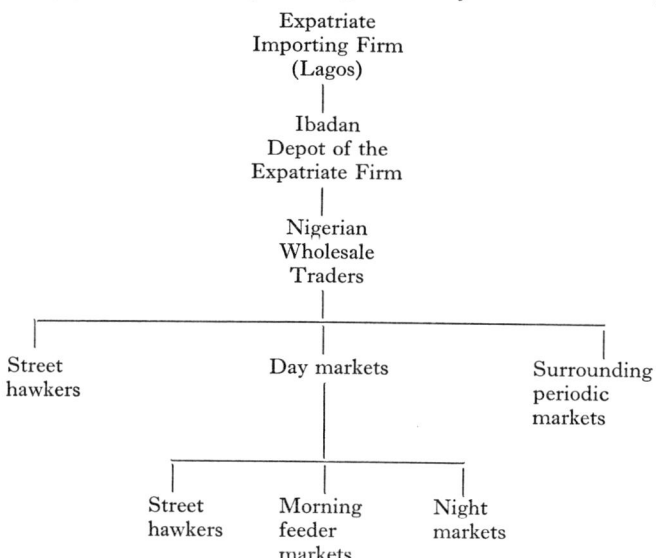

The source area of Ibadan as far as local foodstuffs are concerned stretches northwards into the far north of the Northern Region and southwards to the coast; but, except for palm oil, it does not reach into the Eastern Region of Nigeria, and excludes for most purposes, too, the Mid-West Region. Westwards, there is today only very limited and local movement of foodstuffs across the international boundary. To the geographer, this north-south elongation of the source area for foodstuffs is interesting in that the variety of environments—both natural and social—is much greater in this direction. In particular the latitudinal climatic differences allow a wider range of commodities to be grown. It is also true, of course, that the road and rail network encourages economic relations between Yorubaland and the north rather than between Yorubaland and her eastern neighbours. But this is not true for the Dahomey section of the country, with which there is at least one good road connexion. In this case, the international boundary has been made, especially since Independence, to function more efficiently as a political boundary, but at the same time has made economic exchange much more difficult than it ever was in the past.

The Growth of Retail Shops

Mention has already been made of the tendency for small permanent shops to develop around many of the market places of Ibadan. But in between Dugbe market at one end of the commercial core and the Gege-Oritamerin-Oja Iba market complex at the other end, quite independent areas of indigenous street and shop trading have developed over the last twenty years or so. These street-trading and shop areas, however, deal almost exclusively in non-perishable articles, especially imported manufactured articles of one kind or another. Gbagi, in particular, specializes very much in imported textiles, the women selling their goods on the sides of the streets in front of textile shops which, admittedly, are still dominantly European or Indian owned. The small Nigerian shops in Agbeni Street, on the other hand, sell a much wider variety of goods, though again imported non-perishable goods predominate. Agbeni Street is in fact the chief street for African shopkeepers in Ibadan, as Lebanon Street and New Court Road are for European, Lebanese and Indian shopkeepers. More recently, small Nigerian shops have spread farther westwards and north-westwards along Amunigun and Onireke Streets.

The interest of this element in the commercial core of Ibadan lies in the fact that it illustrates the various stages of trading from permanent or 'continuous' marketing, through street trading and small-scale indigenous shops to the large-scale European and sophisticated African shops. Current trends in the changing structure of the commercial core appear to be (i) a relative increase in wholesale trading in the day markets; and (ii) an increase in the number and size of permanent retail shops owned and run by Nigerians.

The commercial core, including as it does the largest markets of Ibadan, street-trading areas, indigenous and large expatriate shops, and the chief motor park and railway station of Ibadan, is a highly congested area and constitutes a serious problem for planning in the city. Of the markets, only Dugbe is in any sense a planned market site. Like the older markets of many Yoruba towns, for instance Itoku market in Abeokuta, the Gege-Oritamerin-Oja Iba markets of Ibadan are for the most part confused lines of stalls stretching along the streets and paths of the market site in between heavily congested dwellings. Agbeni shops are similarly lined alongside the main road leading from Gege to the Ogunpa Motor Park, and Gbagi 'market' is no more than an area where street traders squat down in front of European and Indian shops.

This last problem, that of the Gbagi traders, has been frequently discussed by the town authorities. In 1962 the Council considered moving Ogunpa Motor Park to some less congested part of the town and building at Ogunpa a new retail market for textiles, to which the Gbagi traders would have to move. This plan was formed in response to a petition of 1962 from Lebanese and Indian shopkeepers, who contended that they were 'not opposed to these women buying and selling . . . ; nor are we afraid that, taken together, they might constitute serious competition in our field [sic] . . . ; but what we do object to is that they constitute themselves into a nuisance . . . by making such awful noise when they advertise their wares by crying '*Gbanjo, Gbanjo!*' . . . and by using the walls of our shops, and the drains alongside, as their urinals.'[1] So far, however, nothing has been done.

In Oja Iba market, however, plans to construct a properly planned market site with permanent stalls, adequate access roads, and proper sanitation, have been drawn up. Certainly at the moment physical conditions in the market are as bad as any to be found in the most isolated market in rural Yorubaland. But improvement at Oja Iba, though generally desired, is made peculiarly difficult by its long existence as the oldest market in the town. Still controlled quite firmly by local chiefs, who collect rent directly from the customers, Oja Iba lies outside the immediate jurisdiction of the City Council; and until the Council is empowered to collect fees of some kind or another from the traders, plans for the development of the market site are unlikely to be implemented.

Conclusion

It has been observed elsewhere that the trends observable in the retail trade of Yoruba towns, and especially perhaps of Ibadan, are in many ways comparable to those that occurred in Western European towns during the eighteenth and early nineteenth centuries.[2] Yet whatever changes do take place, and in particular however rapidly Nigerian shops develop in the commercial core, and however completely markets like Oritamerin take over the wholesale trade in foodstuffs, there is no doubt that open markets will for long continue to dominate the retail structure of Ibadan. It is perhaps too easily assumed that markets are out of place in a modern city; and it is often forgotten that the change from markets to shops in most European towns took place only slowly over a century or so. Moreover, it is by no means certain that open markets are not ideally suited to the prevailing physical, social and economic conditions

[1] File No. T.49/3 of the Ministry of Trade and Industry, Ibadan.
[2] Hodder (1963).

of Yorubaland. Town planning in Ibadan can perhaps only realistically be developed on the assumption that markets will continue to dominate the retail structure. Ibadan markets are not unfortunate anachronisms. The periodic markets make possible the distribution within Ibadan of local food products and the products of craft industries from over a wide area. The morning feeder markets allow easy trading contact between the town and the surrounding rural areas and their market rings. Local night markets provide the Yoruba household with much of its daily cooked food requirements. The large wholesale sections of the day markets make possible the distribution within the town of local foodstuffs from a very wide area stretching northwards to beyond Kano. Finally, the retail sections of the great day markets still serve, and will probably continue to serve, as the main souces of all kinds of commodities for the bulk of the population of Ibadan city.

10

EDUCATION EXPANSION AND THE RISE OF YOUTH UNEMPLOYMENT

by ARCHIBALD CALLAWAY

As a thriving centre for education at all levels, Ibadan leads Nigeria and even West Africa. Every morning during term some 50,000 boys and girls make their way along its winding streets to the 150 primary schools dotted throughout the city. Almost 4,000 pupils train at the 25 secondary modern schools, while another 5,000 study academic subjects in the 16 secondary grammar schools. Over 2,000 students from all over the Federation (and a few from foreign countries) take undergraduate and post-graduate courses at Nigeria's first university, the University of Ibadan. Nearly 500 more attend the Ibadan Branch of the University of Ife.[1] More than this: teachers and nurses get instruction in the city's teacher training colleges and hospitals. Ibadan also has a technical college, a co-operative college, and schools of agriculture and forestry.

This diversity extends to many types of 'unofficial' education: Koranic schools where malams give religious instruction to young Muslims, private 'colleges' which give coaching in G.C.E. subjects, typing and shorthand institutions, radio and television repair workshops which offer technical courses, and sewing centres for training young seamstresses. No one knows how many lights burn at night for those who study alone, tackling correspondence courses in a wide variety of subjects in order to achieve further qualifications. Such intense eagerness for education reflects the widespread desire among the young to find their place in the modern economy.

In Nigeria at present there is great need for professional and other skilled persons to help promote social and economic development. Ibadan's impressive educational institutions contribute markedly in their training. At the same time, Nigeria has many young people with basic education who are unable to continue their schooling or to find jobs. Again, the city of Ibadan, with many primary and secondary modern school leavers uncommitted to productive work, illustrates this difficult contemporary problem.

This chapter will trace briefly the growth of Ibadan's education facilities and will discuss the prevalence in recent years of unemployment among school leavers.

[1] University enrolments for academic year 1963-4.

The First Hundred Years

In the middle of the nineteenth century, Ibadan's first school on Western lines met in Kudeti under a large shelter covered with palm leaves. Here sixteen boys and girls of varying ages were taught by a Nigerian master (later ordained the Rev. Daniel Olubi) to read the New Testament, the Catechism, and the Commandments in Yoruba, and to speak some words of English. This was the day-school opened in 1853 by the C.M.S. Mission under the direction of the Rev. David Hinderer. Some months after the school had started, his wife Anna wrote rather pensively in her diary, parts of which have been published and give a vivid account of Ibadan life during this period, 'Our school does not increase at present, people are afraid to send their children; they think 'book' will make them cowards, but those we have are going on very nicely.'[1] From these inauspicious beginnings, the Ibadan scene has changed completely. Almost exactly a hundred years later, the groundwork was being laid for universal primary education in the Western Region.

To begin with, in Ibadan, as in the rest of the southern part of Nigeria, Western-derived education depended exclusively on the initiative of Christian missionaries, both foreign and Nigerian. Schools for children, as well as Sunday and evening classes for adults, were formed as a natural accompaniment to founding churches. No school fees were charged in this initial period. Inducements of clothes and other gifts, in fact, were occasionally presented to parents and children. Some of the pupils were orphans, others the children of captives. The first Christian converts were often gathered in from the fringes of society. It is interesting to note, however, that the Bale of Ibadan favoured the first mission by granting land and that the Iyalode gave a warm welcome to Mrs. Hinderer.

The first C.M.S. Mission at St. David's, Kudeti, later opened two branches: St. Peter's in Aremo and St. James's at Ogunpa. During the latter part of the nineteenth century, intermittent Yoruba wars were raging, and for some years the missionaries were cut off from the outside world. Before the end of the century, however, both the Wesleyan Methodist Mission and the Roman Catholic Mission had started work in Ibadan, and in 1905 the former founded the first teacher training college in the city, now known as Wesley College.

Classes were first held in church buildings, which were constructed through the collective effort of the local Christian communities. Later when school buildings were proposed, the same principle of self-help

[1] Hinderer (1872), p. 86.

continued. Teachers' salaries were paid from church funds. Gradually school fees were introduced—but they were nominal, about five cowries per pupil per year in the latter part of the nineteenth century.

During the early decades of the twentieth century, the demand for education gradually grew stronger. An awareness was spreading that those who went through primary schools were stepping into wage-paid jobs with the government services, the expanding commercial firms, or as teachers and catechists. Some of the voluntary agency schools which met stringent government standards were assisted by grants-in-aid, but even without such assistance many schools, both mission and 'private venture', emerged to meet the gathering enthusiasm for formal education. Parents were now willing to pay fees (which were high in proportion to their total incomes) in order to see their sons get ahead.

Ibadan's first secondary school, the Ibadan Grammar School, was founded in 1913 by distinguished members of the three C.M.S. parishes.[1] It began with twelve students, and its principal was a university graduate, the Rev. A. B. Akinyele. Some years later the Roman Catholic Mission and the Wesleyan Methodist Mission both established grammar schools, and in 1929 the government built Government College, which opened first as a teacher-training institution and was later changed to a secondary grammar school.[2]

In the early thirties, in response to an appeal by non-Christians, the Native Administration created several schools. At the same time, the Islamic Mission, pioneered by Chief Adeoye Omiyale, opened two Islamic primary schools, one at Odoye and the other at Ibuko, where Muslim children could gain a Western education without parents being concerned about Christian proselytizing. Alhaji Y. S. Ola Ishola and Chief S. A. Salami were other prominent leaders in this movement. More recently, other Muslim denominations, such as the Ahmadiya Movement, Ansar-Ud-Deen, and Nawar-Ud-Deen, have established both primary and secondary schools in Ibadan.

After this period of growth in education facilities, the world-wide depression of the thirties hit Nigeria. Prices for export crops fell, commercial activities were curtailed, and funds for education were cut back. But even through this difficult period, parents made determined efforts to keep their children in school. In his report for 1932, the Director of Education, Mr. E. R. J. Hussey, stated: 'A proof of the widespread desire for education lies in the fact that one of the last economies

---

[1] Mabogunje (1963).
[2] For a revealing discussion on the growth of the literary tradition in Nigeria's secondary grammar schools, see Ajayi (1963).

of Southern Nigerian parents is in school fees.'[1] The voluntary agencies were forced to reduce teachers' salaries, and the consequent bitterness of these teachers began to express itself in political nationalism. With the increase in the number of secondary school leavers and the downturn in business prosperity, the first warnings also appeared—of primary school leavers unable to get jobs.

This slack period in educational development continued during the war years, and it was only after the Second World War ended that the pent-up demands for more extensive primary schooling, as well as increased opportunities for higher education, found their expression. In 1947, for example, the Native Administration initiated nine primary schools in parts of Ibadan which had previously been inadequately served. Voluntary agencies, Catholic, Protestant, and Muslim, were also rapidly expanding their primary education and starting secondary schools. Private individuals were making an important contribution in creating schools to meet the rising pressures for education in Ibadan. In 1948 they came together to form the Independent Schools' Proprietors' Association with Chief T. L. Oyesina as president.

The year 1948 was important for higher education: the University of Ibadan opened with a nucleus of students transferred from Higher College, Yaba. The Nigerian College of Arts, Science, and Technology with three main branches (at Ibadan, Zaria, and Enugu) was later established to give post-secondary training in arts, science, teacher training, and in technical and commercial subjects. (With the coming of Independence in 1960, the three branches came under regional control and formed part of new regional universities. On the site of the old Nigerian College, the Ibadan Branch of the University of Ife took in its first students in 1962.)

This post-war period was one of intense political manœuvring. A series of constitutional changes took place as the colonial government attempted to keep up with the growing forces of nationalism. In education, the importance of these changes was the gradual decentralization of control from Lagos to the three regions. With the Education Ordinance and Code of 1948, which provided for three regional deputy directors of education, Ibadan became the centre of education planning and administration for the Western Region. This Ordinance also put into effect a plan for extensive education development and considerably higher government contributions towards education under a new system for grants-in-aid devised by Sir Sydney Phillipson.[2] The further con-

---

[1] Quoted in Hilliard (1957), p. 138.
[2] Phillipson (1948).

stitutional revisions of 1951 and 1953 placed primary and secondary education—planning, administration, and financing—completely in the hands of the Regions.

Free Primary Education

In Ibadan, this period leading to regional self-government was one of great hopes. The high price of cocoa plus the accumulated reserves in the Marketing Board funds placed the possibility of intense economic development on the horizon. Political optimism combined with the belief in a rising rate of economic growth formed the background for a great surge of vitality among the educated men and women of the Western Region. Spirited discussions, a sudden release of constructive ideas, the strong desire to chart a course for the new nation—out of this setting came the plan for universal primary education.

The feeling of tremendous urgency in stepping up education as an instrument for economic and social change prompted the newly-elected leaders to move ahead with a bold design. In July 1952 Chief S. O. Awokoya, then Western Nigeria Minister of Education, tabled in the regional legislature his proposals for reorienting the education system to meet the development needs of an independent Nigeria.[1] Although the dramatic focus of this new policy was on universal free primary education, it called for an all-out expansion of the whole range of educational institutions. The first priority was for teacher training, to meet the expected flood of new primary pupils.

The 1954 Education Act provided the administrative framework for the new educational pattern. Local Authorities were made responsible for primary schools, secondary modern schools, and teacher training colleges (but not for grammar schools). The act showed concern for safeguarding the interests of voluntary agencies and the rights of individual conscience in religious matters. Although previously the word 'compulsory' had often been used in conjunction with universal free primary education, this word was dropped. It was considered that forcing unco-operative parents would have been unpopular politically and it was also recognized that if all children of primary age were to attend school, the region could not provide the facilities.

In January 1955 free primary education was launched throughout Western Nigeria. Some 380,000 six-year-olds entered school for the first time—as it happened, more than twice the number that had been estimated on the basis of the 1952 census. The total enrolment in the region's primary schools in 1955 thus rose to 812,000, an increase of

[1] Awokoya (1952).

over 360,000 from the previous year. An immense mobilization of resources had taken place: sites for new schools had been secured, often with difficulty; nearly 3,500 new schools had been opened, the division of schools between voluntary agencies and Local Authorities having been arranged with a minimum of friction; over 12,000 new classrooms had been built and furnished, either as extensions to existing schools or in entirely new schools.[1]

After this first lively year, the enrolment in Primary I dropped considerably. The high figure of the initial year was believed to have been caused by the enrolment of children both over seven and under six years of age (in the absence of birth certificates). The next years, however, showed the steady rise expected in relation to population increase. By 1960, when all school-age children were involved in the new system, the numbers in primary schools in the region reached well over a million (1,124,000)—more than double the 1954 total. During these buoyant years, the city of Ibadan shared proportionately in the construction of new schools and the expansion of existing institutions.

At the same time as free primary education was started, 180 secondary modern schools were opened throughout the region to provide an additional three-year course for those unable to go on to grammar schools, either because they lacked finances for the higher fees, or because they could not pass the entrance examinations. This course was designed in two parts, academic and practical, but because of lack of suitably trained staff and of necessary equipment, few of these modern schools have been able to offer any solid vocational training. The number of these schools rose by 1960 to over 530, with an enrolment of 75,000 students, and by 1963 to 700, with 110,000 students. Although the government provided building grants for publicly owned secondary modern schools, these schools are otherwise self-supporting, with teachers' salaries and maintenance costs coming from the fees paid. Many of these schools are under private ownership; a wide variation in academic standards prevails.

This period during the fifties stands as a landmark in the progress of Nigerian education. In particular, the achievement of those planners who believed in the principle and in the possibility of universal free primary education, and who proceeded to put this ideal first on paper and then on the ground in the form of new and well-equipped classrooms for the hundreds of thousands of children coming to school for the first time, can be recognized as an immense act of faith in the trans-

[1] Annual Report of the Department of Education, Western Nigeria, 1954-5 (Ibadan: Government Printer, 1955).

forming powers of formal basic education. The scheme provided the means for equality of opportunity for primary schooling to boys and girls everywhere in the region: in city, town, or remote village.

Such rapid development, however, led to new strains on government and new stresses on individual families. Because of the underlying belief that the economy of the region would continue to flourish, financial difficulties were not clearly foreseen. The costs of the expansion of primary education were carried largely as a direct charge on government budgets through grants-in-aid for both capital and recurrent items—for classrooms, equipment, and teachers' salaries. To some extent, this became a substitute for the component of community self-help previously encouraged through mission and other local leadership. Thus, overall public recurrent expenditure on education by the regional government rose to absorb over 40 per cent of the annual budget (with over two-thirds of this for primary education). This has decreased the possibilities of public expenditure for other forms of development which could provide employment for the rising numbers of school leavers.

Other problems have become pronounced as a result of the introduction of free primary education. With the vast numbers of untrained teachers, the shortening of the primary course from eight years to six, and automatic promotion (except for a few in each class), an inevitable fall in standards has taken place. Concerned about complaints that the new education cannot be compared with the old Standard VI certificate, the government is placing much emphasis on teacher training by improving regular training college programmes and by offering special vacation courses in English and other subjects.

Since the massive expansion of primary education up to 1960, numbers have levelled off and the government has been encouraging a gradual consolidation to raise the standards and at the same time to cut down unnecessary expenses. As more teachers have completed training courses, they have taken the places of untrained ones. In some cases, classes have been combined and the number of teachers reduced. In those areas with inadequate enrolments to fill classrooms, schools have been merged—with care taken to prevent religious controversy.

The most serious problem, however, is unemployment among school leavers. The young men and women who attend schools in villages reject the traditional occupations of their parents and hopefully migrate to the cities in search of wage-paid jobs. With the rapid expansion of basic education, the numbers of job-seeking youths have increased sharply. But the economy is not growing at a rate high enough to provide immediate employment for more than a small proportion of these school leavers. Ibadan, a political, administrative, and commercial centre, attracts many migrant school leavers who remain unemployed. Many of Ibadan's own sons are without jobs. The predicament of these school leavers reveals a major lack of balance between the education process and the developing economy.

Unemployed School Leavers in the City

What are the present dimensions of unemployment in the city of Ibadan and how do these school leavers fit into this picture? Who supports them while they search for work? What are their living conditions? How realistic are they? Are these school leavers mainly Ibadan youth or are they migrants from other parts of the country?

To answer these and other questions, a sample survey of households in three representative sections of the city was undertaken in October, 1964. Interviews were conducted with the heads of every tenth household in these areas. The objective was to gain an insight into the employment, unemployment and under-employment of the labour force as a whole, and to view the unemployment among school leavers against this background of economic activity and inactivity. The survey thus explored not only the occupation and employment of members of the household (all men and women from the age of 14 to retirement) but also the intensity of employment (over the working day, the working year, the working life) in order to derive a meaning for under-employment and for rural-urban relationships of each household. The results confirm, supplement, and bring up to date the findings of earlier studies relating to the employment problem of school leavers in the city.[1]

The survey covered three selected areas in Ibadan: Agugu, Orita-merin, Ekotedo.

[1] The first survey—which included the city of Ibadan—was undertaken in 1960 and concentrated on final leaving classes in primary, secondary modern, and secondary grammar schools throughout the Western Region; school leavers were selected from the rolls of the previous three years; they were sought wherever they were in the Federation, interviewed, and their employment experience recorded; at the same time, the principal commercial, industrial and government employing units in Lagos and the Western Region were visited to gain information on projected employment needs. In 1961 over 1,000 school leavers actively seeking work—at the employment exchange, the few large commercial establishments, and government offices—were interviewed. Again, in 1963, similar but more detailed studies were made in Ibadan, as part of a wider investigation in the principal cities of the Federation, by selecting on a pre-arranged pattern and interviewing 400 unemployed school leavers. In the same year, principals of primary, secondary modern and secondary grammar schools (chosen on a 20% design) were asked to discuss the employment experience of leaving classes for each of the previous five years to determine to what extent the employment problem of school leavers had become more acute.

Agugu, together with Oke Ofa, Ode Aje, and Oje, represents 'traditional Ibadan', the activities of its people largely unaffected by modern influences. This area, with the exception of Oje, which has some families from other parts of Yorubaland, is inhabited almost exclusively by Ibadan people who maintain a close identity with rural areas surrounding the city. Many families have farming interests. The area has a sprinkling of craft industries, but no large business enterprises. Major markets include Agugu—a daily market distributing farm produce brought in from the countryside, and Oje—the cloth market which brings traders from weaving areas as far away as Iseyin and Ilorin, alternating on an 8-day cycle with a smaller market.

Oritamerin, including Alekuso, has a population with origins in Ibadan and other Yoruba towns as well—Ijebu Ode, Abeokuta, Oyo, Ilesha. Here there are craft enterprises, such as blacksmith shops and weaving, and a few trading concerns with permanent premises. But Oritamerin is known mainly as a major food distribution centre: yams and yam flour, cassava, and *gari*, beans, peppers, and so on. Women's occupations are tied in with food preparation and trading in the farm products from the three nearby markets of Ayeye, Oja Iba, and Gege. Men are mainly self-employed or small wage-earners in various occupations; there are a few junior civil servants.

Ekotedo, which includes Adamasingba, is a newer part of the city where not only Ibadan and other Yoruba families live, but also migrant families from the Mid-West, the East, and the nearer provinces of the North. Many different ethnic groups are represented. Here there are more street-side workshops for photographers, tailors, mechanics, furniture-makers, and retail shops of various descriptions. Here also live a higher proportion of steady wage-earners.

For the purposes of this survey, a household is defined as a family unit which habitually shares a common food preparation. Such households are found in traditional, semi-modern, and modern compounds (classified architecturally).

A man is defined as unemployed who is over the age of 14, who is not continuing his education full-time, who is neither incapacitated nor elderly (over an approximate 60 years of age), and whose earned income during the previous nine months was insufficient to meet personal (not family) imputed food costs. A single girl is also considered unemployed on this definition, but no married woman is viewed as unemployed unless she has professional qualifications by examination—such as a nurse, teacher, or stenographer.

Apprentices to indigenous traders, artisans, or craftsmen are classified as employed, provided a formal understanding, verbal or written, exists between master and apprentice (or between business woman and girl apprentice). Although regarded as employed, these apprentices often receive less money and other returns for their work than is required to cover their food costs—if, indeed, there is any money payment at all.[1]

Taking the three areas of the city together, the heads of 686 households were interviewed. Of these households, 566 are in traditional-style compounds, 32 in semi-modern compounds, and 88 in buildings of modern design and construction. These households, with an average size of six, which is approximately the same for each of the three areas, comprise a total population of 4,450.

The number of persons per room averages four: Agugu with over six, Oritamerin with four, Ekotedo with somewhat over two. The average monthly rent per room, in situations where rent is paid, is around 12s. 6d. for Agugu and Oritamerin and £1 5s. 0d. for Ekotedo, where more buildings are of modern design and more households have electricity and pipe-borne water inside the compound.

Of this total population in households visited, some 46 per cent (2,047) are younger than 14 years of age. From the remaining 54 per cent (2,403) are subtracted those attending full-time or secondary modern and grammar schools and other post-primary education institutions. Also subtracted are those either disabled or too elderly for continuous work. (In fact, many elderly people are often found to be involved in small trading, small craft industries, or farming.) This leaves some 2,100—or 47 per cent of the population in the households visited—within the labour force. These are the men and women who are capable of working and whose efforts should help national economic development, whether in transport, market, workshop, farm, office, or building site.

This number shows a small majority of men over women, especially so in Agugu and Oritamerin areas, a majority that would have been more pronounced but for care taken during the survey to discover where women (temporarily absent at family farms in villages some miles from the city) spend most of the year; in cases where most of their time is centred in the city household, they are included as part of that household. Again, young men in the labour force are somewhat greater in number than young women, reflecting in particular the heavier migration of male school leavers to the city.

Of the female labour force, a small number of young women are

[1] Callaway (1964).

wage-earners. They work in pools' offices, or as salesgirls in trading establishments; a few have factory jobs; some are teachers and nurses. Many are apprenticed to women traders and seamstresses. The rest (principally married women), while caring for their children, are mainly engaged in small trading in local markets, along the streets, or in their own compounds.

Some 15 per cent of the female labour force are unemployed. (Married women are not counted as unemployed unless they possess special qualifications and have no work.) Almost all of these unemployed young women have attended primary schools, some secondary modern schools as well. The general complaint is that there are no jobs for them. Nor do they find it easy to gain apprenticeships. A substantial number of these unemployed (some two-fifths) are taking further training in non-recognized institutions such as typing schools or dressmaking classes. Almost half of these unemployed young women have attended schools in Ibadan city; over one-quarter come from outer Ibadan (within the Province); and the balance have migrated mainly from other Yoruba villages and towns. A few have come from Mid-Western and Eastern Nigeria and the southern provinces of Northern Nigeria.

Of the male labour force, nearly three-quarters have some form of employment. Taking the three areas together, around one-fifth of those employed are wage-earners with jobs of varying degrees of permanence and income: clerks, local government, police, male nurses, artisans, labourers. Three-fifths are self-employed as traders, tailors, herbalists, small building contractors or suppliers, blacksmiths, farmers. (While Agugu has 70 men whose predominant occupation is farming, Oritamerin has 13 and Ekotedo none.) The remaining one-fifth (over 200) are employed as apprentices to indigenous traders, mechanics, blacksmiths, and artisans of all kinds. By far the majority of these apprentices are school leavers.

Over one-quarter (28 per cent) of the total male labour force in the households visited are unemployed. That is, they have not earned sufficient during the previous nine months to cover personal food costs—so far as this fact can be established from close inquiry about sources of income and support. Of these male unemployed, three-quarters (78 per cent) are school leavers. Almost all of these unemployed school leavers have had full primary schooling; many have completed the secondary modern course of three years; three are withdrawals from secondary grammar schools; two have earned West African school certificates, two have passed through trade schools. Several are married and are being supported by relatives with help from wives' earnings.

The median age of these unemployed school leavers is 19. Some 53 per cent are less than 20 years of age; 35 per cent are between 21 and 25; the rest are over 25. The distribution between ages 15 and 25 is fairly even. How long have these school leavers been unemployed? Some 35 per cent have been seeking work in the city for less than one year; 21 per cent for between one and two years, 26 per cent for between two and three years, and 13 per cent for more than three years. A comparison between the dates of leaving school and of arriving in Ibadan shows that, particularly with those coming from outside the Province, there is often a delay of a year or more before migrating.

What working experience have these unemployed school leavers had? Fifty-eight per cent have never had a job; 26 per cent could prove they have worked once; while those remaining have held more than one job. Of those who have never worked, nearly half are under the age of 20. Those who have held jobs once, twice, or even more often, for varying stretches of time, express feelings of living in a world of uncertain employment. This is an important factor in interpreting the meaning of unemployment: the continuous threat that even when a job is obtained, it may not last long. Obviously where there is an abundant supply of 'applicants', the threat of dismissal helps to discipline those employed, but is also creates a climate of insecurity.

Many of the more mature unemployed school leavers are those who have held apprenticeships with indigenous masters, some holding government trade test certificates as well as 'diplomas' from their former masters. But after completing their apprenticeship training, they have been unable to start work on their own or to get jobs (perhaps as artisans) and so earn enough money to pay their food costs. A few of the unemployed claim to have had 'on-the-job' training with larger firms.

The generalization can thus be made that the widespread unemployment in Ibadan centres on young men and women who—because they have completed from six to nine years of schooling—have heightened expectations about their future. There is no valid reason why these youths so classified as unemployed should be characterized as underemployed persons. Some may do a few chores in the households where they are living; they may help younger relatives with homework when they return from school. A few from the Ibadan area make occasional journeys to family farms, but there is no evidence that they are taking a purposeful part in farm operations. They go to the employment exchange, and they visit employed members of their families to get tips on job possibilities. They are actively seeking work with all the means at their disposal. These young people could be said, of course, to be in the period of transition between leaving school and taking up adult responsibilities. But what are the psychological results of several years' looking for work? What are their future prospects? This group is new on the political horizon. These young people have come to their maturity in an independent Nigeria, and they look to the government for hopeful signs of new industries or new projects for modern agriculture. They read the daily newspapers and are highly conscious of the changing political scene.

These school leavers were asked, 'Why do you have difficulty in getting a job?' Some of the replies were:

'Because many job-seekers come from other regions to look for jobs in the big towns.'
'Because of my education and qualification.'
'There is nobody to help me.'
'My luck has not yet shined.'

They were also asked, 'How do you think more jobs could be provided?' They invariably mentioned the government:

'Except government opens more trade centres.'
'Government should open more factories and farm settlements for new school leavers.'
'Only government knows what to do to avert the situation.'

School leavers are realistic enough in assessing their own personal economic situations, but understandably less so in appraising the regional or national economic scene. The government is in the centre of the drama, and school leavers call for action—sometimes in partisan political terms.

The Drive for Self-improvement

Forty per cent of these male unemployed school leavers are taking some kind of further education either in unofficial training institutions or by correspondence. The most popular is learning to type. For one hour of tuition a day each weekday there is a charge of 5s. or 6s. a month; for two hours a day, 10s. or 12s. a month and so on. This training of one hour a day enables the young unemployed school leaver, if he is a migrant, to justify his continued stay in the city, not only to his parents back in his home village but also to the relatives who give him food and shelter. The R.S.A. (Royal Society of Arts) examinations held regularly each six months always attract a massive turnout of young aspiring men and women hoping to win the certificate that might help to gain a job.

In Ibadan there are no less than 327 typing institutions, some with only two or three typewriters, some with as many as twenty. Because so many of the unemployed school leavers attend these 'schools', a 10 per cent sample design was worked out and 32 proprietors were interviewed. The typing schools have been started in recent years by civil servants, clerks to big firms, a few school teachers, a few enterprising school leavers who themselves have had training in the same system. These schools draw not only those without jobs, but also those with some kind of work who want to improve their prospects. Some take clients only in the afternoons and evenings, when the proprietor himself is present to give the coaching. Many operate all day with typewriters clattering from early morning to late at night and echelons of pupils coming and going at the end of each hour. A senior pupil may supervise the trainees during the owner's absence during the day; in return he will have his fees waived and perhaps other compensation as well.

Other skills can also be learned part-time from qualified tutors: for instance draughtsmanship, radio and television engineering, and signwriting. Fees are well established; for example, 'radio and T.V. engineering' for 2 to $2\frac{1}{2}$ hours each weekday costs £1 5s. 0d. a month. Most artisan skills can be learned part-time from a master or journeyman by special arrangement, with fees set by a competitive market.

There is little difficulty in distinguishing between the various kinds of indigenous apprenticeships and the workings of these private schools where skills are taught. All require a fee to be paid, but the difference depends on the time spent per day as well as the nature of the daily experience. Regular coaching for G.C.E., typing and shorthand training provides instruction for only an hour or two a day for each trainee, with fees paid monthly. Apprenticeship is a long-term arrangement (whether by written contract or not) in which the trainee surrenders his labour for a period of from two to five years and learns by spending his whole day on the job. Often he pays an annual fee to the master, and at some point he may receive wages or food and shelter from the master.

The pressure by so many unemployed school leavers for self-improvement through these non-recognized institutions emphasizes the inequality of opportunity for education at higher levels: in secondary grammar schools and technical institutions. Such opportunity depends on whether or not parents and relatives are able to pay high fees over a period of up to five years.

The Dynamics of Migration

Some 15 per cent of all unemployed male school leavers in the households visited have come to Ibadan from Mid-Western and Eastern Nigeria; most of these live in Ekotedo.[1] Some 35 per cent have migrated from villages and towns in Western Nigeria: for example, from Abeokuta, Ogbomosho, Ijebu Ode, Ondo. The remaining half have their origins in Ibadan or its surrounding area. They have received their primary and secondary modern schooling either within the city itself or in villages and townships in Ibadan province.

The reasons for these migrations to the city are mainly economic; school leavers are moving towards what seems to them a better opportunity. Three-quarters of all school leavers who catch a lorry to the city in search of work have fathers who are predominantly farmers. They come from villages and towns (often with some delay after their final year of schooling) and stay with relatives in the cities. Ibadan, because of its dominant role as an expanding administrative and commercial centre, has become a magnet.

When a boy completes primary school in a village, he often sees around him little possibility for self-improvement. The family farm probably consists of fragmented plots growing the usual food crops: probably yams, cassava, maize. In some areas, these subsistence crops are the only ones. In more fortunate areas, there may be tree crops as well (such as cocoa, palm, or rubber) or ground crops (such as tobacco, groundnuts, or rice) which bring some cash returns. But if this school leaver follows his father to the farm, he will be doing something that he could have done without having gone to school at all. Both he and his parents have greater hopes. He cannot see any possibility of creating, unaided, any marked change in the pattern of crops grown, or in the system of farming itself, which might bring a higher and more steady income. Very likely there is a school farm plot, measuring perhaps an acre or less, where he and his classmates were required to spend some time each week hoeing and slashing with a matchet. If this farm training has taught him improved methods, still there is little encouragement for him to put these practices into effect or later to establish himself on his

---

[1] Three further areas within the city, Elekuro, Inalende, Mokola (without Sabo), were surveyed in the same way as the former three with somewhat similar overall results. The principal difference is in Mokola where a high proportion of migrants from other regions live. Of these unemployed school leavers, 50% received part or all of their education in Eastern Nigeria, 13% in Mid-Western Nigeria, 5% in the southern provinces of Northern Nigeria, 20% in Western Nigeria other than Ibadan Province, 7% in Ibadan City and districts, the remaining 5% in schools elsewhere in Ibadan Province.

own. Again, the school leaver may be one among several sons of his mother, who in turn may be one among several wives of his father. Depending on the succession rights and his place in the family—if, for instance, he is the third son of the second wife—the school leaver may have little prospect of making an independent living by staying in the village. All he can see in front of him are years of hard work with elementary tools, duties varying with the change of seasons, and little chance of financial progress. And because of the conservative traditions of villages in many areas, he sees ahead many years of bowing to the elders before he gains a voice in village affairs.

With the expansion of medical facilities and health education in recent years, the survival rate within families has risen, both of young children and of older people. In situations where land is scarce, the fallow period has been shortened and the fertility of the soil has declined. When family land cannot be extended, the school leaver may in fact be surplus to the labour requirements of the farm. With existing tools and farming methods, the output from the family holding would not increase through the addition of his unit of labour. There is, therefore, no economic value in his continued presence. In such instances, it may be only reasonable from a national economic viewpoint that the school leaver should migrate to seek his fortunes elsewhere.

Lines of migration from village to city have gradually become established. Some years ago, for example, a school leaver arrived in Ibadan and was able, during a period of commercial expansion, to get work and set up a home. Then some of his relatives followed, using his rooms for a base, until they too found the means for a livelihood. They in turn granted hospitality to more young job-seekers from the same village. But now the situation has become acute: more and more school leavers are coming to the city and very few jobs are available.

This family system, based as it is on reciprocal obligations, eases the transition from the village for the school leaver. But it places a heavy burden on the relative, who may be earning only £10 a month to support himself and his wife and children. He may live in only one or two rooms and in some cases the school leaver may have to sleep in the corridor outside. Budget studies in Ibadan show that minimum costs of food for one youth come to around £1 10s. 0d. to £2 a month (with the lower cost for an Ibadan youth who consumes food from family farms). If this is subtracted from the monthly pay of the relative for a period of a year or more, it is easy to understand why the school leaver may become less welcome. He may then go to another relative or he may travel to another city to try his luck.

Taking the country as a whole, the proportion of school leavers who migrate from any particular area depends on the level of farm income, the availability of fertile land, and the date of the spread of education. At one extreme are areas where there is heavy population pressure against limited land and where education has been introduced at an early date; here 90 per cent or more of the school leavers will follow the already marked lines of migration to the cities. Young people from such a background persist indefatigably in their effort to find jobs, even as general labourers. For them there is no alternative: they cannot make a living by returning to the family farm. At the opposite extreme are those areas with fertile land in plenty and a relatively late diffusion of education; under these conditions, many school leavers remain on the farm because there are opportunities at hand and because there are usually few, if any, relatives with footholds in the cities. Between these two extremes are many villages and minor towns from which a varying proportion of school leavers migrate to seek their fortunes.

These school-leaver migrants often maintain close ties with their home villages. Even at a long distance and over a long period of time, they usually retain their share of land, no matter how small or fragmented, handed down through traditional processes of succession. A person who is successful in his career in the city generally builds a house in his village for his retirement and, in the meantime, for the use of his relatives. He may contribute to the development of the village through clan unions or improvement associations.

Here some distinction should be made between the long-range migration of school leavers coming in from many parts of the country and the perpetual movement that takes place between Ibadan and its outlying rural areas. Especially in the older parts of the city (Agugu, Aperin, Aremo, Eleta, for example), families are tied in with the production and marketing processes of surrounding farms. Farmers live within the city and travel out to their farms, lying at distances of a mile or so up to 15 or even 20 miles away. Some of these, of course, exercise absentee-management and attend the farms only at peak seasons of the labour year. At the same time, other members of the family may spend most or all of the year in the village near the farmland. Women members of such households usually help with the production of minor food crops and with the marketing: bringing a wide variety of items by head porterage to the city markets. They carry wood and charcoal for fuel, clay pots for water storage, palm wine in calabashes, vegetables and fruit and other farm products.

There is always a great deal of coming and going between the family compounds in Ibadan and the family compounds in the villages. For Christian or Muslim holidays, naming ceremonies, or wedding festivities, the whole family may gather together in the city. Other traditional celebrations take place in the village and the gatherings will meet there.

When young men and women complete their years in the village schools in the wide area surrounding Ibadan, they usually move to the city to go on with secondary education or to look for jobs. During July 1963 the headmasters of 25 of the 38 primary schools in Southeast Ibadan District Council area were visited. From school rolls it was established that 3,860 pupils had passed through Primary VI in the previous three years (2,660 boys, 1,200 girls). Estimates were made that some 940 of these were full-time students (390 at secondary grammar schools, 550 at secondary modern) mainly in Ibadan city. A few of those unable to continue their education remained on the farm or took up apprenticeships locally, but most of the school leavers came to the city to search for work. For these young people, there is relatively little permanent movement back to the village. They do not want to commit themselves to the peasant agriculture of their fathers. In any case, their parents and relatives expect them to find something better.

Expectations and Reality

In the city of Ibadan there are at least 20,000 young men who have completed six to nine years or more of formal schooling but are uncommitted to productive work of any kind.[1] Within the definition used in the survey, they are unemployed school leavers. Some of these will move away from the city back to their home villages or townships; a few will pass on to stay with relatives in other cities; but the majority will remain and persevere in their search for work. As each year passes, more school leavers arrive in the city and the backlog of unemployed youth grows.

By the nature of its disciplines, modern basic education creates a break with traditional life and occupations. Traditional education provided for the continuity of culture and the maintenance of a relatively unchanging way of life. Modern education opens minds to the forces of progress. Some years ago, when only a few completed primary schooling, school leavers were able to get jobs in the modern economy. But now the

---

[1] Taking the three sections that were explored in the survey (which covered, on a 10% sample design, a total population of 44,500) as a representative cross-section of the 30 sections of Ibadan, then an estimate of unemployed males in the City's labour force is 30,000. Three-quarters of these can be assumed to be unemployed school leavers. A substantial number of the remaining one-quarter are youths with less than full 'Primary VI' or with no schooling at all.

large numbers who pass through 'Primary six' and secondary modern school find themselves in that confused area between the rejection of the old occupations and the finding of new patterns for making a living. Their horizons have been widened, their expectations raised. These expectations are for personal and family gain and, to a certain extent, for higher status. They are consistent, nevertheless, with the driving force required to diversify and to develop further the Nigerian economy. Not only do these school leavers themselves have these hopes about the kinds of rewarding jobs they may find, but so do their parents and relatives who have contributed funds for their education. That these young people should remain without work, without a first step towards a career, represents a condition of deeply felt concern throughout the entire society. Unemployment among school leavers, then, should be explained within the context of heightened expectations set against the hard facts of the process of economic development.

How realistic are these unemployed school leavers? Their willingness to revise their ideas about the kinds of jobs they will take is directly related to the level of family income. It is these alternative earnings (opportunity cost) that must be examined in order to explain the behaviour of jobless youth in the city. If the school leaver comes from an area where land is sufficient and where cocoa or another crop brings in a cash return, then he may shun work as a general labourer; he would rather return home. But if he comes from an area where there is definite population pressure against available land and where he is surplus to the family's farm enterprise, he will very likely take any job, no matter how menial, to keep going. And he will continue to hope and to search for something better.

How does competition among these applicants express itself in the employment market? First, there is the official employment exchange where some applicants re-register each week. Next, there are the unofficial employment markets—the queues that form, for example, behind Mapo Hall, where contractors' trucks swoop in the haze of the early morning to select labourers paid by the day. The work might be to headpan earth at a building site; rates of pay range from 2s. 6d. to 4s. a day. These school leavers may group outside the gates of a commercial firm which hires daily general labour. In these cases, school leavers who are physically strong compete for jobs on the same basis as adult men and women. And lastly, there is the network of family relationships where help comes through the individual initiative of a relative or through the collective effort of a family meeting or clan union. 'Finding the price of a job' is a familiar, however unpleasant, aspect of the job lottery. Any apparent advantage that school leavers with their origins in Ibadan may have in competing on the city's labour markets is offset by the intensity of these migrant family enclaves in finding openings for work for their members.

What are the signs of the tightening 'job market'? They can be found in higher qualifications demanded of applicants to the police force, retail firms, banks, and so on; in the lengthening time spent between school leaving and finding work; in the rising numbers of applications for wage-paid jobs; in the fact that former teachers (untrained) are now without work and that former apprentices are now jobless; in that pressure is being brought to bear upon improving skills in the many unofficial educational institutions of the city. The indications for the next few years are becoming clear. Among university graduates, competition for key positions will be intense, and many will have to be prepared to accept such jobs as teaching in isolated rural areas. Promotions will come slowly. Secondary grammar school leavers will need to adjust their hopes accordingly; employment opportunities for them in the modern economy will be scarce. Finally, secondary modern and primary school leavers will have even less chance than at present for wage-paid work.

Investment in Basic Education

Given that unemployment among school leavers is so widespread in Ibadan—as in all cities and towns in Southern Nigeria—was the decision in the 1950s to provide free primary education desirable? What social and economic returns can be expected from such heavy investment in basic education?

The signal achievement of free primary education has been in going far towards creating equality of opportunity at the basic education level for all children in the Western Region, regardless of family income or locality. It could be argued, of course, that this primary education is neither free nor universal. Parents still must pay from £2 to £6 a year to cover costs of uniforms, books, and such incidental expenses as collections for school harvest festivals. And in most areas a varying proportion of children do not attend school. But the programme did cut the direct costs to parents and did provide education facilities in areas which had previously lacked them because of the erratic expansion of earlier years.

Apart from the political motives that sparked the scheme, there was the belief that the exposure of young people to modern schooling would raise the quality of the future labour force. Already some evidence has accumulated to show that primary education does raise productivity in the markets and workshops, in transport, on building sites, and even on farms. Many proprietors of small enterprises prefer school leavers to those who have not attended school at all: tailors and carpenters want apprentices who can make accurate measurements and keep rudimentary accounts; traders need assistants who can keep records and calculate. The position with farming is not so clear, but given opportunities, selected and willing school leavers are likely to be more ready to innovate new crops and to try new methods. Another benefit from the high proportion of school-age children attending school is the resulting greater mobility of labour; this competition for available jobs can be a spur to the economy, provided, of course, that procedures for selecting merit are given a chance to work.

When the plan for free primary education was proposed, what was not sufficiently foreseen was the effect of primary education in converting a state of youth under-employment in villages into a state of youth open unemployment in the cities and towns. The normal flow of rural migrants to the cities has been multiplied many times. Again, the commitment of such high public costs for primary education in relation to the total budget was not fully anticipated. With such large allocations to primary education, these finances have not been available for enlarging other parts of the education system, such as secondary grammar and technical colleges, or for expanding other parts of the economy.

Any long-term appraisal of the benefits and disadvantages of a widely based education system will depend largely on policies worked out now—policies for reducing the burden of financing primary education, for improving the quality of teaching in conjunction with curriculum reform, for balancing rural and urban development, and for providing jobs for school leavers consistent with the needs of the growing economy.

11

GOVERNMENT AND POLITICS IN IBADAN

by GEORGE JENKINS

On 15 August 1893 an Agreement between the chiefs of Ibadan and the Acting Governor of Lagos was signed, which incorporated Ibadan, the little Egba village which had become the scourge and protector of Yorubaland, into the British Empire.[1] Today, as the capital city of the Western Region and a centre of economic, educational, religious, and scientific activity, Ibadan is second only to Lagos. This chapter traces the development of Ibadan's political system from the inception of colonialism to the beginnings of independence.

Nineteenth century Ibadan had rejected the constitutional pattern of other Yoruba cities based on sacred, hereditary monarchy, and gave political authority to men who showed the qualities of bravery, wealth, leadership, youthful vigour and experience which the city needed in its early, difficult years. In the course of time, as the military power of certain lineages grew, and as they accumulated hundreds of warrior-slaves, the city's political leaders were recruited from the heads (*mogaji*) of these powerful lineages. Thus, the kinship unit, which supervised agricultural land and acted as the lowest civil and criminal court, as well as being the basic military unit, also became the source of civic leadership.

The *mogaji* were recruited into one of several chieftaincy lines. That of the cavalry chiefs became moribund with British rule and no longer exists today. The young men's line was responsible to the Balogun, or head of the war chiefs' line. In addition to these military lines there were the Bale's town chiefs' line and a line of women chiefs, who were responsible for the government of the town during the absence of the war chiefs. Within each line, the junior chiefs advanced toward the more prestigious and influential senior titles upon the death or deposition of an incumbent. Every freeman might become a *mogaji* and hence a junior chief, and every chief, according to his performance in war and in seniority among the other chiefs, might eventually become the

[1] I am grateful to the Program of Comparative Politics and International Relations of Northwestern University, Evanston, Illinois, for a grant from Rockefeller Foundation funds to conduct the research on which this chapter is based, and to the Nigerian Institute of Social and Economic Research and the University of Ibadan for their generous support in its execution.

Balogun. Since the most senior chieftaincy title, that of Bale (lit.: father of the town) was reserved for the retired Balogun, every freeman had the theoretical opportunity of becoming Bale. In this sense, Ibadan was a democracy.

The senior chiefs from each line constituted the central Council, which recruited *mogaji* into the various lines and promoted them through the ranks. The Council also dealt with foreign policy and war, the control of the subordinate towns of the empire, and the control of lands and of the gates to the city. It also acted as court of original jurisdiction in political crimes and as appeal court for the lineage courts. With the exception of the *ajẹlẹ* system, little existed of a formal bureaucracy. There was no formal, central treasury. The messengers, the soldiers, and the wealth of the individual chiefs and lineages were also those of the polity. This was the essential achievement, and the essential problem, of the Ibadan constitution: to channel the lineage-based power of its citizens toward socially acceptable and useful purposes. Military success and political power were thus closely related, and the city-state of Ibadan and its empire were ruled by chiefs who were warrior-politicians. Within a single lifetime Ibadan had grown from a troublesome camp of 'soldiers of fortune' into a capital city governing dozens of subordinate towns. The fact that the British were able to control Ibadan after 1893 with so little violence may be taken as a sign of the workability of the existing constitutional order.

Ibadan was also an urban political order. By 1893 it had a population of perhaps 190,000 and served as the centre of the economic, religious and social life of the surrounding rural areas. Here were the shrines, here were celebrated the rituals of marriage, birth and death. To live in Ibadan was to be a citizen or a slave, but not a peasant. In spite of the fact that nearly everyone is engaged in agriculture for at least a short period during the year, most Ibadan men prefer to identify themselves according to their urban activities and occupational status.

British Impact: 1893–1903

Although the Yoruba powers and the British had been negotiating for some time in an attempt to halt the Yoruba wars, the Ibadan Agreement of 1893 resulted from the threat of force and the fear of military reprisal as much as from diplomatic persuasion. In 1892 Gilbert T. Carter, the British Governor of Lagos, sent a military expedition against Ijebu Ode, the capital of the Yoruba group which controlled trade between the coast and the interior, for violating their treaty of peace, friendship and commerce with the British. A few days after this force had captured

Ijebu Ode, Carter wrote to Ibadan that he had taught the Ijebu: 'a lesson which it is not likely they will ever forget and they fully realize what the power of the Queen of England is able to do if it once put in motion.'[1]

Nor was the lesson lost on Ibadan, and after some negotiations and assurances, and at the urging of the Ibadan Anglican catechists who advised the chiefs on their relations with the British, the Agreement of 1893 was signed. The Agreement provided for peace (to be ensured by the Governor's Hausa constabulary and his political officer—the Resident—stationed at Ibadan), commerce (to be extended eventually by a railroad), and arbitration of disputes between the signatories (in the last instance solely by the Governor). These provisions led, in the years to come, to the loss of Ibadan's independence.

The British found it frequently necessary in the first few years to stress their determination to enforce the Agreement by military power. In March 1894, hearing that Ibadan had invited the northern city of Ilorin to help expel the British troops, Carter wrote: 'You cannot imagine that you would be able successfully to withstand the power of the British Government which you would be fighting against, for you have to consider not only Lagos, but the power that is behind it.'[2] In the same letter he stated bluntly his intention to dominate Ibadan generally beyond any specific provisions of the Agreement. 'I feel sure that you will not impose upon me the necessity of using harsh measures, but the Government of Ibadan *must* be carried on in the way I wish and I shall not hesitate to apply compulsion if such a course is thrust upon me by the headstrong action of your Government.'[3] By August Carter spoke simply of the 'English occupation' of Ibadan.[4] By 1897 an uneasy but mutual recognition of the changed power relations between the signatories began to emerge. The Ibadan chiefs, who had hoped the Agreement would provide a temporary peace, open trade routes and perhaps gain a powerful (British) ally for Ibadan against her enemies, now largely accepted the fact that they were militarily thwarted. The British also shifted to a less belligerent pose. Relations became more peaceful, but remained marked by suspicion and imperial condescension. In the courts, which the British administrators now spent much time attempting to supervise, plaintiffs who brought cases

---

[1] Carter to Ibadan Authorities on 8 June 1892 in a file of Historical Papers in Mapo Hall collected by the late Olubadan Sir Isaac B. Akinyele, while a clerk to the Bale in 1916.
[2] Governor to the Bale on 7 March 1894, Historical Papers.
[3] *Ibid.*
[4] Carter to the Secretary of State for Colonies on 15 August 1894 in Lagos Interior, Colonial Office 147/95.

of sorcery were ridiculed and the chiefs who were willing to hear them were threatened with report to the Governor for encouraging what in British eyes was foolishness. Yet Ibadan people who believed in the efficacy if not the morality of 'juju' could see in the British action only a breakdown of law and order. Concerned largely with such 'abuses' of 'good government' as slavery, 'juju' and the 'secret' lineage courts, the British never asked how Ibadan maintained itself as a viable, urban polity, and the Ibadan chiefs could not understand why the British wished to interfere in such matters.

A third group of political leaders, from which grew the forces which eventually were to overthrow both the chiefs and the British, was beginning to form around the nucleus of the African agents of the Anglican Church Missionary Society. The C.M.S. mission at Ibadan, because of its geographical and organizational separation from Lagos, was largely in the hands of Yoruba and Ibadan catechists, who, during the protracted negotiations surrounding the Kiriji War, acted as a sort of international civil service, translating and writing letters, delivering messages and negotiating differences between the Ibadan chiefs and the British. Their relations to both chiefs and British were therefore close. However, at the time of the Ijebu Ode expedition, when the Ibadan chiefs seriously considered expelling the Christians at the request of the Ijebu, in return for opening the roads through Ijebu country for Ibadan munitions, the C.M.S. agents, in Christian resignation, left their fate in the hands of the chiefs rather than turning to the British for protection. No stigma of British imperialism was attached to the Christians, and their participation in local affairs was increasingly welcomed. In 1903, for example, Rev. James Okuseinde and a layman became official members of the council.

Frustrated Enlightenment: 1904–13

In 1897 a civilian Resident was appointed, who began to meet regularly with the Council. At his insistence licensing fees and tolls were introduced to supply a civic revenue, and the first municipal projects were begun, which were, somewhat unfortunately, a new barracks for the Governor's Hausa constabulary and a jail. The Council Treasury was known for years as the Prison Fund. A more concerted effort was made by Captain Elgee, Resident from 1903 to 1913. Elgee's goal was to raise Ibadan 'up to the higher standard of municipal life'.[1] Elgee's method was to improve the economic structure of Ibadan so as to increase the

---

[1] Elgee to the Colonial Secretary of 4 November 1904 in 797/1904 Conf. in the Mapo Papers.

standard of living and to provide a basis from which civic revenue could be extracted. Each of his projects was discussed in Council and in committees for agriculture, education, health, etc.

One of these projects was an attempt to improve rubber production. A reserve had been established in 1899 in which tapping would be controlled to protect the trees; the rubber was taxed at a rate of two shillings per head load to provide a civic revenue. The son of the Rev. Olubi, a C.M.S. pastor, was appointed Head of the Forestry Department to supervise these arrangements. Within a year he had beaten a man so badly for disobeying the rules that Resident Elgee warned him he might have to face manslaughter or murder charges. In 1912 Olubi's attempt to lease ten square miles of the reserve to an English firm was quashed by court action. Olubi was later jailed for three years on another manslaughter charge. The chiefs never felt the reservation of the land or its supervision outside of the Council was justified. '... we gave the Government a little land and they took more and more and more...'[1] Government had promised an inspector to examine the rubber forest, but he had not come, and the people accused the chiefs of being responsible for the whole affair.

In 1905 Elgee opened a school for the sons of the chiefs. He purchased the supplies himself while on leave in England, toured the southern United States to learn more about 'Negro education', and tutored the schoolmasters daily at the Residency. However, the school committee did not function and schoolmasters came and went almost annually, one because of 'successive reports that he was useless in that capacity'.[2] At the mission schools, the chiefs had seen that schoolboys carried water and chopped wood, tasks fit for women and slaves, but not for future chiefs. If their sons learned Christian notions of peace and monogamy, would they be fit to guard the honour of their fathers' houses? It was not surprising, therefore, that a ruling that each chief should place two of his sons in the school was broken by the Bale himself. In 1911 the Council transferred the school to the Government's Department of Education for 'lack of attendance'. As a result, illiteracy remained high in Ibadan and the sons of slaves were as often educated as those of chiefs and the *mogaji*.

Other projects went the same uncertain path to ignominy. The British Cotton Growing Association, despite the bitter protests of the chiefs, was given 5,000 acres for education in improved cotton growing techniques. As the chiefs had warned, the land proved unsuitable for

[1] Council Minutes of November 1904.
[2] Council Minutes of 16 September 1911.

cotton and by 1910 when transferral of the tract to the Department of Agriculture was begun, less than 100 acres had ever been devoted to its culture.

After great cajoling, pupils began to attend a European-supervised pottery school to learn how to use the potter's wheel. Only later was it discovered that the proper clay for throwing on a wheel did not exist in Ibadan. The projects of enlightenment did not provide a satisfactory experience in new governmental activities in Ibadan.

To make things worse, the constitution began to collapse. It was earlier pointed out that the Council consisted of the senior chiefs from the various lines, primarily from those of the Bale and the Balogun. According to the constitution, the Balogun, or head of the military line, was entitled to become Bale after proving his leadership in the battlefield. When peace was imposed in 1893, Balogun Akintola, who had not yet proven himself in battle, believing the British still might leave Yorubaland, declined the office of the Bale. Since it was unthinkable that one of his subordinate chiefs should be promoted over him, the office was filled from the Bale's line for the first time. A second, more opportunistic innovation followed immediately. When Akintola's successor was willing to become Bale without having gone to the field, it was pointed out that although the Bale ought to be the ex-Balogun, no Balogun had ever held the post. Only his juniors who had survived him had become Bale. To the continual and traditional competition among the military chiefs for success in war and position in the council was thus added a conflict between the two most important lines over the criteria for appointment as Bale. With the *raison d'être* of the military structure eliminated by peace, the relevance of chieftaincy as a constitutional form began a long and undignified decline.

The British became increasingly involved in disputes among the chiefs, at first attempting to act as impartial referees. After 1907, however, when Bale Dada committed suicide rather than accept the 'resignation' which Captain Elgee enforced upon him, an unheard-of method of surrendering office, the British assumed a more active part in the selection and control of chiefs. This was done in two ways: first, by consultation with the Alafin of Oyo as to who would be the 'best' chief, and second, by the practice of withholding the 'recognition' of the Governor which was necessary before a chief could receive a salary. The Governor thus insisted that Apampa, successor to Dada, would not be recognized as Bale until he had first publicly accepted the Alafin as his overlord. Subsequently, all questions of promotion were referred to the Alafin, who acted upon the advice of the District Commissioner of

Oyo, Captain Ross. The Alafin, it was hoped, would provide correct and impartial information concerning the propriety of promotions while legitimizing through his royal sovereignty those who had been selected. The result, however, was the loss of autonomy in traditional affairs to Oyo. The Christians were dropped from the Council, and the attempt to direct the evolution of indigenous institutions toward new goals dissolved in confusion. A commentator in 1912 could only lament that the Ibadan system of government seemed to be:

'... neither fish, fowl, nor good red herring; neither African, nor European, nor Europeanized-African. All real influence has been taken out of the hands of the Bale (head-chief) and nothing has been substituted for it. Treated at intervals with unwise familiarity and with contemptuous disregard, the present Bale, a man obviously unfitted for his office, has no authority over his chiefs ... The town and the inhabitants are obviously out of hand ...'[1]

The Reign of Captain Ross: 1913-31

The frustrating attempts at 'enlightenment' at least left the British and the Ibadan alike in agreement that something had to be done to overcome the excesses and disappointments of the first twenty years of British rule. The British efforts were directly supervised by Governor-General Lugard through Captain Ross, whom he had selected to succeed Elgee as Resident, and Ross's assistant, S. M. Grier, whom Lugard had brought down from Northern Nigeria to implement 'indirect rule', a form of local government Lugard had instituted there.

According to Grier, a basic fault of the Ibadan polity was the dilemma of the Bale. 'His position appears to be that of a President of an unruly Republic, and history seems to show that his tenure of office is as short or shorter even than is the case of a South American Republic.'[2]

Should this trend continue, he argued, Yorubaland would 'fall under the control of the semi-educated native and alien native'. This he deplored. By strengthening the ties between Oyo and Ibadan, Grier thought that a more 'complete' form of rule by the chiefs could be re-established, obviating the need to rely on the emerging literate group and thus avoiding the difficulties Captain Elgee had experienced with the personnel of the Forestry Department and the Bale's School. As Grier wrote: 'I have sufficient faith in the Yoruba people to believe

[1] Morel (1912), p. 80.
[2] From a draft of a report by Grier for the Commissioner, Ibadan Province, dated 28 January 1914, Confidential No. 2 in file C 18, kindly made available to the author by the Ministry of Local Government, Ibadan. In fact, only seven Bales ruled from 1830 to 1893. From 1893 to 1912, the first two decades of colonialism, however, there were eight Bales.

that their chiefs can still be taught to govern them justly and in accordance with their own laws and customs.'[1]

Ibadan, however, only had a *balẹ*, not an *ọba*, and since Yoruba constitutional theory places all *balẹ* under an *ọba*, Grier argued that Ibadan ought to be under the Alafin of Oyo, who would be the channel for the indirect rule of the empire which Ibadan had constructed. Under this arrangement, Captain Ross and the Alafin came to rule Ibadan very directly indeed. While Ross refused to allow the Bale and his senior chiefs to be sued in open court for divorce, he frequently threatened to cut off their salaries if they did not provide free road labour or if they did not personally supervise the cutting of grass along routes the Governor was to travel. Ross insisted that all Ibadan prostrate to him and slapped the faces of those who refused.[2] Rumours of financial 'deals' between Ross and the Alafin, of sumptuous gifts exchanged between the two direct rulers of Ibadan, irritated and depressed the Ibadan people.

Animosity between the British and Ibadan grew during the First World War. Grier once wrote to the Bale saying that, 'In a Yoruba country where all men are liars, without definite evidence it is difficult to know the truth.'[3] It was even thought unwise to make a public appeal for Red Cross funds. It was believed by Ross and Grier that a plot existed to discourage Ibadan enlistments in the army. One of Grier's 'political agents' reported the following remarks had been made by a follower of Balogun Ola about a European as he passed on a motor bicycle in 1917. 'Look at the bastard. What is he doing here? He is only meat for the Germans. Have you not heard that the Germans are only twelve miles from Kano and will soon drive them all out? This is why they are trying to get all these recruits . . .'[4] It was also said that the Balogun was the only chief to oppose payment of a stipend from the Ibadan Treasury to the Alafin. The other chiefs seeking to dissociate themselves from Ola's stubborn independence accepted Grier's suggestion one day that if they wished the Balogun removed, a signed petition stating their reasons should be sent to him by that afternoon at three o'clock so that it might catch the night train to Lagos where the petition was awaited. The petition was duly delivered.

---

[1] *Ibid.*
[2] Akinyele (1946a), p. 85, refers. A petition reprinted by Akinyele, pp. 115-19, was sent to the Governor complaining of Ross's practice, which contributed to the deposition of the Bale. Memories of these practices are still vivid in Ibadan, but administrative officers who served under Ross after 1927 deny any knowledge of them.
[3] Grier to the Bale on 26 January 1917, in a Correspondence Book at Mapo Hall.
[4] Grier to the Bale on 15 June 1917, in a Correspondence Book at Mapo Hall.

'The Balogun is not straightforward ... his evil dealing is a cause of general unrest to us all ... we fear that if we are too late to take this measure ... evil may fall upon the Town, causing thereby loss of innocent lives and property which is sure to be so, if the rebellion can be successfully raised against the British Government by the Balogun.'[1]

A few days later Ola was called before the Council and told that in the Alafin's opinion he had been rejected by the people of Ibadan. Ola accepted the fact that he had been rendered helpless. He committed suicide in his own house rather than accept banishment. Eight years later Bale Shitu was caught in the same web of conspiracy among his chiefs, the Alafin and the British officers, and ably abetted by his own stubbornness, was sent to exile.

In violation of professed principles, the chiefs were effectively excluded from the governing of the city during the period of 'indirect rule'. Shitu expressed his astonishment in 1925 that Ross had deigned to consult him concerning the expenditure of Council funds. Curiously, the clerks and translators, nearly all 'alien natives', became increasingly influential. Ross continued to rely heavily on them for daily administrative matters. Gin, bushmeat and money flowed into their hands from persons seeking to have land inquiries deferred, relatives released from jail and court cases adjusted. When a delegation from the Egbe Agba O'Tan (Historical Preservation Society), a new political society, protested against this corruption to Ross shortly after he had made what one of the Egbe members termed a 'touching' plea for the inculcation of honesty in the schools, the Resident admitted his knowledge of such practices, but said it was impractical to combat them as it would undermine the authority of the chiefs he was committed to uphold.

The Egbe Agba O'Tan was formed by a group of Christians in 1914. Isaac B. Akinyele, then a clerk in the Ibadan Treasury and the Olubadan of Ibadan from 1955 to 1964, was a founding member with his brother, the now retired Bishop of Ibadan, Rev. Alexander B. Akinyele. Their friend, Akinpelu Obisesan, a product of missionary education, became its Secretary. The Egbe Agba O'Tan had as its purpose 'to make research of the past, and retain the existing wisdom and knowledge of our Forefathers'.[2] Later, a few economic ventures such as the production of sugar were considered, and a serious attempt was made to manufacture roofing tiles. The project eventually collapsed over the inability of the

---

[1] A petition from the chiefs dated 13 August 1917 in a Correspondence Book at Mapo Hall.
[2] Minutes of the inaugural meeting of the Egbe, then known as 'The Knights of Yorubaland', on 30 January 1914. My thanks to Chief Obisesan for his permission to use these documents then in his possession.

members to organize the necessary capital and their fear that the financial backing promised by Salami Agbaje, one of the wealthiest of Ibadan's merchants, might give him undue control over the enterprise.

By 1920 Ibadan was in full revolutionary fervour. Under the influence of the Lagos nationalists, and angered by Ross's administration, members of the Egbe in 1921 felt Ibadan needed its own newspaper to put its case before the world. Since the Egbe was a secret society it could not engage openly in such political activity. A 'Committee of Gentlemen', later called the Native Aboriginal Society, therefore met to organize a press. Rebuffed by T. H. Jackson, editor of the *Lagos Weekly Record*, they turned to Ikoli of the *African Messenger* since they had 'no idea of journalism'. Several letters were exchanged with Ikoli which pleased them greatly since they feared the slights of their compatriots in Lagos.

The practical question was again that of finance. Salami Agbaje solved this problem by purchasing a press and materials for a total of £745 according to Akinpelu Obisesan, who noted: 'No doubt Agbaje will one day be called "King of intelligent Natives". He has proved himself able to lead without motive to cheat. His benefaction and patriotism combined with his spirit of enlightenment go to prove that he is able to lead.'[1] Yet if Agbaje owned the press, who would control it? According to one Society member, Agbaje was 'the most covetous, avaricious and selfish man Ibadan had ever known'. Might not the Government influence him 'to deprive us (of) the liberty of printing'? Agbaje's answer was to surrender the press 'unconditionally and absolutely' to a committee appointed by the Gentlemen. Unfortunately the Committee, consisting of ten Muslims and ten Christians to provide the public basis such a venture required, was almost a 'committee of the whole' of the élite group Ibadan could muster. Relations among the members were too close to allow the Committee to function as an organization. Several of the members were in debt to Agbaje or worked for him and they feared the additional bond to him that the press represented. Obisesan was suggested as the editor, but he refused to work under the manager after he had criticized Obisesan for his part in the tile-making venture. The manager resigned and by the end of the year the enterprise had collapsed. The Christians, not being chiefs, were always under suspicion by Ross, and in contrast to their role of the first twenty years of colonialism, were excluded from all political affairs.

[1] Akinpelu Obisesan Diary of 17 June 1921.

Native Authority: 1931-52

While the reign of Captain Ross is remembered as the period of 'slap my face', the five years' residency of H. L. Ward Price from 1931 to 1936 are remembered with affection. Ward Price spoke Yoruba and disliked the Alafin, who, upon hearing of Ward Price's appointment, protested at being placed under 'a Syrian'.[1] The most important constitutional change of the period was the reversal of Ibadan's dependence upon Oyo. Ward Price first made a few symbolic changes—he moved his own office from Oyo to Ibadan into the Governor's lodge without warning the Governor, and had the wife of one of his junior officers paint a picture of the Bale to be hung at Mapo Hall next to that of the Alafin. In 1934 Ibadan and its towns were separated from Oyo and the Ibadan Council became the Native Authority with the power and responsibility for Ibadan affairs. In 1936 the title of Bale was changed to that of 'Olubadan', meaning 'Head of Ibadan', which carries some of the connotations, if not all the legal rights, of an *ọba*. Ward Price divided in order to allow Ibadan to rule.

During the next twenty years, much of Ibadan's political power rested with a political society which had grown out of the Egbe Agba O'Tan. The Ibadan Progressive Union, again largely composed of educated Christians, inherited the historical and traditional concerns which had infused the Egbe, and like the Egbe, it quickly grew from a literary society into an effective political body. Within a few years, the Union, whose membership included many men who, Ross had once told the Governor, were 'of no importance', was the most influential body in the city.

There is a custom in Yoruba society whereby a father returning from a journey brings gifts for his children. When Ward Price returned from his first leave while serving in Ibadan, the I.P.U. asked for three gifts: piped water, electricity and the return of educated councillors to the Council of Chiefs. Ward Price was pleased to grant their request to re-institute councillorship, which had lapsed since the time of Rev. James Okuseinde. Isaac Akinyele and J. O. Aboderin, their candidates for this office, were accepted by the chiefs. Schoolmaster J. L. Ogunsola, D. T. Akinbiyi, a wealthy trader, Akinpelu Obisesan and other educated men followed them. Since the Council had no executive officer to administer day-to-day affairs or to co-ordinate activities among the departments, the councillors performed these functions. As 'executive

---

[1] A mistaken conclusion drawn from Ward Price's swarthy complexion. Although he was born of English parents in Chester, some of his subordinates looked down upon him as a Welshman, or as a West Indian, and referred to him as 'a Cheetah'.

councillors' they received a salary, attended weekly meetings and spent a substantial part of their time on Council business. Most of the Council's policy planning was done by committees of the councillors and a few of the literate chiefs, while the Council as a whole acted as a final deliberating and approving body.

Upon completion of their three year terms, Akinyele and Aboderin, although not from chieftaincy houses, were honoured with titles in return for their good services. Akinbiyi and J. L. Ogunsola were eventually made heads of their own houses and began the slow advance through the ranks. It appeared for a time that councillorship might provide a new and politically relevant channel of recruitment into the chieftaincy lines, slowly infusing them with younger, educated men. Isaac Akinyele, for example, did become the Olubadan of Ibadan; Chief Ogunsola, at the time of his death in 1964, was third in line of succession to the Olubadanship. During the 1940s, however, other political societies began to demand the extension of the nomination privilege, which had hitherto rested with the I.P.U., to their own groups; and since the increased number of councillors could not be accommodated in the chieftaincy lines, the idea was dropped.

More important than their infusion of the chieftaincy ranks was the introduction of a new conception of politics. As younger men and as councillors without final authority, the I.P.U. councillors generally avoided the disputes among the chiefs. Their energies were devoted to the planning of the water and electricity schemes, the new residential lay-out on the Ijebu bye-pass, the attempt to build new offices for the Council, and municipal transport. Their contribution was to establish the idea that development of various projects ought to be the substance of the council's business and to reduce the significance of the problems of personalities and authority which had marked the era of Ross. Thus effective control returned to Ibadan-born and Ibadan-resident men.

The selection of councillors from the Union was necessarily from the educated élite, but its standards of literacy, public service, and political influence could be, and were, emulated. The most powerful of the other societies which developed was the Ibadan Patriotic Association, a federation of many smaller societies organized by Belo Abasi to provide popular support for his father, Olubadan Okunola (1930–46). Representation on the Council was soon extended to the Association, and the selection of councillors and members of a broader Advisory Board was made largely from these groups, until 1943, when the first selection from territorial wards was introduced. Even under territorial representation, which was often nothing more than the appointment by a powerful chief of the ward's representative, the I.P.U. men fared well, evidence that they were indeed looked up to as leaders. At the outbreak of the Second World War, in contrast to World War I, these and other groups were praised by the Resident for: '... spontaneous demonstrations of their loyalty to the Empire which exceed the expectation of one who never for a moment doubted where their feelings lay.'[1] Air-raid wardens, canteen hostesses, a Win the War Fund and a Greek Relief Committee were organized almost overnight. The proliferation of such groups during the 1940s paved the way for mass participation in local affairs in the next decade.

From 1949 to 1952 Ibadan was embroiled in complex constitutional and political changes. For some time the administrative officers had urged upon the chiefs the creation of an office of administrative secretary to assume the executive functions the councillors had hitherto performed. They had also urged the chiefs to delegate considerably more autonomy to the towns of the empire. Both of these proposals were steadfastly opposed by the chiefs.

Although the post of administrative secretary was still unapproved, Adegoke Adelabu was anxious to be appointed to it. He was at one time scholarship holder of the I.P.U., had become the first African manager for the United Africa Company and an inspector in the Co-operative Union of Cocoa Producers (whose president was Akinpelu Obisesan). By 1949 he was well known for his command of the English language, a talent that the Olubadan, his junior chiefs and some of the *mogaji* lacked.

During the years since the attempt to establish a newspaper under the aegis of the Egbe Agba O'Tan, Salami Agbaje had become a member of the Legislative Council of Nigeria, a chief of Ibadan and a President of one of the Ibadan courts. Chief Agbaje was probably the wealthiest man in Ibadan in 1949, and much of his wealth was distributed in loans to various traders and chiefs in Ibadan. Some of them owed him as much as £800. Now, as one of the four most senior chiefs, he was in a position from which he could attempt to succeed to the title of Olubadan. Fear of his power, jealousy of his success, disgust over an alleged lack of generosity, and the fact that Agbaje was not a native of Ibadan, led to the contrivance of a set of charges against him, the purpose of which was to deprive him of his title and his hopes for succession to the Olubadan's office. To formulate these charges, the chiefs enlisted the talents of Adegoke Adelabu, in payment for which Adelabu claimed he was promised the post of Administrative Secretary. To examine the charges

[1] Annual Report for Ibadan Province, 1939.

against Chief Agbaje, a Commission of Inquiry was established, which also inquired into allegations by British officers of inefficiency and maladministration on the part of the Council. These allegations were corroborated by the I.P.U. and other groups which were later to become associated with the Action Group party.

The results of the Commission were unforeseen by any of the participants.[1] Commissioner Butcher cleared Chief Agbaje of all charges; he recommended that the post of secretary be immediately established (it was subsequently filled by a British officer); and he urged that the northern reaches of the old Ibadan empire, known subsequently as Oshun Division, be removed from any further control by the Ibadan Council. The Hayley reform committee for constitutional revision eventually accepted these recommendations and greatly expanded the number of elected councillors.[2]

These local changes were being made against a background of political change throughout Nigeria which impinged increasingly on the local scene.

Parties and Politicians: 1952–63

During the post-war period, the new medical, educational, governmental and commercial facilities attracted many immigrants to Ibadan. The most objectionable of these 'strangers' in the eyes of the Ibadans were the Ijebu, against whom historical memories were still alive. Now, they offered economic competition to the emerging Ibadan trading and commercial class, many of whom were members of the Ibadan Progressive Union. A large number of Ijebu settled in the Ijebu Bye-pass Layout which the council and the I.P.U. councillors had planned in the late 1930s to relieve population pressure in the heart of the old city. Fear of economic competition and charges of land-grabbing were made against the Ijebu, who were organized into the Native Settlers' Union, under the General Secretaryship of Obafemi Awolowo. Awolowo was also the founder of the Action Group, a political party with nation-wide ambitions. At the time of the Agbaje dispute he had supported the desire of Oshun for separation, a move opposed by all factions of Ibadan. Thus, by 1952, ethnicity, economics and party politics were greatly intermingled.

The I.P.U. men, after some hesitation, aligned themselves with the Action Group, a party of lawyers, doctors, teachers and business men. Their hesitation, however, gave Adelabu, who had, from his part in the

[1] Nigeria (1951).
[2] Nigeria (1952).

Agbaje dispute, gained some popularity if not the administrative secretaryship, and who had been elected to the Western Regional House of Assembly in 1952, the opportunity to organize a mass political party called the Mabolaje. This he affiliated with the National Council of Nigeria and the Cameroons party which opposed the Action Group. Adelabu's Mabolaje was made up almost entirely of Muslim illiterates. Running on a platform of the popularity of their leader, dissatisfaction with the I.P.U. (on whose shoulders Adelabu laid the responsibility for the Hayley recommendations) and the lowering of taxes, the Mabolaje candidates swept into office incurring election expenses that averaged only a half or a third as much as their wealthier, literate, Christian opponents.

The 1954 Council was the first in Ibadan to operate under the new Western Region Local Government Law. The Council was now a local authority of the Regional Government, in which power over all local government matters was vested. The Council was composed of the senior chiefs, who sat by right of tradition, and councillors, elected through party contests in territorial wards. Party lines were sharply observed in the Council and in the committees in which the Council did most of its business. Adelabu was elected Chairman of the Council and of each of its standing committees. Matters considered in committee were brought to the Council for approval and its decisions were implemented by the Council's civil servants. From all of this the chiefs were largely excluded.

To end the half-century of dispute among the chiefs, promotion had been made automatic upon the death of a senior chief. Wealth, talent and political skill no longer mattered. The number of titles in each line had been extended to twenty-three and by the time the *mogaji*, who were usually already old men, had advanced through this lengthy apprenticeship to the senior titles, they were frequently too old or too tired of politics to provide vigorous leadership.

One exception to this general rule was Chief Isaac Akinyele who, by 1954, had risen to the title of Balogun, and was the likely successor to the Olubadan's office. Chief Akinyele disapproved of Adelabu's political style and supported the programmes of the Action Group Regional Government to which the Ibadan Council, dominated by the N.C.N.C., was responsible. As Chairman of the Council, Adelabu attempted to have Chief Akinyele deprived of his title and of his position as Chief Judge of the Ibadan courts. He was thwarted in this effort since the Local Government Law did not give the Council power over the traditional rulers and in 1955 Chief Akinyele succeeded as Olubadan, thereby becoming the first Christian, and the first educated, ruler of Ibadan, at precisely the time when the powers of the office reached their lowest point.

The Adelabu Council, however, had its own difficult path. Its boisterous leader was soon charged with maladministration and corruption, which the Nicholson Commission of Inquiry was called to investigate.[1] Although few of the failures of the Council were found to be 'substantial', and although the one criminal charge that was brought against Adelabu in the courts was dismissed, the Regional Government demanded his resignation from the Council. When the Council refused to suspend him and four of his councillors, the Council itself was dissolved and replaced in 1956 by a Provisional Council appointed by the Regional Government in consultation with the Ibadan Action Group leadership. Most of these Provisional Councillors were members of the I.P.U. In contrast to Adelabu's Council, the members of the Provisional Council were all educated men. Olubadan Akinyele was elected Chairman and President. The conflict of party between the local and regional levels was thus temporarily resolved.

Adelabu attempted to recoup his losses by running for a seat in the Western House of Assembly in 1956. So certain was he that he could lead the Regional N.C.N.C. to victory that he had cloth made with his picture over the title 'Adelabu, Premier of the Western Region', from which his supporters could make costumes to celebrate their victory. The Action Group, however, won the election and Adelabu became the Leader of the Opposition. He was planning the 1958 local elections in an attempt to return to the Ibadan Council when he was killed in a car accident. Some officials feel that the riots which broke out the following day, in which many Action Group supporters were murdered, were in part the result of earlier N.C.N.C. plans to protest against an increased tax levied by the Provisional Council and were triggered to unexpected violence by Adelabu's untimely death.

Although the N.C.N.C. won the 1958 elections, the renewal of the conflict between the local Council and the Regional Action Group Government, and the bitter factional struggles over the successorship to Adelabu's position as leader prevented the N.C.N.C. from taking advantage of their victory. In the 1959 Federal elections, the national N.C.N.C. leadership awarded the party label and financial support to A. M. F. Agbaje, the lawyer son of Chief Salami Agbaje, but Adeoye Adisa, also a lawyer, captured Adelabu's following, and with the financial backing of the Northern People's Congress of the Northern

[1] Nigeria (1956).

Region, carried the Mabolaje to victory. The Adisa group returned to the N.C.N.C. in 1960 for the Regional elections, but their diminishing strength at the polls manifested clearly the internal difficulties of the party.

By the time of the 1961 local elections, the local Action Group election machine, under A. M. A. Akinloye, was well organized. It was supported by almost all of the senior chiefs and it benefited from the persuasive electoral talents of Chief S. L. Akintola, the Western Region's Premier. A few weeks prior to the election, an earlier plan to separate the city of Ibadan from the immediate farm areas surrounding it was resuscitated. From the area of the old council were created six rural councils, and the Ibadan City Council. Left intact, the Action Group feared the rural strength of the N.C.N.C. would be insuperable. By dividing the city from the rural districts they could hope for a more modern and urban city council under Action Group control. Several of Adelabu's closest supporters joined the Action Group for this election, and the rest of the N.C.N.C. was torn by personality and organizational differences. Many N.C.N.C. candidates complained bitterly that the Action Group resorted to unfair campaign tactics—that goats were tied outside their houses during the night to implicate them in theft, that thugs were brought in from outside of Ibadan to intimidate N.C.N.C. supporters, that beatings and bribes went unchecked by officials. Rather than contest under such circumstances, the N.C.N.C. 'boycotted' the election at the last minute, telling their people not to legitimize the 'reign of terror' with their votes. Typical ward returns gave the Action Group candidate 1,500 votes to 50 for the N.C.N.C. candidate. Some N.C.N.C. candidates insist the boycott would have been perfect but that the Action Group stuffed both ballot boxes to give the appearance of a fair election. All forty-six Council seats were taken by the Action Group, once more aligning the Regional and the Council parties.[1]

One outcome of the 1962 crisis in the Action Group was the formation of the United People's Party by Premier Akintola. A. M. A. Akinloye, then Chairman of the Council, led a comfortable majority of the members into the United People's Party and party unity between the Regional Government and the Council was maintained. Enthusiasm over the new party varies and some Councillors admit their loyalty to it is highly conditioned. 'The Chairman got me elected and I follow him', said one. Another remarked, 'I'm really a sympathizer of the Action Group, but where are they now? What committee appointments do they get?'

---

[1] In fact, the majority of the N.C.N.C. councillors elected in 1958 had already switched to the Action Group; but this had not been recognized at the polls.

The support accorded the Action Group in 1961 by an electorate which Adelabu had once ruled with demogogic ease, and the subsequent turn of the Action Group councillors to the United People's Party suggest the uncertain nature of party politics in Ibadan. Without Adelabu, who could turn personality into votes, without the lavish financial means enjoyed by the Action Group, even victory for the N.C.N.C. in Ibadan is too expensive if the result is only to provide opposition members in the Regional House and a Council out of step with the Regional Government. No party has been able to assure itself of its future nor has it been able to assure councillors of re-election. Their qualifications and their political accountability impose further limitations on them. At present, only the three lawyers on the Council are professionally trained and while most of the rest are literate, few possess any technical qualifications which would give them any special insight into the problems of health, town planning and water supply, which the city faces. The councillors, and the doctors, teachers, engineers and lawyers who avoid Council politics, alike attribute this to the nature of the electorate, which is still essentially illiterate, with an average annual income of considerably less than £100. Their immediate world is one of market stalls, butchers' licences and land leases, problems which they insist their councillors help them solve. To be elected may cost from £50 to £300, and an annual outlay of a like amount to pay fines, doctors' fees, and make small loans for his constituents is probably the rule. Since most of the councillors claim an annual income of less than £100 per annum they must recover the difference from political gifts and fees. Few constituents would deny them the right to these perquisites, and the councillors admit that their committee assignments help them to meet their expenses. ('Do you think the "X" Company did not say "thank you" to the finance committee for a £50,000 contract?') Less than ten per cent of the present councillors have served a previous term, and at each election the old Council, with whatever virtues or ills it may possess, is turned out to provide a new group of men with the opportunity of serving.

The political way of life of the councillor has two consequences for other kinds of political leaders in Ibadan. Constituency concerns and petty fixing arrangements are looked upon as the councillors' business. Politics as policy planning in such areas as improvement of the markets, the new municipal bus system, the abattoir and other large-scale projects is left largely to the Council's civil servants. In order to preserve this great latitude from 'political' and technically unqualified intervention, the official must spend much of his time in meticulous respect of the councillors' concerns with individualistic constituency problems. As a result, the qualified officials Ibadan now has in its service have inadequate time for the planning which they are capable of doing. While some of them are frustrated by the immensity of the tasks that confront them, others are frustrated because it is so difficult for them to approach these problems as vigorously as they wish. Their position at present is doubly difficult in that the fiscal problems of the Regional Government prevent them from pursuing the plans they have developed. Through its control of grants and the tax structure the Government can effectively control the financial position of the Council. The estimates for the year 1963–64 were based on the loss of £125,000 in taxes to the Regional Government, leaving only £35,000 to be expended for new capital works. Salaries consume £315,000 of the total estimated expenditure of £778,000.

Qualified, educated, professional people in Ibadan generally abhor 'politics'. To face an election, with its self-advertisement and the necessity of meeting the masses on their level, is a task many of them carefully avoid. Even if one were elected, he would have to deal with other politicians, party caucuses, and, worst of all, the trivia of Council affairs. Said one lawyer, 'Should I serve on the Market Committee and allocate stalls?' Although the Provisional Council could boast a qualified engineer as Chairman of its Works Committee, the present Council holds little interest for him. When elections were held in 1958, after the term of the Provisional Council expired, the Provisional councillors did not contest. If Ibadan suffered thirty years ago from a certain provinciality of her educated elements, today it does not even have them at her immediate disposal.

It is doubtful whether the chiefs will have any significant future contribution to make to Ibadan politics. During the nine years of Olubadan Akinyele's rule, chieftaincy gained in prestige, but the rapidly expanding power of the political parties outran any possibility of a revitalization of their leadership. The electoral process effectively excludes the chiefs whose positions and authority rest on age, kinship and ascription. For a chief to lose an election would be an intolerable blow to his dignity. At best, he can support electoral candidates of his choice. Thus, while every political party, and the chiefs themselves, agree that the chiefs should 'stay out of politics', at election time their ability to persuade the voters remains an important, if diminishing, factor. The prejudice against education which kept most chiefs' sons out of school fifty years ago means that today there are few well-educated chiefs capable of preserving the traditional forms while coping with new problems. Unfortunately, most of them are neither young men nor senior chiefs and it is doubtful whether they can revitalize chieftaincy institutions.

Ibadan may learn to accommodate itself to non-chieftaincy politics, but it will do so only if it can retain some financial independence from the Regional Government. The Council's financial weakness makes its politics uninteresting for many people, as we have seen, and it makes the Council and the type of political leader who emerges to represent Ibadan on the Regional level heavily dependent on Regional Governmental and party authority. Nor are the prospects for fiscal independence, based on taxation, immediately promising.

Taxation was begun in Ibadan in 1918 when each adult male was required to pay seven shillings to the chief, acting as tax collector, to whom he owed allegiance. The Council thus had no more control over its tax collectors than it had over the chiefs, and the chiefs had little power to compel payment, since tax payers were free to shift their allegiance and their tax collector as they desired. Tax was collected during the cocoa harvest season when money was available, but the system was an inefficient one. In many years most of the tax was collected after the legal date.

The practice of 'tax raiding' was therefore begun, whereby streets and compounds were cordoned off, and all who were unable to produce a tax receipt were threatened with arrest and prosecution. About a third of the registered tax payers paid only under threat and officials estimate that 25–30 per cent of the taxable citizenry is not inscribed on the tax rolls at all. Tax evaders in the 1950s included government ministers, Council employees, missionaries and university professors as well as thousands of less illustrious persons.

Three reforms were proposed. The first was accepted in 1952. It deprived the chiefs of their tax-collecting powers and established committees of residents in each ward to register and assess tax payers. The result, however, was a decrease in tax payers during a period of population increase and continuing charges of corruption and late payment, a pattern perhaps not unrelated to the fact that the committees were selected by the political parties. By 1956, when no less than 535 government employees were on the default list, it became clear that even cordoning off the entire Secretariat at the end of the day, forcing defaulters to pay as they left the premises, was no longer a practice conducive to law and order and that the reform had served largely to remove the chiefs from their positions as collectors.

Due to legal problems it was not until 1961 that the second reform could be instituted. Under the Pay-As-You-Earn system, tax was deducted for all wage and salary earners at the source of income, regardless of size of income. This system was operated by the Regional Government on behalf of the Council, since the Government had more efficient book-keeping and enforcement procedures at its disposal. By 1962–63, 88,000 of the Ibadan 118,000 tax payers were paying £300,000 of the £373,000 annual tax to governmental collectors. Whatever gains might have accrued to the Council from increased efficiency were lost when the Regional Government, because of its own financial straits, returned only £104,000 to the Council. Allowing the Regional Government to reform its tax structure had been expensive for the Council.

The third reform failed even to get an adequate public hearing. In 1948 it was proposed that additional revenue might be gained on a property tax. No serious action was taken by any Council until 1954, when Adelabu accepted the idea but then proposed to tax only the buildings of the Lebanese shop owners, which was ruled to be racially discriminatory, and Government buildings, which was ruled to be beyond the powers of the Council. In 1957 the Provisional Council, forced to raise the income rates in order to make ends meet, turned to the property tax, as did the elected Councils in 1958 and 1961. Eventually a scale was worked out by which all houses would be taxed, but the majority of Ibadan's one storey mud-houses would be taxed at a rate lower than that of existing income rates. Taxes on modern buildings would more than make up the difference. Presumably such a plan would find great support with the masses of the voters and therefore with the councillors. Such was not to be the case. Thirty minutes before a public meeting to explain the scheme, Olubadan Akinyele cancelled the meeting, some say after threats of a violent reaction to the plan had reached him. Whether the threat was a false one, or whether the voters thought this was a prelude to tax on lands, or whether the vast body of taxable but unregistered persons feared they would now be caught by a more efficient scheme, is unknown. Perhaps the ward tax committees, whose services would no longer be required, opposed the meeting. Whatever the cause, this failure to establish an independent financial base meant that the Council became increasingly dependent upon a Regional Government whose own affairs were entering a period of unprecedented uncertainty.

12
RELIGION IN IBADAN

A. TRADITIONAL RELIGION AND CHRISTIANITY

by E. B. IDOWU

'Where?'
'There?'
'Here?'
'Yes, there!'
'Clear the place; not too wide; enough to take only six persons; five others with me.'

It was the chief *babalawo* who was addressing some of those in attendance.[1] The occasion was the founding of Ibadan. Lagelu and his retinue were seeking divine sanction before they occupied the land. Therefore a chief priest and five others were brought to the proposed site and a divination was about to take place.

When the bush had been cleared, the six *babalawo* sat down in a circle; the tools of divination, consisting especially, among other things, of a divining board, sixteen *ikin* (consecrated palm kernels) and a small gourd containing *iyẹ-irosun* (wood dust of the irosun tree), were laid on the ground; the *iyẹ-irosun* was spread on the divining board, and the *ikin* placed in position. Then the chief *babalawo* struck the ground with the *ikin*, saying:

'O Orunmila... Lagelu and his folk are here today. Their expressed intention is to found a habitation here, on this site. Is it approved for them to settle on this site? Will this be a land of blessing, a fruitful place, where they will increase and multiply?'

Then he manipulated his tools of divination and, as a result, the *odu* called *Ọsẹ Meji* appeared on the divining board.[2] He declared this to be a propitious omen. Thus Ibadan was founded that day on the approved site; and *Ọsẹ Meji* became the guardian *odu* of Ibadan.

We have reconstructed in the above paragraphs the foundation ritual which marked the beginning of the city. In every case when a Yoruba town is founded, there must be a consecration ritual. The oral traditions concerning Ibadan persistently tell that the guardian *odu* of Ibadan manifested itself distinctly on at least four occasions at the beginning of

---

[1] See Idowu (1962), pp. 7ff.
[2] Idowu (1962), p. 8.

the history of the city. It revealed itself first on the occasion of the founding of the town; then the oracle directed that a certain offering should be made, and the main item in this consisted of 200 snails. When the snails were brought to the *babalawo*, he sprinkled the *iyẹ-irosun* on which the *odu* had been printed on them; then he scattered them in several directions, with the words 'Creep as far as you can, over a very wide area.' That was the behest of the oracle, he said; the town would be as wide as the extent to which the snails crept. The snails, we are told, travelled far and wide in all directions; hence the ever-expanding size of Ibadan!

The second occasion on which the *odu* occurred, according to the oral traditions, was when the dwellers of the new town were settling down. According to the practice of the Yoruba, they consulted the oracle about what should be done to make the place prosperous for them, especially so that they might increase and multiply. This time the oracle told them that the 'hill-spirit' of the locality would be the tutelary genius of the new town, and that Lagelu and his folk should enter into a covenant with the spirit by sacrifice. This done, they immediately began to increase and multiply. The tutelary genius became known as *Oke Ibadan*.

The rate of the growth of the population gave the leaders of Ibadan some anxiety. How could they preserve this growing population, how could they protect the people from harm and danger, so that they did not die but remained in health? Again, the oracle gave a direction. *Ọsẹ Meji* told them that they should make an offering, and their protection would be assured. That was the third occasion.

Then there was a siege of Ibadan. The oracle was consulted and *Ọsẹ Meji* appeared again: the fourth occasion. The oracle this time directed that an offering of 200 snails, lances, and spears should be made. This gave them victory over the enemies: the lances fought for them in the rear, the spears in front, and the snails continued to creep away in all directions, thus ensuring the expansion of Ibadan. On this occasion, the name *Ọsẹ Meji* was translated as 'Double Victory', implying the victory of the Ibadan people twice in one day over their enemies.

These oral traditions are interpreted as meaning that Ibadan was founded under divine sanction, is under divine protection, and that this ensures its ever-expanding area and its ever-increasing population. Later immigrants to the town have successively recognized the deities of the earlier founders.

RELIGION IN IBADAN

The Traditional Religion of Ibadan

The traditional religion of Ibadan appears to rest heavily on two cults. The first is that of *Oke Ibadan* and the other, that of *Egungun*.

The history of *Oke Ibadan* has naturally gathered legendary additions over the years. It is certain, however, that the cult is that of a tutelary divinity, the genius of the city. Tradition persists in saying that *Oke Ibadan* is a goddess. She is therefore known as the 'Mother with immense breasts' (*Olomu-oru*), a reference both to her personality and to her prolificity, so innumerable are her children; she is believed to be the goddess of fertility and procreation. It is in connection with this attribute of hers that the traditional history of Ibadan merges with that of Erin. For according to a tradition, a person from Erin was directed to make an offering to *Oke Ibadan* in order to have children. As a result of the offering, Erin became populous and prospered.

There has been a suggestion that the cult of *Oke Ibadan* originated from an earlier cult of an ancestor. This is probably due to the fact that *Oke Ibadan* came to be identified rather closely with the founder of Ibadan, who became her priest, and that a confusion of identity has therefore taken place here. The memorial festival of an ancestor is usually observed as a subsidiary one to that of the local tutelary divinity. Where the ancestor has been the priest of the tutelary divinity and has also been a person of very strong character, it is not unusual that the divinity and the ancestor become so closely associated that the distinction between them is blurred or disappears.

The festival of *Oke Ibadan* is an occasion of universal rejoicing and merriment for the whole of Ibadan. It used to be a period of complete holiday when work and trade in the markets were forbidden. It was then also attended with simulated moral laxity and excesses. Perhaps it is true that some promiscuity was practised and connived at during the period; such a symbolic ritual commonly features in festivals connected with fertility cults.

The cult of *Egungun* is definitely associated with the ancestors. The word *egungun* in the singular number means 'the spirit of an ancestor'. *Egungun* has its basis in the strong belief of the Yoruba that death is not the end of man; that those who departed from this earth in consequence of the phenomenon called death have only gone to live in another 'world', the 'After-Life'; and that there is a spiritual link between the deceased and those who are still on earth. Consequently, communion and communication must be maintained between the two worlds. The ancestors in the world beyond have considerable powers because they

LIFE AND WORK

have been released from the handicaps of the physical world; they continue to bear their titles of relationship: father or mother; and they are believed to be spiritual superintendents of domestic affairs, especially with regard to the assurance of prosperity and the preservation of moral values. The ancestral cult means to the Yoruba that the family life of this earth has been extended beyond the physical milieu to the spiritual. The *egungun* either remains an invisible spirit to be approached at the domestic or communal shrines, or it may be represented symbolically by a re-embodied form, a figure completely covered by a robe and sometimes wearing a mask, speaking in a piping falsetto. This figure is known as *ora ọrun*, a sojourner from heaven.

The *Egungun* festival usually lasts a whole week in the month of June. This too is a time of general merriment. The festival precedes the harvesting of yams, which is another way of saying that new yams can only be eaten when the ancestors have first partaken of them. Here, again, the significance of the ancestors in the family hierarchy is emphasized in the ordering of the life of the community.

But whereas these two pillars of the traditional religion have so much hold on the traditional life of Ibadan, we find that the cults of the 'gods many and lords many' of Yorubaland are well represented in the city. These include the cults of the divinities, as well as the cults of certain semi-divinities, who are descended from original divinities and certain deified priests or ancestors. We have observed above how the hybridization between a divinity and an ancestor happened in such a way that the attributes of the divinity were absorbed by the ancestor.

Among the principal divinities found in Ibadan is *Orişa-nla*, with his consort *Yemowo*, and their variations under the names of *Ogiyan*, *Olufọn*, *Ikire*, *Alaşọfunfun* and *Iya mapo*. *Orişa-nla* is the archdivinity of Yorubaland; he is designated as deputy to *Olodumare*, and is the creator god and the divine symbol of ethical purity. *Ọrunmila* (often called *Ifa*, which is really the name of the system of divination connected with his cult) is the oracle divinity who is a *sine qua non* in the traditional religion of the Yoruba; *Eşu* is the divine messenger, an inspector-general and a liaison officer between heaven and earth, ubiquitous and given to mischief; *Ogun* is the god of war and of the chase, of the smithy and of all who deal in mechanical things of iron and steel; *Şango* (now the prevalent name for the thunder and lightning divinity) is the expression of 'the wrath' of *Olodumare*; *Yemọja*, the goddess, is believed to be the mother of *Şọpọna*, the divinity whose scourge is the smallpox, and of *Şango*; *Ọya* is the able consort of *Şango*, the mainstay of her husband in every way; and *Ọsanyin* is the tutelary divinity of doctors. Of those

238

which are crosses between divinities and ancestors we have *Oriṣa-oko*, a very prominent and popular divinity in Ibadan, who is the god of agriculture; and *Oduduwa*, a goddess or a god-ancestor, depending upon which tradition is prevalent in each locality in Yorubaland; in Ibadan, he is believed to be god-ancestor.[1]

Basically, of course, as in all Yorubaland, the ultimate end of worship is the Supreme God, *Olodumare*.[2] All the divinities and ancestors are believed to have been brought into being by him and are here to serve his behest and purpose.[3] The divinities and ancestors, though apparently autonomous in respect of their functions, are in fact theologically never ends in themselves, but means to an end. The alpha and omega of life and worship is *Olodumare, Olọrun* or *Ẹlẹda*, depending upon the context in which one is speaking or thinking of him. He is the author of moral values and the ultimate determiner of destiny.[4]

Christianity in Ibadan

The work of the Christian Church in Ibadan began with the visit of David Hinderer, a C.M.S. missionary, in 1851. He and his wife, Anna, made the city the scene of their missionary activities for several years; and it was through their zeal that the C.M.S. began and founded there the Anglican Church. The Methodists followed in 1888, although it was not until 1891, with the stationing in the town of the Rev. C. B. Macauley, that a settlement was really established. In 1895 the Roman Catholic Church made a beginning. The Baptists came in 1906, the Salvation Army in 1921, and the Seventh Day Adventists in 1926. The churches founded during this period have now grown considerably in size and number, and several other small bodies have been added to them.

Christianity in Ibadan is divided into four groups. Its distinctive features are marked by the way it is expressed by the various churches. These churches may be grouped under the following four headings:

(1) Those which are called by the generic title 'Protestants'. Among these are the Anglicans, Methodists, Baptists, and the Salvation Army.

(2) The Roman Catholic Church.

(3) Those which are generally described as the African Churches. These include the African Church (Incorporated), the United African Church, and the United African Methodist Church.

[1] Idowu (1962), pp. 22-9.
[2] *Ibid.*, pp. 30-56.
[3] *Ibid.*, Ch. 7.
[4] *Ibid.*, Ch. 12, 13.

(4) The 'Independent Churches', the most prominent components being the Cherubim and Seraphim Church and the Christ Apostolic Church.

The Protestant and the Roman Catholic churches are European-related; that is, they were introduced into Nigeria by European and American missionaries and still depend to a large or small extent upon the European mother-churches for maintenance both by way of financial aid and the supply of staff. All the churches in these two groups show a marked loyalty to the traditions of the mother-churches from which their missionaries came. They maintain a strong link with these mother-churches, and hold so fast to the imported traditions that they wear a rather disturbing European complexion. Today they are aware of the undesirable effect of this situation and are now trying to make their patterns of working follow indigenous forms more closely and ensure that Nigerian clergy and church workers play the dominant role.

The African Churches came into being, partly in consequence of the objection made by certain Christian Nigerians to the domination of the church by white missionaries, and partly on the grounds of discipline in connection with Christian practice. They are made up of splinter-groups from the Anglican and the Methodist churches. All the break-away movements occurred in Lagos, formed into separatist churches, and have now spread all over Nigeria and beyond. The first introduction of an African Church into Ibadan took place about 1914.

The African churches are neither related to, nor dependent upon, any European bodies in the sense in which the Protestant and the Catholic churches are. From the very beginning all their leaders, ministers and laymen, have been Nigerians, and their organizations have been handled entirely by indigenous leaders. Nevertheless, it is somewhat disappointing that the African churches have little that is specifically African in the ordering of their organizations and worship. It would appear that from the very beginning, they have had the notion that the way to be 'respectable' was to conform in their every outward expression to the ways and practices of the various orthodox bodies from which they originally seceded. Thus, those which originated from the Anglican church faithfully use the clerical vestments, the hymn book, and the liturgy of the Anglican church; those who originally came out of the Methodist church follow the Methodist practices in the pattern of worship and the ordering of church life, their ministers wearing the black Geneva gowns, or whatever happens at the time to be in vogue among the Methodists.

It should be admitted, however, that the African churches have made a definite step forward in the direction of the indigenization of the church in Nigeria. They promote to some extent the use of traditional music and songs at worship, although only as appendices to the main liturgies, which are largely those that are being followed by the European-related churches. Furthermore, the African churches have declared openly their inability to see why they should give up certain traditional ways and adopt instead Christian values, with particular reference to the Christian home and family life. Specifically, the question of polygyny or monogamy is an issue about which they leave the individual Christian to decide for himself, except that some of the churches have demanded that their ministers (but only these men) must be monogamous. There are signs, however, that at least one of them is reconsidering its stand on the issue, especially now that the question of relationship with the other Protestant bodies is being seriously raised.

The Independent churches embrace a number of organizations, the origin of which was a spiritual phenomenon which occurred in Yorubaland between 1918 and 1930. It was another sign of the revolt of the spirit of certain Christian Yoruba against the European complexion of the church in Nigeria, with her prefabricated liturgies and traditions. These liturgies were found wanting in that, generally, they did not minister adequately to the spiritual temperament of the people. These Christian Yoruba were spiritually very sensitive and thus found the worship of the Church rather arid and unsatisfying. There awakened in them therefore a craving for something more original and spontaneous. Again, Christianity, as introduced by the Europeans and Americans and as practised in Nigeria, appeared to them to be an incomplete religion: it was something which began within the walls of the church building and ended there, a thing therefore which did not reach every area of life and could not support a person under all circumstances. To such people, Christianity in its European form had little spiritually and was therefore a traitor to its own basic tenets.

As a result of the spiritual crisis which was experienced by these few Christian Nigerians, a spiritual restlessness began within the orthodox churches. Small groups began to form themselves here and there, being variously named 'prayer groups' and 'prayer bands', or described as 'faith-healing groups'. By 1925 the movement had taken a definite shape. This was the year in which the Seraphim Movement, later called the Cherubim and Seraphim Movement, and now known as the Cherubim and Seraphim Church, first began. Then followed, in 1930, the movement led by Joseph Babalola, which resulted in the Apostolic

Church, now known as the Christ Apostolic Church, and that led by Josiah Ositelu, which culminated in the Church of the Lord. These three bodies have since proliferated, or splintered and multiplied under various names.

The first definite manifestation in Ibadan of the spiritual phenomenon which resulted in the formation of the Independent Churches may be said to have occurred in 1924, although we have reason to believe that it began there much earlier. Almost all the churches and sects which came into being as a result of the 1925 to 1930 movements are now represented in the city.

The Independent Churches have certain common characteristics. At the beginning, they all held tenaciously to the belief that faith in operation through prayer was sufficient for the purpose of healing any manner of sickness. This was, in fact, their most distinguishing mark. On the whole, this is still their general official position, although some of them have moved gradually from this position and have reached the point of arguing that since medicine is of God's creation, it can be used provided it is done within the context of prayer. All the churches attach importance to visions, revelations and predictions. They are all given to somewhat boisterous and ecstatic behaviour at worship, and to frank and uninhibited evangelistic zeal.

The Independent Churches are a step beyond the African Churches in the movement towards making the church an indigenous one. In their case it is more definite and more spiritually spontaneous. They have a tendency towards syncretism, however: they use the Psalms as charms; more often than not, their rituals have a magical overtone, while their vision-seeing, prophetic predictions, and imposition of ritual acts or penances, serve as substitutes for certain elements connected with the traditional system of divination. But there can be no doubt that their contribution towards the church is of a permanent value. In particular, their use of hymns and lyrics locally composed, spontaneously expressive of personal faith, set to traditional tunes and accompanied with traditional instruments, indicates a form of worship which has the effect of reaching the emotional depths which the imported liturgies can never reach.

The Christian churches have always worked through three media— the medium of evangelism, that of education, and that of healing. These have all been used and are still being used in Ibadan.

At the beginning, the Christian gospel did not find a ready reception in Ibadan; the local chiefs were very suspicious that Christianity might jeopardize their influence and authority. Furthermore, Islam had already found favour with the local leaders of Ibadan and had entrenched itself among them before the coming of Christianity. They saw in Christianity a rival faith to their own. Eventually, however, the gospel made headway. The result can be seen today in many church buildings, large and small, all over the city; in the thousands of practising and worshipping Christians who fill the church buildings to capacity, especially on Sunday mornings; and in the Christian influence which indisputably permeates the whole community.

The lot of Christian education was not at the initial stage easier than that of the preaching of the Gospel. It was difficult to persuade parents to send their children to school, even though education was offered free of charge. This was due partly to the suspicion and antagonism mentioned previously, and partly to the fact that parents felt they could not spare their children for the amount of time that school education demanded, as this appeared to them to be a waste of valuable time and man-power. Notwithstanding, the church's programme of education was eventually accepted, and it became successful. The result is that, today, at least seventy-five per cent of the work of education in the city of Ibadan is in the hands of the churches—through their kindergarten schools, through the very large number of primary schools, each of which at present offers a six-year programme of education, through several secondary grammar schools and higher school certificate classes, through teacher training colleges for men and for women, and through theological institutions for the training of ministers and lay agents of the churches.

It is certain that the educational programme of the churches has had a considerable effect on the life of the community as a whole. In every walk of life in Nigeria there are men and women of outstanding calibre who owe their training and upbringing to one or another of the churches' educational institutions. There is at least one Christian hospital in Ibadan: that of the Roman Catholic church situated at Oke Ofa. There are also several dispensaries and first-aid posts which are operated by the churches. A good example is the Wesley College dispensary which for many years now has been serving Elekuro area and beyond not only in the treatment of minor ailments or injuries but also in maternity and child welfare.

Religion and Life

Man's concept of the supersensible world and his relationship to the divine has always determined his mode of life. Traditionally, the Yoruba have their way of life determined by covenant-relationships: with the divinities immediately and with the supreme deity ultimately. But whereas the moral values accepted in each locality depend on the character of each local tutelary divinity, the norm and binding force of the universally accepted moral values come from the Supreme God.

We have observed above that the traditional religion of Ibadan rested apparently on the two cults of *Oke Ibadan* and of the *Egungun*. Generally, the influence of the fertility cult is reflected in the lives of the people, while there are also evidences of the hereditary characteristics of the ancestral patterns of behaviour. Those ancestors were not always, during their life-time, models of predictable behaviour; and this trait must have been forced upon them by their circumstances in the new place of abode. They had to become tough and to be quick-thinking, in order to meet all the emergencies with which they were confronted in their struggle for existence or for supremacy over some of their neighbouring towns. During the *Egungun* festival, it is not infrequent that quarrels develop between rival *Egungun* leaders and their followers; and these continue all the year round to disturb the rhythm of daily life.

There is, however, unmistakable evidence that the people recognize a set of moral values which is infinitely higher than that which is implied in the two traditional cults. This is inculcated partly through other cults which demand higher standards of ethical and spiritual life. There is, for example, *Orisa-nla*, who represents ethical purity, and *Sango*, who reminds man constantly of the 'wrath' of *Olodumare*. More especially, this is due to the inevitable ethical urge implanted in every person by the supreme deity. To this, expression is given frequently by every person in Ibadan in such sayings as *Olorun ko o* or *Olorun ko fẹ bẹ*— 'God forbids it' or 'God will not have that'.

With the coming of Christianity, the people of Ibadan were inevitably confronted with new moral values, or, rather, with the basic values governing human existence and relationships as presented and interpreted by the new religion. By its tenets, Christianity demanded high standards of living, and it was, therefore, by implication, revolutionary. This was one of the first things that struck the people when the gospel was first preached, and its lessons introduced, in Ibadan. For this reason, Christianity had the power either to attract or repel, depending upon the spiritual disposition of those who came into contact with its message. Where it attracted, it brought converts into the fold of the church and started a community of people who were beginning a new spiritual and moral life; where it repelled, it evoked antagonism and persecution.

RELIGION IN IBADAN

Interactions of Religions

When Christianity came to Ibadan, the traditional religion was already getting old and tired. There was a yearning in the hearts of the people for a new way of life, for something more forceful, more satisfying, and less cumbersome to the spirit. Islam had already arrived as a religion of greater enlightenment, cleaner living, and superior power. It had been uncompromising in its monotheistic demand, although, by and large, it afforded satsfactory substitutes for some of the things it took away from its converts.

Christianity came with the demand that only one God should be worshipped, through Jesus Christ, and that the demand of this one God was the whole of life, surrendered without reserve in self-dedication and implicit obedience. In its own way it was uncompromising, and began by asking that the house should be swept clean of all that it judged, in consequence of the tenets of the faith or through the eyes of its foreign missionaries, to be of the devil. It was presented in a clean vessel: a new, foreign vessel. The early converts accepted all that it taught and demanded, and sought to sever connexions with the past and often, as far as was possible, with their environments. Many of them adopted foreign customs as taught by, or exemplified in the lives of, the missionaries. The missionaries found the schools very useful in their relentless campaign against all that they regarded as 'heathen' ways. Children of Christian homes who received education in Christian schools sought to live up to the 'new' dignity which being Christians conferred upon them. Gradually, those who became 'enlightened' through the Church were turning away indiscriminately from the traditional ways.

Looking back today, one can see that the early method of evangelism had its faults. For example, it resulted, by some miscarriage of purpose, in creating for the Africans a dichotomy in life which was unknown to them before. Somehow, their old life became unrelated to the new. Before long a conflict arose in their minds. With the more sincere converts of the first generation, absolute faithfulness to the demands of Christianity as taught by the missionaries was the rule, but this could not equip them to cope with all strains and stresses. 'Blind faith' worked its miracle, however, and many remained faithful to the end. There were those, however, to whom the temptations and spiritual conflicts became too much; there were complete or surreptitious lapses. Thus, while the Church went on increasing and multiplying, the traditional religion kept making assaults upon her in various ways, reclaiming some of those whom Christianity had at first won from it.

It was not very long before there came a generation of Christians who found Christianity, as practised, to be inadequate. Therefore, while many of these have remained as much as possible 'faithful' members of the Church, there have been those who have had no qualm in seeking the guidance of the oracle or the ministration of a priest of the traditional religion in regard to certain vital issues of personal life.

As we have observed, the 'spiritual' movements of the 'twenties and 'thirties began as a result of the inadequacy of the European form of Christianity; and in some of the churches which the movements have brought into being, we see unmistakable marks of the interaction of the traditional religion and Christianity upon each other. In the worship and practices of these churches, there are elements of the old cults, like ecstasy, divination and sacrifice, ritual music, the seeking of seclusion by the sick or suppliants in the temple, charms and incantation, all used in adapted and refined, 'Christianized', forms.

With the coming of vigorous nationalism, the syncretism took a reverse direction. Christian structural elements are now being employed in the reconstruction of resurgent traditional cults. Thus we have the Reformed Ogboni Fraternity, which is only the old cult in a 'reformed' structure, or the *Orunmila* Church, with a liturgy cast in a Christian mould.

It would appear that the present-day educated Ibadan man who has come under the influence of Christianity and yet has not accepted or has discarded its spirit is a worse man morally and spiritually than the Ibadan man in his pre-Christian days. That would certainly be the claim of the traditional elders. They make frequent observations to this effect, because there are unwholesome happenings today which would have been either impossible or punished severely under the system of the purely traditional religion.

Nevertheless, we must observe that there is abroad now a spirit which frowns at the excesses of, and all that is now adjudged as immoral in, the old cult practices. For example, even the simulated moral laxity connected with *Oke Ibadan* festival does not now meet with the general public approval, and all *Egungun* must behave themselves, at least when out and about.

The Future of Religion in Ibadan

This is a speculative paragraph; but a word or two is necessary. As I have said above, the traditional religion in its indigenous form is on the way out. But as a result of nationalism and the inspiration of other higher religions, it appears to be coming back in a resurgent or recrudescent form. Has the traditional religion only stooped to conquer? Is the current tendency towards resurgence going to result in something of permanent value?

Christianity is handicapped by the fact that the Church is a house divided against itself: a consequence of the faulty evangelism which characterized its beginnings in Ibadan. Its effect on the life of the people is therefore not altogether as it should be. There is, however, an effective scheme for a United Church in Nigeria; and there is also a drive towards the adequate training and spiritual equipment of the ministry of the Church. These two factors of unity and integration in the life of the Church, and of effective ministry, are bound to stand Christianity in good stead.

In the spiritual struggle for the life of Ibadan, Christianity has an intrinsic advantage over the traditional religion; it only needs to remove the defects which have become attached to its outward expression to become completely suited to Nigerian life.

B. ISLAM[1]

by F. H. EL-MASRI

Introduction of Islam to Yoruba Country

The date of the introduction of Islam to Yoruba country is uncertain; the earliest reference occurs in a work by Ahmad Baba of Timbuktoo (d.1627) entitled *Al-Kashf wa'l-Bayān li Aṣnāf madjlub al-Sudān*; in this work, Ahmad Baba put Yorubaland among the areas where 'unbelief predominates and Islam is rarely found'.[2] This would seem to imply that some Muslims had by this time penetrated Yoruba country, perhaps from Hausa country to the north. Both Johnson and Parrinder, however, suggest later dates for the introduction of Islam; Johnson puts the time of the spread of Islam into Yoruba country as the 'close of the eighteenth century', while Parrinder suggests that Islam was introduced 'from the latter half of the eighteenth century'.[3] The important thing to note about the spread of Islam, however, is that it had already become a factor in the country before the Fulani Jihad of 1804. By the end of the eighteenth century and the beginning of the nineteenth century, Islam had gained a foothold even as far south as the coast, where European travellers bore witness to the flourishing state of Muslim communities. Most of these Muslims were, however, slaves of Hausa origin who, despite their status, were described by the Lander brothers in 1830 as 'respectable and (are) never called on by their

---

[1] This chapter results from a series of meetings with the learned malams of the central mosque in Ibadan, which began in December 1961. A chance discovery of Uthman Dan Fodio's *Ihyā'al-Sunna* amongst their manuscript collections stirred my interest in their methods of transmitting knowledge. This led to inquiries into the history of the older-established families of teachers and proselytizers and gradually into the wider study of the growth of Islam in Ibadan.

The chief Imam arranged weekly Sunday meetings for me with some twenty elder shaikhs of the city. The oral evidence contributed in both Yoruba and Arabic was written and compiled in Arabic by the Deputy Chief Imam, Ahmad al-Rifai in May 1962.

As a means of verification, their accounts were cross-checked with other groups of Muslims outside the central mosque organization, such as members of the Ansar-Ud-Deen and the Ahmadiyya Communities as well as al-Hajj Adam Abdullahi al-Ilori of Agege who compiled a short work on Islam in Yorubaland.

I should like to extend my thanks to all who have helped to make this work possible, particularly Dr. Bolanle Awe who lent considerable assistance in the revision of the material.

[2] There are two MS copies of this work in Morocco and one in Paris. The work was often quoted by Uthman Dan Fodio to determine which people of the Sudan were unbelievers against whom a *Jihād* could be waged. The above quotation is reported by Dan Fodio in his *Bayān* (W. E. N. Kensdale, *A Catalogue of the Arabic Manuscripts Preserved in the University Library, Ibadan, Nigeria*, 1955–1958 (82/54).

[3] Johnson (1957), p. 26; Parrinder (1956), p. 33.

masters except when required to go to war, supporting themselves by trading for slaves which they sell to Europeans.'[1]

Islam was in general introduced to Yoruba country by peaceful means. Both Johnson and Parrinder bear witness to the fact that it was spread by traders and mendicants visiting Yoruba country from Muslim lands. The process of contact between these Muslim areas and Yoruba country has, however, not yet been a subject of serious investigation and, in spite of the dates given by Johnson and Parrinder, it is difficult to determine how far back this contact occurred. There is no doubt that there must have been very early trade contacts between Kanem-Bornu and the Habe (or Hausa) kingdoms, where Islam had taken root since the eleventh century, and the neighbouring Nupe and Yoruba countries. According to Ifemesia, there were three main routes between these areas: (1) the Kano-Badagry land route, (2) the north-south main road from Kuka, the capital of Bornu, to the Benue, (3) the Niger-Benue waterway which connected at different points with the main avenues.[2] A close study of these trade routes and of the trade being carried on along them may throw some light on the extent of the impact of Islam in Yoruba country. In this regard, a linguistic comparison of Hausa and Yoruba languages, a study of the influence of Islam on Yoruba traditional religion,[3] as well as the examination of oral traditions should be of great value.

Beginnings of Islam in Ibadan[4]

Since Islam has been a factor in Yoruba country from the end of the eighteenth century, it is not surprising that right from its foundations (c. 1829), Ibadan had numbered among its inhabitants some Muslim converts under an Imam called Gunnugun. They were, however, few in number and were only nominally Muslims, since they maintained to a large extent their pagan practices; their knowledge of Islam was meagre and imperfect.

True Islamization only began in the early 1830s when learned Muslim teachers came from Hausa country through Ilorin and started to preach in Ibadan. Notable among the first preachers were Ahmad Qifu and Uthman b. Abu Bakr: the first came in the reign of Oluyedun within the first few years of the foundation of the town, and he was reputed to

---

[1] Lander (1832), p. 37.
[2] Ifemesia (1959), pp. 13–16.
[3] Cf. Idowu (1962), pp. 100–101.
[4] For this section, the manuscript compiled by Ahmad al-Rifai which is now kept in the Library of the University of Ibadan has been extremely useful.

RELIGION IN IBADAN: ISLAM

be a grandson of one of the Alafins of Oyo.[1] The other, Uthman b. Abu Bakr, came during the period of the ascendancy of Bashorun Oluyole.[2] He was originally from Katsina and had settled in Bornu. He left Bornu with some of his people with the intention of going to one of three towns, Ijebu Ode, Abeokuta or Ibadan. It is related that Bashorun Oluyole had been told by one of his priests that a foreign Shaikh whose prayers were always answered, would come to Ibadan, and that if he arrived, he (Oluyole) should take pains to accommodate him. Thus, when Uthman arrived, he was received very hospitably and lodged near Oluyole's house.

Uthman b. Abu Bakr eventually became the first truly Muslim Imam of Ibadan in 1839, a post which he held till his death in 1871, when be was succeeded by Ahmad Qifu. By 1871, Islam had gained a large number of adherents in Ibadan, particularly through the proselytizing activities of itinerant shaikhs; these came especially from Ilorin, which had become the chief Muslim centre for learning and spiritual guidance in Yoruba country. This did not, however, mean the establishment of any official religious connection between the Fulani-dominated town of Ilorin and Ibadan; in most cases these preachers came, as private individuals, to preach in Ibadan of their own volition.

It was one such missionary from Ilorin, Shaikh Abu Bakr b. al Qasim, who laid the foundation of Islamic learning in Ibadan.[3] He was himself a native of Ibadan whose father had settled in the course of his trade at Ilorin, where Abu Bakr received a good grounding in Muslim education; so well versed was he in all branches of Muslim learning that he was invited back to Ibadan by the Muslim community when Are Latosa was still the leading chief in Ibadan. He settled on Oke Aremo in the north-east of the town and there started a school which was frequented by Muslim students from all parts of Yoruba country; he taught them Arabic grammar, philology, theology, Qur'anic studies and prophetic traditions. It is, however, in the field of scholarship that he made his most notable contribution. He produced many distinguished

---

[1] Are Onekakanfo Oluyedun was one of the earliest war chiefs of note in Ibadan; he came to power before Oluyole, and must thus have been in power in the first few years of the 1830s.
  Johnson (1957), p. 186, relates a tradition that Alafin Abiodun of Oyo (c. 1775–1805) bestowed honours on a Muslim by giving him one of his daughters in marriage.
[2] Bashorun Oluyole became the dominant military personality in Ibadan from c. 1836, to the time of his death in 1847. The first Hausa who arrived in Ibadan during his reign lived in his house in front of Iba Market.
[3] Haji Adam Abdullahi al-Ilori of Agege, a graduate of Al-Azhar University in Cairo, and author of a short work on *Islam in Yorubaland* claims that the standard of education laid down by Shaikh Abu Bakr was as high as that of the traditional Muslim universities.

pupils such as Aminu Allah, a refugee of the Ijaye War, Malik b. Husayn from Ikoyi Ile, and Harun, son of Matami, a chief in Oshogbo. All these men were also notable teachers and preachers and they continued the intellectual tradition laid down by him; one of them, Harun, used in fact to assist him by translating his interpretations of the Qur'an from Hausa into Yoruba and eventually succeeded to his intellectual leadership in the community. But apart from teaching and preaching, Abu Bakr was also responsible for broadening the religious experience of the Muslim community of Ibadan in other ways; a notable example was his attempt to organize in Ibadan a pilgrimage to Mecca. Unfortunately he died on the way, in Ibariba country to the west of the present boundary of Nigeria, but he had paved the way, and by the end of the century, Ibadan pilgrims were going to Mecca.[1]

Indeed, Harun dominated the intellectual and spiritual life of the town right from the death of Abu Bakr till the time of his own death in 1935. He eventually became the mufti, or jurisconsult, of his time, the final authority on any religious disputation. Like his master, he produced most of the distinguished scholars of the period. He tried to improve the quality of learning in Ibadan and to keep in touch with intellectual developments in the Muslim world generally by encouraging scholars from other places to come and stay at Ibadan; in fact such scholars came from as far afield as the Sudan and Sokoto, and were often maintained financially by Harun. He also sent his own students to other Muslim centres such as Ilorin. A notable student of his was Al-Shaikh Salih b. Abd al-Qadir (1871–1909), who went to study arithmetic under Shaikh Muhammed al-Busiri of Ilorin. As a result of all this intellectual activity, Ibadan became an important centre of Muslim learning, and attracted students from all over Yoruba country who went back home to lead the Islamic movement in their various towns.

Harun also played an important part in the spiritual development of the Muslim community in Ibadan. In 1922 he became the Imam of the central mosque in Ibadan;[2] this, as well as other important posts in the Muslim hierachy, were, by the end of the nineteenth century, acquiring

---

[1] The pilgrim route was from Ibadan to Oyo, Iseyin, Shaki, Kishi, Ibariba and Sokoto; this north-western route was taken because the more direct eastern route was unsafe. From Sokoto the route went east to Fasher in the present Republic of the Sudan, then to Nuhud, Khartoum and Sawakin in the Eastern Sudan. Haji Adam, *op. cit.* claims that the number accompanying Abu Bakr to Mecca was twenty and that a gang of robbers attacked the party and killed Shaikh Abu Bakr.

Haji Abdullahi Aliyu, one of the informants on Abu Bakr's death, went on pilgrimage in 1897 and came back successfully six and a half years later.

[2] See below for the role of the central mosque in the Muslim cummunity in Ibadan, and also Cohen above, pp. 126.

a position of significance in the national life of the town. The reason for this development was largely the close association in the nineteenth century of these Muslim leaders with the war chiefs, who patronized them because of the belief in the efficacy of their prayers and talismans to give protection in times of war. The Imamate in particular was a post of great prestige and was closely contested by the leading Muslim teachers of the day; in this case the close association with the secular authorities has persisted, and today the Olubadan, as traditional ruler of Ibadan, turbans the Imam-elect. As the Imam of Ibadan from 1922 to 1935, Harun had to assist his shaikhs who were mostly his own students; his deputy was Muhammed Olatusa, whom he chose to explain the Qur'an during the Ramadan season, to preach in the mosque before the Friday prayers and to give the sermon at funerals. At other times, his shaikhs gave the interpretation of the Qur'an in private houses; this practice was discontinued in the reign of Bashorun Apampa, and the shaikhs moved to the courtyard of the great mosque, which became the centre for Qur'anic exegesis.[1]

Islam in Ibadan today

The tradition of learning and spiritual development set down by Harun and his predecessors still persists today. Since this is a different tradition from that contained within the structure of the indigenous society, it has tended to make the Muslims a distinct group in Ibadan. This is, however, not to say that the relationship between them and other foreign-inspired religious groups is not cordial. Indeed, the relations between Muslims and Christians in Ibadan are very friendly. They eat together except when food forbidden by Islam, such as pork, is offered; they visit the sick and bury the dead together, except when prayers over the dead are said; the people following the other religion then stand at a distance. They donate when collections are made to build churches or mosques, and take part together in religious ceremonies, congratulating one another for *Id* or Christmas. Some strict malams of the central mosque may frown at such close contacts with the Christians when religious traditions are involved; they may even quote a hadith attributed to the Prophet Muhammed forbidding it. Nevertheless, the cordial relations between Muslims and Christians continue and deepen. The treatment of pagans by Muslims on the other hand, noticeably differs. Muslims refrain from eating with pagans and do not, as a rule, attend their funerals.

---

[1] It was during the rule of Bashorun Apampa (1907–10) that quarrels broke out between the Muslims and the Pagans who accused each other of abusing their religion.

LIFE AND WORK

Most of the Muslims in Ibadan now are orthodox, following the Maliki rite, though, among the malams, the Tidjaniyya brotherhood seems to be more popular than the Qadiri. It is significant that the 'deviant' forms of Islam, such as the *shi'a*, have not found their way southwards from North Africa. According to Hodgkin, the coming of the Almoravids to the Western Sudan 'checked the possibility of the spread southwards from the Maghrib of the "deviant" forms of Islam, and transmitted to the emerging Muslim states of the Western Sudan its own particular conception of "orthodoxy"—Maliki rigourism, respect for "fugahā", hostility to kalam'.[1] The only non-orthodox group in Ibadan are the Ahmadis who believe in the prophethood of Mirza Ghulam Ahmad of Qadian (d. 1908). This movement was first introduced to Ibadan from Lagos in 1923, and was split in 1940 into the Sadr Anjumani (Qadiani) and the Ahmadiyya movement-in-Islam (Nigeria). The two branches are highly organized and have been actively engaged both in preaching and in the educational field; and had it not been for their theological differences with the orthodox group, they would have led the Muslim community in Western Nigeria.

The orthodox Muslims acknowledge the Chief Imam of the central mosque as the spiritual head; they are all members of the central mosque and the main organization for their spiritual development is centred round it.[2] Under the Chief Imam, there are two important posts; one is for interpreting the Qur'an during the month of Ramadan and for preaching in general, and the other is for reading the sermon before the Friday prayers. The Chief Imam and his two assistants are selected for life by a 'council of scholars' (*Dīwān al-'Ulama*) which is the committee that runs the affairs of the central mosque. This council is composed of six *mogaji* and four malams (*'alim*) all of which are hereditary posts from the old families of shaikhs who first came to Ibadan and established their fame through preaching there. The Chief Imam should be a scholar noted for his learning and character, but should also come from one of the old families, though he need not necessarily be a descendant of a chief Imam.[3] There is no financial provision for the main-

---

[1] Hodgkin (1962), p. 323.
[2] A new central mosque is now being rebuilt on the same site at an estimated cost of over £300,000. The foundation stone was laid by the Sultan of Sokoto and a special stone was sent by the Chief Imam of Medina; the Olubadan of Ibadan was the chairman at the ceremony which was attended by the Premiers of Northern and Western Regions, ministers, *oba*, and other leading religious and political men of the two regions.
[3] In fact a list of the Chief Imams of Ibadan seems to indicate that the title gradually became confined to a few families; see the table at the end of this chapter.
   The man who would most likely be a Chief Imam today is Ahmad al-Rifai; no ancestor of his was a chief Imam but his family is included in the council of scholars with the title of '>*Alim* (malam).

RELIGION IN IBADAN: ISLAM

tenance of the Chief Imam, his two assistants and the members of the Council of scholars, but they gain their subsistence from the *Zakat* and *Ṣadaqat* (alms) collected from the community of the central mosque. Other sources of income are contributions paid to the officiating *mogaji* and other scholars when they pray at naming ceremonies, marriages and funerals.

Although the activities of the central mosque are confined to the religious field, there is provision elsewhere for education of children in the Islamic tradition. There are many circles of children around a malam or an ex-pupil of his, reading chapters of the Qur'an or the Hadith or old religious texts, most of which are commentaries on the *Mukhtaṣar* of Khalil, the main textbook on the Maliki law in West Africa. The majority of these books are hand-written, being copied either from printed books obtained from the only two bookshops dealing in Arabic works in Ibadan, or from manuscript material. Very often the pupils do not stay long enough to master these texts or get any proper knowledge of Arabic. They abandon their studies soon to join a profession. There are only about four primary schools in Ibadan where pupils remain till the age of sixteen and become proficient in the reading and writing of Arabic. The only career open to such pupils when they finish their course is to teach in one of the above-mentioned circles. Some parents, however, send their children to Ilorin or to the Arabic centre at Agege for further Arabic education. Such pupils seldom have a chance to learn how to read and write in English. On the other hand, the Muslim children who go to government and Christian missionary schools have western education but they do not know Arabic and their religious knowledge in Islam is weak.

The need to combine a sound Muslim education with an equally sound education along western lines has given rise to an interesting development in the Muslim community. Within the ranks of the orthodox Muslims a number of organizations have sprung up mainly to develop Western education of the Muslims within a Muslim context. This trend in the structural organization of the orthodox Muslims has been attributed partly to the failure of the central mosque to meet the educational requirements of the Muslims, and to confine itself only to the religious field, and partly to the pressure being put on Muslim children to become Christians in Christian schools.[1] The largest of

---

[1] Cf. a pamphlet published by the Ansar-Ud-Deen Society, 1 June 1961, pp. 2–3, states that 'Prior to the inauguration of the Society, only two or three Muslim schools were being run. The Christian Missionaries, on the other hand, dominated the educational life of the country, and pressure was being exerted on some of the Muslim pupils attending the Christian schools to convert to Christianity.' Some

these organizations is the Ansar-Ud-Deen Society which was founded in 1923 in Lagos and was introduced to Ibadan in 1937; others such as the Young Nawar-Ud-Deen Society and the Islamic Missionary Society soon followed.

It is, however, too soon to judge the success of this educational experiment. The Muslim primary and grammar schools established by these organizations are handicapped in the teaching of Arabic and Islamic knowledge by the absence of qualified teachers. In meeting this difficulty the Department of Arabic and Islamic Studies of the University of Ibadan is making some contribution. It now runs a one-year Certificate Course in Arabic in which teachers from these schools are given an intensive course in Arabic language, preliminary English and theories of education. The successful candidates in this one-year course may return later to the University for a further year's advanced course to qualify them for teaching Arabic and Islamic knowledge up to the standard of the General Certificate of Education Advanced Level in grammar schools.

The foundations of these organizations have also posed one major problem within the orthodox Muslim community as a whole. Although all orthodox Muslims consider the Chief Imam of the central mosque as their spiritual head and regard themselves as members of the central mosque, yet the development of these associations has encouraged a certain amount of parochialism; the tendency now is for every small organization to have its own mosque; the central mosque has valiantly tried to resist the establishment of mosques for Friday prayers as it has the effect of minimizing the amount of income and prestige the central mosque enjoyed when all Muslims attended it on Fridays. Its stand here is supported by the Maliki school, which insists on one single mosque for every town so that all Muslims can assemble in one place on Fridays.[1] The central mosque has, however, lost the battle and there are fifteen mosques for Friday prayers in Ibadan, as well as about five hundred for the five daily prayers.

In a way all these activities are an indication of the growing strength of Islam in Ibadan; a large percentage of the inhabitants are Muslims

> young members of the central mosque also felt the need for more positive action towards the advancement of the Muslims. An Ibadan Muslim Progressive Committee emerged from within the central mosque, and in collaboration with members of other Muslim organizations, launched the campaign for constructing a large central mosque. They intend to enter next into the educational field and establish modern schools.

[1] The creation of new mosques resulted in legal proceedings to stop the Hausa Sabo Community from saying the Friday prayers at Sabo.

RELIGION IN IBADAN: ISLAM

and are making an impact on the life of the community in many fields, apart from those of religion and education, which have been described. This makes all the more glaring the fact that there has as yet been no comprehensive study of the social, economic, political and religious life of the Muslims in Ibadan; this is an interesting field which calls for a special investigation.

Table 12B.1: List of Chief Imams of Ibadan since the introduction of Islam to the city*

1st Imam	? –1839	Abdullahi (Gunnugun)[1]
2nd Imam	1839–1871	'Uthman[2] b. Abu Bakr (Basunnu) native of Katsina or Dindi
3rd Imam	1871–1872	Ahmad Qifu, native of Bornu.[3]
4th Imam	1872–1884	Harun Agbeni.[4]
5th Imam	1884–1886	Sulaiman Alagufon[5] a native of Bida.
6th Imam	1886–1896	Ibrahim Gambari[6] native of Zaria or Bornu.
7th Imam	1896–1911	Abdullahi Basunnu, son of 2nd Imam.
8th Imam	1911–1922	Muhammed Lawal Qifu, son of 3rd Imam.[7]
9th Imam	1922–1935	Harun Matami.
10th Imam	1935–1940	Ali b. Muhammad (Ajagbe Afasegbejo), grandson of the 4th Imam.
11th Imam	1940–1940	Muhammad Bello b. Yusuf Inakoju.
12th Imam	1940–	Mahalli (Adisa Basunnu), son of 7th Imam,[8] his grandfather was also the 2nd Imam.

* Comparisons with the list of Parrinder (1956), p. 201:
[1] His origin is unknown but Parrinder says he was from Sokoto.
[2] Parrinder calls him Ismaili.
[3] Parrinder calls him Jibrila.
[4] Parrinder calls him Tijani Afasegbejo; Harun had a son by the name of Sanusi Afasegbejo who did not become an Imam.
[5] Parrinder calls him Garuba Alagufon, he also cites him as a native of Ilorin.
[6] Parrinder calls him Sulaiman and native of Kano; in fact Ibrahim had a son by the name of Sulaiman who was not an Imam.
[7] As the eighth Imam Parrinder puts Yusuf Inakoju. Yusuf was a great scholar, but he did not become an Imam at all. Thus Parrinder's list totals 13.
[8] Parrinder puts his first name as Ayinde.

IV. THE FUTURE

13

THE PROBLEMS OF A METROPOLIS

by A. L. MABOGUNJE

The previous sections in this book have shown the way in which Ibadan has grown since it was re-founded in 1829 as a predominantly Oyo city.[1] The story is of a city continually attracting to itself people of different ethnic origins. At first, as Ibadan rose to be the capital of an ever-expanding empire, most of the immigrants into the city were either young men seeking a life of adventure in the military activities of Ibadan, or slaves, male and female, brought in as booty from these frequent engagements. These earliest additions to the city's population were usually absorbed into membership of existing compounds or lineages, so that heterogeneity, from the start, has characterized the Ibadan population.[2]

With time, this heterogeneous strain deepened. After 1893, when the British arrived, still more people flocked into Ibadan. They came from Ijebu and Egba provinces; they came from Oyo, Ife and beyond Ilesha. They were all mainly Yoruba-speakers although belonging to different sub-groups. They came this time mainly for trade and kept themselves apart from the earlier population. Then the railway was constructed. By 1912 it linked Ibadan to Northern Nigeria and by 1927 to Eastern Nigeria. Henceforth, all Nigerian ethnic groups—Hausa, Fulani, Kanuri, Ibibio, Ibo, Edo, Urhobo and Tiv—flocked into Ibadan. Non-Nigerians—Lebanese, Syrian, Indians, and Europeans—also came: the population of the city became truly cosmopolitan.

This heterogeneity of population meant a complexity of needs which the city was now expected to satisfy. Whilst the earlier immigrants were satisfied with living in family compounds, sharing the pleasures of urban existence with their kin, the later comers had no such inclinations. Having only a limited circle of relations in the city, they demanded individual living quarters, perhaps a single room, an apartment or even a detached, single-family house. Where once the compound could survive with an indifferent system of conveniences, the immigrants demanded an ever-increasing range of improved household utilities, for which they were prepared to pay higher rents. And where once the age-group or occupational guilds provided the forum for activities outside the family circle, the new city provided a wide range of activities

---

[1] Bolanle Awe; see above, p. 11ff.
[2] Barbara Lloyd; see above, p. 59ff.

based on common employment, common political affiliation, common recreational interest and attendance at the same church or mosque.

Still more pressing were the needs following the modern technological innovations introduced by the Europeans. At first there was simply the need of setting up a modern administrative machinery; of producing a corps of educated élite to consider various development plans and give deliberate decisions about them, and of providing this élite with airy, spacious and structurally safe office buildings. Then there were the needs of the railway system which, within Ibadan, involved the operation of a station, loco-shed, engineering depot and marshalling yard. These were needs which, apart from calling for more educated men, specifically required the provision of an adequate water supply and the generation of electricity. Commerce and banking operations also made their own demands for land, special types of housing, men with special types of training, and improved means of transportation within the city and between it and other centres. The latter demand, especially that of speedy transport and movement from city to city, required new conceptions in the developments of housing, and is forcing the pace of change in the older part of the city.

This complexity of needs is thus transforming the structure of Ibadan from that of a simple, traditional African city into one more differentiated in its parts and increasingly more difficult to co-ordinate in terms of its efficient functioning. The major places of work are located peripherally to the major residential districts. The residential districts, in turn, differ considerably, both in their physical appearance and in the character of their residents. Each district is, as it were, visibly stamped in the image of the social and economic expectations of its populace. The result is a confusing criss-crossing of daily movements, both of people and vehicles, into and out of work areas, between and beyond residential districts.

On more than one occasion, the administrative machinery designed to regulate and foster the efficient functioning of the city has had to be changed in recognition of the need to reflect the increasing complexities of the city. Until 1893 the city was ruled by a line of civil chiefs, usually relatively old men, whose days as members of the more attractive and respected line of military chiefs were over. When the British administrative control of the city began in 1893, the idea initially was to have a British Resident who would work with the traditional council of chiefs to stimulate the introduction of modern innovations and development. But the chiefs were interested not in innovations but in power struggles among themselves. As a result, many of the innovations in Ibadan before

1931—that is, the railway, the production of rubber, the creating of a forest reserve, the opening of a school supported by public funds—were the results of direct coercion on the part of the British Residents.

By 1931, however, Ibadan was already producing its own modern élite, which began to make its influence felt in the administration of the city. The élite at first operated through a political association, the Ibadan Progressive Union, and were absorbed into the administration through the system of nominated councillorship. The councillors advised the chiefs of the need for development and performed various services connected with council administration. As Jenkins observed, 'their energies were devoted to the planning of the water and electricity schemes, the new residential lay-out on the Ijebu bye-pass, the attempt to build new offices for the Council, and municipal transport. Their contribution was to establish the idea that development of various projects ought to be the substance of the council's business and to reduce the significance of the problems of personalities and authority which had marked the era of Ross.'[1]

Soon the idea of the Council becoming the forum for discussing the development of the city gained ground. By 1943 a system of selecting councillors on the basis of wards in the city was introduced and by 1949 the way was opened for mass participation in local affairs. The beginning of internal self-government in Western Nigeria further encouraged this trend, and the passage of the Local Government Law in 1953 democratized the composition of the Council. In 1961 the administration of the city was separated from that of the districts. The instrument which established the present City Council indicated that the Council should consist of sixty-six members, four being nominated female members. The present Council is thus overwhelmingly dominated by elected members who were chosen on the basis of the forty-six wards into which the city was divided.

Modern democratic representation in the Council has not been an unmixed blessing for the city. Whilst it has broadened the base of authority and involvement in the city administration, it has tended to encourage the election to office of the less educated and the less enlightened. By and large, the rough-and-tumble of local political life has dissuaded many of those whose experience and training could have helped the city along the road of development and modernization from presenting themselves for election. The result is that Ibadan today misses the devoted concern of the early councillors. Instead, much of the activities of the Council is bogged down in the petty trivialities of

[1] Jenkins, above, p. 224.

councillors trying to derive immediate benefits from their office. And as Jenkins pointed out 'petty fixing arrangements are looked upon as the councillors' business'.[1]

The Trend up to 1980

It is against this background that one must look at some of the changes imminent in the situation of Ibadan. For, as the capital of Western Nigeria, its character as a metropolis is bound to be greatly emphasized in the next two decades. This emphasis is bound to result from the greater move towards industrial development in the city. Although it is true that industrial location in Western Nigeria has been strongly orientated towards Ikeja, a town now more truly a suburb of Lagos, there are indications that this trend may be reversed soon. The orientation towards Ikeja was initially to prevent the Federal Government from extending the boundary of Lagos, the Federal capital. This would have been at the expense of Western Nigeria. The cost of paying back to the Western Nigerian Government for a viable industrial estate at Ikeja close to the Lagos boundary would have been so overwhelming that this was considered a sufficient deterrent to the extension of the boundary. There is no doubt, however, that the Ikeja estate succeeded so well in attracting industries precisely because of its proximity to Lagos. By 1958, when the Estate was being developed, Apapa, the major centre of industrial concentration in Lagos, was already becoming crowded. New industries, desiring a location near to the port of Lagos, were only too willing to move to Ikeja.

Today the strained political relation between the Federal and the Western Regional governments, which had underlain the earlier call for the extension of Lagos boundary, has lessened. Moreover, there is the growing realization that a policy of concentrating industries in Ikeja does not help to resolve the more pressing problem of unemployment in the major cities of Western Nigeria. This realization is obliging the Regional Government to give more positive encouragement to industrial location in Ibadan. At present all that this means is that a decision has been made to establish a well-planned and adequately equipped industrial estate to the north-west of the city. Plans are already afoot to acquire an area over 1,000 acres in extent located along the western portion of the projected ring-road skirting the city. How soon this estate will be ready is not known, but that its effect on the growth of Ibadan is bound to be decisive is clearly beyond any doubt.

The experience of Greater Lagos has shown how phenomenal an

[1] Jenkins, above, p. 230.

increase of population can follow in the wake of industrial development. From a city of only a little over a quarter of a million in 1950, Greater Lagos had, by 1962, shot well over the one million mark. Its area, too, within this twelve-year period, more than doubled. However, it may be unrealistic to expect that Ibadan will show the same rate of growth. In the first place, it is only a regional capital, not a national capital with a strong attraction to it of people from all parts of the country. In the second place, Ibadan, with its resident population of 650,000 (1963), has a greater back-log of under-employed urbanites waiting to be gainfully absorbed by industrial development; so that the attractive strength of new industries in terms of migration into the city from other places is bound to be much less.

Nonetheless, industrial development would witness a rapid growth in the city's population and area. In any case, if the present rate of annual increase—3·2 per cent—is sustained, Ibadan should pass the one million mark by 1977. This will be a population more heterogeneous than ever before and therefore much more differentiated in terms of its social and economic characteristics. In a situation of growing wealth and enlightenment, the prospect of these trends in the development of the city does not make for enthusiastic expectations, for there are certain problems which they are bound to aggravate. These problems are broadly of two types, namely those related to the efficient functioning of the city and those related to the efficient administration of the city.

Problems of a Functional Nature

By efficient functioning of a city is meant three things: the provision of an adequate standard of public services, so that the essential economic, social and cultural activities of the city can be carried on vigorously and without hindrance; the smooth and unrestricted flow of people and vehicles along the roads of the city at all times of day; the stimulation and sustaining of a feeling of belonging, and of loyalty, to the city. The individual city-dweller must feel directly committed to fostering the continued growth and development of the city.

At present the level of public utilities in Ibadan is far from adequate for its present population. Less than 10 per cent of all houses in the city have water installed, and average daily consumption of water per head is less than 10 gallons (cf. Lagos with an average daily consumption of about 30 gallons). Yet, in spite of this, there are periods of acute water shortage each year, especially during the months of December, January, and February. There is no doubt that the 4 million gallons maximum output per day of the Ibadan Water Works is already proving too small for the demands being made on it. This volume of output is, however, in itself an achievement, since the construction of the water-works involved the creation of a lake or reservoir by diverting the headwaters of a number of very small streams flowing into the Ogunpa stream. An improved water supply for Ibadan is already projected; it involves damming the much bigger Oshun River, some 20 miles from Ibadan. When this scheme is completed, it is expected to furnish a maximum output of 16 million gallons of water per day, which should serve the need of the city for at least the next decade.

The same story of rapidly rising demand is told in the supply of electricity. Between 1959 and 1964, units sold rose from 25 to 41 million, a 60 per cent increase in the short period of five years. The consumption by commercial and industrial enterprises, whilst it represented only 60 per cent of total units consumed in 1959, rose to 75 per cent of the total in 1964. Indeed, these primary users more than doubled their consumption in the period. All indications are that the rate of growth of electricity consumption in Ibadan is likely to continue to increase rapidly. Since, however, the city's supply is now integrated into that portion of the nascent national grid based in Lagos, its growth is bound to be circumscribed by the efficiency of power production at Ijora. At present, Ibadan suffers with Lagos from the rather frequent breakdown of power supply, with incalculable effects on industrial productivity.

In terms of educational and health facilities, Ibadan's metropolitan status is clearly demonstrated. Within Western Nigeria it is the only city with a full range of educational institutions from the kindergarten to the University. In 1963 the city possessed over 200 primary schools, about 50 secondary modern and 20 secondary grammar schools, some 8 teacher training colleges, a Technical Institute and two Universities. Total enrolments in educational institutions of all kinds are well over 100,000. The presence of so many facilities for obtaining higher qualifications generates other related activities, such as the provision of coaching and private lessons, or, sometimes, the running of evening classes for the many people wishing to benefit by them. The Extra-Mural department of the University of Ibadan also runs a number of evening classes for interested individuals, whilst the University of Ife offers evening classes for law students. Both the British Council and the United States Information Service supplement the rather inadequate library facilities provided by the Regional Government.

In a country with limited medical centres, Ibadan again stands out with its dozen or more hospitals and nursing homes, and about the same number of maternity homes and dispensaries. It also has the best-equipped dental centre in the region. The presence of the University of Ibadan Teaching Hospital is perhaps the single most important element in the unequalled medical facilities which Ibadan provides. Over the last decade, this hospital has built up a nation-wide reputation for itself, and it attracts patients from all over the country. However, these facts should not blind one to the almost intractable health problem which Ibadan still presents. Poor sanitary conditions, congestion and large areas of overcrowding have made the work of the preventive and social Health Services more vital for survival in the city than is that of the hospitals. Yet there is no sign that they are winning the battle, and, at a time when everything indicates that the city is at the threshold of much more rapid growth, the problem needs to be attacked squarely and efficiently, both by the Health and the Town Planning Authorities.

Traffic problems in the city are still modest. Compared with Lagos, the number of privately owned vehicles are few. Mass-transit public transport has only begun in the last year, although there are numerous small, Morris Minor taxi-cabs that facilitate movement from one part of the city to another. In the circumstances, traffic congestion problems are limited to short periods of the day and to the Western margin of the city (the Ijebu bye-pass through Oke Ado, the Railway Station, Ekotedo and Mokola). This is an area where the separation of work-places from residences is so distinct that a traffic problem is inevitable. One important determinant of the rate at which this problem is likely to grow is, of course, income. As income rises, the tendency to buy more vehicles, private and commercial, also increases. But other phenomena are equally generated by rising income—increasing rent, rising value of housing and rising cost of labour—all of which tend with time to make the solution of traffic problems more intractable. This is why there is need for a comprehensive review of traffic generation in any consideration of urban planning and development.

The question of stimulating and sustaining a feeling of belonging and of loyalty to the city is one which is of vital significance to the healthy growth of cities in Nigeria. Since in many traditional Nigerian cities the immigrant population often represent the more educated, the more enlightened and the wealthier sectors of the population, opportunities should be provided for it to use these advantages in the interests of the city. But at present two factors operate against this realization. In the first place, the inhabitants of the traditional city feel strongly that, since the city has always been their home, it belongs exclusively to them. For this reason they should be allowed to run its affairs as best they can. Unfortunately, this situation is further encouraged by the elected council system, which gives overwhelming representation to the inhabitants of the traditional city.

In the second place, partly as a reaction against the situation, the immigrants develop a completely indifferent attitude to the affairs of the city. Increasingly, they see themselves as sojourners in a foreign city, and, apart from carrying on their work, they leave matters concerned with efficient administration and development of the city severely alone. Rather, they try to strengthen their relation with their home towns. They find an outlet for their talents in organizing Improvement Unions for their home towns and as often as not travel frequently between Ibadan and the former to participate in the life and progress there.

The existence of so many ethnic unions and improvement unions thus tends to isolate the immigrant in Ibadan. The result is the wasting of the very talents which could make a considerable difference to the development of the city. This is a situation that needs to be investigated seriously. If Ibadan is to reflect its growing cosmopolitan character, greater efforts need to be made to provide opportunities and facilities for both the indigenous and immigrant population to co-operate in the task of transforming Ibadan into a modern, beautiful and economically viable city.

Problems of Efficient Administration

In a sense, the problem of the efficient administration of the city is partly related to the issue raised above. A city wishing to make a rapid transition to modernity needs a group of far-sighted individuals who appreciate, and can efficiently apply themselves to, the work of directing its affairs. But at the moment, the establishment of the Council which directly administers the affairs of the city is greatly weighted against the emergence of such a group. Until 1961 the city was administered along with its rural districts. The rural districts are, of course, populated almost exclusively by native Ibadan whose votes tend to be cast for an Ibadan-born man irrespective of his capacity for this type of work.

In 1961, however, the City was separated from its rural district and constituted into a City Council, but the membership was still weighted against an enlightened, energetic group. The Council is to consist of 66 members: a President (the Olubadan), who may or may not be educated; 15 traditional members, who, holding hereditary chieftaincy titles, may or may not be enlightened; 46 elected members from the 46 wards into which the city has been divided (of these wards, only about 9 are in the immigrant sections of the city); 4 nominated female members.

With a Council most of whose members are uneducated and most of whom see in Council work a means of earning their living, a background to inefficiency in the administration of the city is clearly set. The result is a series of problems, some of which are directly related to the electoral system and others to the calibre of the councillors.

A system which engenders the feeling that the city belongs to a section of the community is bound to lead to nepotism and corruption, as well as to the detriment of efficiency. It has also tended to affect revenue, since it makes possible the mass evasion of tax-payment by the large majority which voted the councillors in and who, because of their relatively low annual income, have to pay the poll tax, not the graduated income tax. The problem of tax collection in Ibadan is a serious one. Although for most wards of the city there are assessment committees to assess the income of the self-employed people with incomes likely to exceed £300 per annum, the organization for collecting the poll tax is so poor that much revenue is lost annually. Periodically, of course, members of the local government police are sent out to check on tax receipts and to apprehend all those who do not appear to have paid their annual poll tax.

In the face of these defects in tax collection, it has been strongly argued in some quarters that a better and more efficient means of raising revenue is by property or tenement rates. Attention is drawn to the immense success that followed the adoption of this system in Abeokuta under the rule of a specially appointed administrator. There is little doubt that this system has many advantages, although some people have pointed out that it may not achieve its end in raising revenue because of the large proportion of low-value properties and the generally haphazard pattern of their arrangement.

However, it must not be assumed that the Ibadan City Council is starved of funds. Indeed, as the following Table shows, the Council has been doing very well for itself in the period 1954–55 to 1960–61, for which we have records. Its revenue grew at a rate faster than that of any local council in the region. But, as the second column indicates, much of this was due to increases in grants from the Regional Government. The table also shows that total expenditure, and especially expenditure on public works, rose at a much higher rate than is true for the whole of Western Nigeria.

Furthermore, Ibadan is specially favoured as far as revenue is concerned. For whilst the city accounts for less than a fifth of the total of those with income less than £300 in the Western Region, it contains, because of its position as the regional capital, more than half of the people with incomes above this figure. This fact underlines the relation of the City Council to the Regional Government. The latter has set up a Regional Tax Board to collect taxes from all those whose assessable income is over £300. Based upon its receipts, the government makes grants to the individual councils. Thus, the more rapid rate of increase in grants from the government to the Ibadan Council is a reflection of the rapid increase in the number of assessable units in this group. But in the last few years there have been complaints of delay, and sometimes of defaulting on the part of the Regional Government which has tended to strain the finances of the Council and to exacerbate its relation with the Regional Government.

Table 13.1

	1 Annual Growth Rate of Total Revenue 1954–61	2 Annual Growth Rate of Grants 1954–61	3 Growth Rate of Total Expenditure 1954–61	4 Growth Rate of Expenditure on Public Works 1954–61
All Councils	2·53%	1·7%	2·58%	2·3%
Ibadan District Council	2·60%	2·3%	2·82%	3·2%

Figures calculated from the Western Nigeria Statistical Bulletin, June–December 1963.

Nonetheless, the relation between the City Council and the Regional Government is somewhat more involved than this. As Ibadan is the capital of the region, the government feels directly involved in giving it an honoured position among Western Nigerian cities. There have been occasions in the past when the Regional Government has taken over specific functions of the City Council, such as tarring roads or issuing vehicle licences. More important is the special concern of the Regional Government for the industrial development of the city. Being not only the capital but also the largest city, Ibadan focuses attention on the growing problem of unemployment in the region. Efforts to increase employment opportunities in the city have not been remarkably successful, but the foundations for extensive industrialization are being laid in the planned improvements to the public utilities in the city. This is particularly true of the water supply which, as mentioned earlier, involves the damming of the Oshun River, estimated to cost over four million pounds.

Nonetheless, the role of the Regional Government in the local affairs of the Ibadan City Council should not be exaggerated. Indeed, it is a role whose importance varies considerably according to the efficiency of the Council, for the Regional Government has as much at stake in making the city worthy of its high status. In this respect, it is unfortunate that the Town Planning Authority is weak and can exert little beneficial influence. The Town Planning Authority comprises a group of enlightened and dedicated people whose function, unfortunately, has been limited to approving building plans. And furthermore it is empowered to pursue this function only in the immigrant half of the city. There is no section of the city administration concerned with planning for the economic growth of the city, with thinking about the social implications of economic development and with problems of social maladjustment and conflict in the city. There is thus no attempt to fit the work of the Town Planning Authority into a wider framework. The result is that even as far as the physical structure of the city is concerned not much progressive planning and improvement is shown.

To sum up, then, the city of Ibadan presents a picture of a traditional pre-industrial Nigerian city adapting itself to the needs and demands of the twentieth century's industrial society. Throughout its recent history as a city, it has served as a metropolis. The scope of the functions it discharges in this respect, however, has constantly been changing and the city in turn has been responding to these changes. In the modern period, Ibadan is already an important commercial centre and a major transport centre. Its prospects for industrial growth are also far from bleak. These developments are already straining the resources of the city and calling attention to the weaknesses of its infra-structure, its social amenities and its administration. In the next decade or two, therefore, it seems obvious that if Ibadan is to play its role as the most important metropolitan centre in Western Nigeria, there is need to overhaul its administrative and planning machinery to achieve greater efficiency.

BIBLIOGRAPHY

This bibliography contains work cited in this volume together with additional uncited works relating specifically to Ibadan. All items dealing primarily with Ibadan have been starred.

Adams, J. (1823). *Sketches taken during ten voyages to Africa between the years 1786 and 1800*, London.
Adejuwon, J. O. (1962). 'Crop Climate Relationship: the Example of Cocoa in Western Nigeria', *Nigerian Geographical Journal*, Vol. 5, pp. 29ff.
Adejuwon, J. O. (1963). *Farming and Farmlands in Ibadan Division of Western Nigeria*, unpub. M.Sc. Thesis, University of Ibadan.
Ajayi, J. F. Ade (1963). 'The Development of Secondary Grammar School Education in Nigeria', *Journal of the Historical Society of Nigeria*, Vol. 2, No. 4, pp. 517–535.
*Akinola, R. A. (1963). *Ibadan: a study in Urban Geography*, unpub. Ph.D. Thesis, University of London.
*Akinyele, I. B. (1946a). *Iwe Itan Ibadan*, Exeter.
*Akinyele, I. B. (1946b). *The Outlines of Ibadan History*, Lagos.
d'Avezac, A. (1845). *Notice sur le pays et le peuple des yebous en Afrique*, Paris.
Awokoya, Chief S.O. (1952). *Proposals for an Education Policy for the Western Region, Nigeria*, Ibadan: Government Printer.
Bascom, W. B. (1942). 'The Principle of Seniority in the Social Structure of the Yoruba', *American Anthropologist*, Vol. 44, pp. 37–46.
Bascom, W. B. (1955). 'Urbanization among the Yoruba', *American Journal of Sociology*, Vol. LX, pp. 446–53.
Bascom, W. B. (1957). 'Urbanism as a Traditional African pattern', *Sociological Review*, Vol. 7, No. 1, pp. 29–43.
*Biobaku S. O., Dina, I. O., Lloyd, P. C. (eds) (1949). *Ibadan*, published for the 3rd International West African Conference, Ibadan.
Biobaku, S. O. (1957). *The Egba and their Neighbours, 1842–1872*, Oxford.
Bowen, T. J. (1857). *Adventures and Missionary Labours in Several Countries in the Interior of Africa from 1849 to 1856*, Charleston.
British West African Meteorological Services, Nigeria. (1955). 'Preliminary Notes on the Rainfall of Nigeria', *Meteorological Notes*, No. 2.
Buchanan, K. M. and Pugh, J. C. (1955). *Land and People of Nigeria*, London.
Callaway, A. (1964). 'Nigeria's Indigenous Education: The Apprentice System', *Odu* (new series), Vol. 1, pp. 62–79.
*Cohen, A. (1965). 'The Social Organization of Credit in a West African Cattle Market', *Africa*, Vol. XXX, pp. 8–20.
*Cohen, A. (1966). 'Politics of the Kola Trade', *Africa*, Vol. XXXVI, pp. 18–36.
Coleman, J. S. (1952). 'The Role of Tribal Associations in Nigeria: Summary', *First Annual Conference West African Institute of Social and Economic Research in Ibadan*.
Dike, K. O. (1956). *Trade and Politics in the Niger Delta, 1830–1885*, Oxford.

BIBLIOGRAPHY

*Elgee, C. H. (1914). *The Evolution of Ibadan*, Lagos: Government Printer.
Epstein, A. L. (1958). *Politics in an Urban African Community*, Manchester.
Forde, Daryll (1951). *The Yoruba-speaking Peoples of South-western Nigeria*, Ethnographic survey of Africa, Western Africa No. 13, London.
Galletti, R., Baldwin, K. D. S. and Dina, I. O. (1956). *Nigerian Cocoa Farmers*, Oxford.
Gluckman, M. (1961). 'Anthropological Problems Arising from the African Industrial Revolution', in A. Southall (ed), *Social Change in Modern Africa*, London.
*Gordon, T. and Lancaster, M. (1961). 'Orisha Houses in Ibadan', *Ibadan*, No. 11, pp. 22-23.
Hilliard, F. H. (1957). *A Short History of Education in British West Africa*, London.
*Hinderer, Anna (1872). *Seventeen Years in the Yoruba Country*, London.
Hodder, B. W. (1963). *The Markets of Yorubaland*, unpub. Ph.D. Thesis, University of London.
Hodgkin, Thomas (1962). 'Islam and National Movements in West Africa', *Journal of African History*, Vol. III, p. 32.
Hogben, S. J. (1933). *The Mohammadan Emirates of Nigeria*, London.
Idowu, E. Bolaji (1962). *Olodumare: God in Yoruba Belief*, London.
Ifemesia, C. C. (1959). *British Enterprise on the Niger, 1830–1869*, unpub. Ph.D. Thesis, University of London.
Johnson, S. (1957). *The History of the Yorubas*, Lagos.
Jones, G. I. (1962). 'Ibo Age Organization with special reference to the Cross River and North Eastern Ibo', *Journal of the Royal Anthropological Institute*, Vol. 92, pp. 191-211.
Keay, R. W. J. (1959). *An Outline of Nigerian Vegetation*, Lagos.
Lampard, E. E. (1955). 'The History of Cities in the Economically Advanced Areas', *Economic Development and Cultural Change*, Vol. 3, pp. 81-136.
Lander, R. and J. (1832). *Journal of an Expedition to Explore the Course and Termination of the Niger*, London.
Lloyd, P. C. (1953). 'Craft Organization in Yoruba Towns', *Africa*, Vol. XXIII, pp. 30-44.
Lloyd, P. C. (1955). 'The Yoruba Lineage', *Africa*, Vol. XXV, pp. 235-251.
*Lloyd, P. C. (1956). 'Land Settlement and Tenure in Ibadan' in 3rd C.I.A.O. (1949). *Proceedings*, pp. 264-268.
Lloyd, P. C. (1959). 'The Yoruba Town Today', *Sociological Review*, Vol. 9, pp. 45-63.
Lloyd, P. C. (1962). *Yoruba Land Law*, London.
*Mabogunje, A. L. (1961). 'Ibadan: Black Metropolis', *Nigeria Magazine*, No. 68, pp. 12-26.
*Mabogunje, A. L. (1962a). 'The Growth of Residential Districts in Ibadan', *Geographical Review*, Vol. 52, pp. 56-77.
Mabogunje, A. L. (1962b). *Yoruba Towns*, Ibadan.
*Mabogunje, A. L. (1963). 'Ibadan Grammar School is 50 next Monday', *Daily Express*, Lagos, March 30th.
*Maclean, Una (1960). 'Ibadan Churches', *Ibadan*, No. 8, p. 20.
*Mellanby, K. (1958). *The Birth of Nigeria's University*, London.

BIBLIOGRAPHY

*Meyerowitz, E. L. R. (1946). 'Notes on the King-God Shango and his Temple at Ibadan', *Man*, Vol. 46, sec. 27, pp. 25-31.

*Mitchel, N. C. (1953). 'Some Comments on the Growth and Character of Ibadan's Population', University College, Ibadan, Geography Dept., *Research Notes*, No. 4, pp. 2-15.

Mitchel, N. C. (1961). 'Yoruba Towns', in K. M. Barbour and R. M. Prothero (eds), *Essays on African Population*, London.

Mitchell, J. C. (1960). *Tribalism and the Plural Society*, London.

Morel, E. D. (1912). *Nigeria, Its Peoples and its Problems*, London.

Murray, K. C. (1943). 'Arts and Crafts of Nigeria: Their Past and Present', *Africa*, Vol. XIV, pp. 156.

*Nigeria (1951). *Commission of Inquiry into the Allegations of Misconduct made against Chief Salami Agbaje, the Otun Balogun of Ibadan, and Allegations of Inefficiency and Maladministration on the part of the Ibadan and District Native Authority: Report by H. L. M. Butcher*, Lagos: Government Printer.

*Nigeria (1952). *Final Report on Ibadan Divisional Reforms: Report by J. F. Hayley*, Ibadan: Government Printer.

*Nigeria (1956). *Commission of Enquiry into the administration of the Ibadan District Council: Report by E. W. J. Nicholson*, Ibadan: Government Printer.

Norris, Robert (1789). *Memoirs of the Reign of Bossa Ahadee, King of Dahomey*, London.

Ottenberg, S. (1955). 'Improvement Associations among the Afikpo Ibo', *Africa*, Vol. XXV, pp. 1-27

Oyerinde, N. D. (1935). *Itan Ogbomoso*, Ibadan.

*Park, E. (1963). 'Taffy Jones, First Town Engineer of Ibadan', *Nigerian Field*, Vol. 28, pp. 103-114.

*Parrinder, G. (1951). 'Ibadan's Annual Festival', *Africa*, Vol. XXI, pp. 54-58.

*Parrinder, G. (1953). *Religion in an African City*, London.

Parrinder, G. (1956). *The Story of Ketu, an Ancient Yoruba Kingdom*, Ibadan.

Phillipson, S. (1948). *Grants of Aid of Education in Nigeria*, Lagos: Government Printer.

Proudfoot, L. (1959). 'Mosque Building and Tribal Separatism in Freetown East', *Africa*, Vol. XXIX, pp. 405-416.

*Saunders, J. T. (1960). *University College, Ibadan*, Cambridge.

Schwab, W. B. (1955). 'Kinship and Lineage among the Yoruba', *Africa*, Vol. XXV, pp. 352-74.

Sjoberg, G. (1960). *The Preindustrial City*, Glencoe, Illinois.

Skinner, Elliot P. (1963). 'Strangers in West African Societies', *Africa*, Vol. XXXIII, pp. 307-20.

Smith, H. F. C. (1961). 'The Islamic Revolutions of the Nineteenth Century', *Journal of the Historical Society of Nigeria*, Vol. II, No. 1.

*Steigenga, W. (1965). 'Ibadan, City in Transition', *Tijaschrift van het koninklyk Nederlandsch Aardrijkskundig Genootschap*, Diel LXXXII.

*Thorp, Ellen (1950). *The Swelling of Jordon*, London.

United Nations, Department of Social and Economic Affairs (1958). *Management of Industrial Enterprises in Under-Developed Countries*, New York.

BIBLIOGRAPHY

Ward Price, H. L. (1939). *Land Tenure in the Yoruba Provinces*, Lagos: Government Printer.

Western Region, Nigeria (1955). *Annual Report of the Department of Education*, Ibadan: Government Printer.

Wilkinson, Thomas D. (1961). 'Agricultural Activities in the City of Tokyo', *Rural Sociology*, Vol. 26, pp. 50ff.

INDEX

Abiodun, Alafin of Oyo, 251*n*
Aboderin, J. O., 223–4
Aboh division of Western Iboland, 97–99
Abu Bakr b.al Qasim, Shaikh, 251–2
Action Group, the, 82, 124, 226–30
Adelabu, Adegoke, 225–8, 230, 233
Adeyemi, Alafin of Oyo, 23, 24
Atonja, Are Onakakanfo, 12-13
African Churches, the, 92, 239–41
African Messenger, the, 222
Agate's compound, 61, 62, 66, 67, 72, 73, 82
Agbaje, Salami, 222, 225–6
Agbeni Street, 49, 176, 186, 188
Ago Taylor market, 177
Agodi residential area, 49, 51, 91, 131, 136–8
agriculture, 4, 5, 15, 27–33, 71, 85, 98, 105, 199, 200, 205–7, 211; cocoa, 7, 9, 29, 32, 33, 47, 132, 156, 174, 195, 205; food crops, 29, 30, 32, 33, 98, 205; palm kernels and oil, 7, 22, 97, 98, 174, 178, 205; physical environment, 27–8; system of shifting cultivation, 28–9; tools, 5, 29, 32, 40
Aguga, 198–201; market, 177–8
Ahmad Qifu, 250–1
Ajadi's compound, 63, 67
Ajayi- Amadu's compound, 63–72 *pass*.
Ajeja's compound, 65–72 *pass*.
ajele, 20, 214
Akinajo's compound, 62–72 *pass*.
Akinbiyi, D. T., 223–4
Akinloye, A. M. A., 229
Akintola, Chief S. L., 229
Akinyele, Rev. A. B., 193, 221; Isaac B., Olubadan of Ibadan, 221–3 *pass*.
Alabata market, 174
Alafin of Oyo, 12, 16, 20, 21, 25, 218–9, 220, 221, 223; *see also* Abiodun, Adeyemi, Atiba
Alagba market, 174
Anglican Church Missionary Society, 192, 193, 216, 239
Apampa, Bashorun, 253
Aremu, O., 175*n*, 177*n*
Asaba Division of Western Iboland, 97–8, 99
Atabante's compound, 62–9 *pass*.

Atiba, Alafin of Oyo, 17–9
Awogu, Miss A., 138*n*
Awokoya, Chief S. O., 195
Awolowo, Obafemi, 226

babalawo, the, 74, 76, 235, 236
Bale (Olubadan), the, 6, 19, 20, 38, 66, 92, 117, 118, 192, 213–23 *pass*., 268; *see also* Akinyele, Isaac
Balogun, the, 19, 66, 213–4, 218; *see also* Akintola, Ibikunle, Oderinlo, Ola
Baptists, the, 92, 239
basketry; *see* industries, craft
black soap; *see* industries, craft
blacksmith; *see* industries, craft
Bodija Estate, 54–5, 137
'Brazilian' style of building, 50–1
British Cotton Growing Association, 217–8
British Council, 45, 266
British in Nigeria 24–5, 39, 41, 86, 87, 99, 117, 149, 214–9, 262–3
building; *see* industries, other

carpentry; *see* industries, craft
Carter, Gilbert T., 25, 214–5
cattle; *see* trade
Christ Apostolic Church, 92, 240–2
Christianity, 48, 72–4, 87, 92, 111*n*, 140, 141, 239–47, 253; and schools, 89, 192–3, 216, 255
City Council of Ibadan, 10, 38, 56, 93–4, 148, 223–33, 263–4, 268–71
civil service, Nigerianization of, 130–3
climate of Ibadan, 27–8
cloth; *see* industries, craft, and trade
cocoa; *see* agriculture
Commercial Reservation, 51, 91
compound, concept of, 5, 46–7, 65–9; life of children in, 76–9, 101, 102, 106–7, 143
cooked foods; *see* trade
Co-operative Society, 45

Dele, Are Ago, 59–63, 81; present chief, 62–3, 66; 's compound, 63–77 *pass*., 81–2
diokpa, the, 109, 110*n*
Dugbe market, 153, 178–88 *pass*.

277

INDEX

Edo, the, 8, 42
education, primary, 9, 143, 144, 191–7, 201, 208, 209, 210–1, 243, 255–6, 266; secondary, 7, 80, 131, 135, 144, 160, 165, 191, 193–6, 200–10 *pass.*, 243, 256, 266; university, technical and further, 41, 89, 132, 135–6, 191, 194, 195, 200, 203–4, 210, 256, 266; *see also* Christianity and schools, Free Primary Education Programme, University of Ibadan, University of Ife
Education Act of 1954, 195
Education Ordinance and Code of 1948, 194–5
Efik, the, 42
Egba, 3, 13, 14, 18, 21–4, 37, 42, 49, 86, 94, 134
Egbe Agba O'Tan, the, 221–2, 225
Egbe Omo Ijebu, the, 92–3
Egbeda market, 173
egungun celebrations, 6, 61, 65, 74, 237–8, 244, 246
Ekotedo settlement, 8, 49–50, 54, 99, 100, 102, 124, 198–201, 205
Ekiti, the, 20, 23, 24
Eleiyele market, 177
Elekuro (Labo) market, 177, 178, 205*n*
Elgee, Captain, 216–7, 218
élite, new educated, 7, 41, 50, 54, 90, 105, 129–50, 262, 263
endogamy, 136
entrepreneurs, 163–8
exogamy, 136, 146

Folashade's compound, 63–74 *pass.*, 79–82 *pass.*
food crops; *see* agriculture
foodstuffs; *see* trade
Forestry Department, 30, 217, 219, 263
Free Primary Education Programme, 48, 79–80, 131, 134, 195–6, 210–1; *see also* education, primary
Fulani, 3, 11, 12–3, 17–8, 20, 24, 97, 249

Galetti, 68, 69
Gbagi traders, 176, 188–9
Gbalefa's compound, 62, 67, 73
goldsmith; *see* industries, craft
Grier, S. M., 219–20

Hādjdj, 126–7
Harun, 252–3
Hausa, the, 8, 42, 50, 117–27, 179, 182–3, 249
Hayley reform committee, 226, 227
Hinderer, Rev. David and Anna, 15, 73, 87, 192, 239
Hogben, 13*n*

Ibadan Patriotic Association, the, 224
Ibadan Progressive Union, the, 223–7, 263
Ibibio, the, 42
Ibikunle, Balogun of Ibadan, 16, 20
Ibo, the, 8, 42
Ibo State Union, the, 113
Ibuko (Bode) market, 177–9 *pass*
Idiape market, 177, 178
Ife, the, 13, 14, 37, 86
Ijaye, 3, 21, 86
Ijebu bye-pass development, 45, 50, 54, 224, 226, 263
Ijebu, the, 11, 13, 134, 136, 145, 146, 159, 160; rivalry with Ibadan, 9, 21–4, 214–5, 216; settle in Ibadan, 14, 37, 42, 49, 85–95, 226; Students' Association, 92–3
Ijesha, the, 23, 24, 42, 49, 94
Ikeja-Mushin estate, 169, 264
Ile Ife, 14, 24
Ilorin, 13, 17, 73
Imam, Chief, 117, 126, 127, 254–5, 257
imported manufactured goods; *see* trade
Inalende settlement, 99, 100, 102, 160, 205*n*
Independent Schools' Proprietors' Association, 194
industries, craft, 5, 9, 30–1, 40–1, 71–2, 88, 90, 105, 153–9, 199, 200; blacksmith, 40, 153–62 *pass.*, 171, 199; black soap, 155, 175–7; carpentry, 32, 33, 40, 71, 153, 155, 159, 163, 165–6; cloth, 33, 40, 154, 155, 157–9, 160, 162, 171; goldsmith, 88, 158, 159, 160, 171; leatherwork, 16, 159, 171; pottery and basketry, 40, 154, 158, 162, 218
industries, other, 32, 33; building, 33, 71, 105, 154; printing, 88, 155, 159, 160, 161, 171; property investment, 90; transport, 71, 89, 105, 154, 155
Isale Ijebu, 87, 90
Ishole's compound, 62, 67, 68, 82
Islam, 9, 48, 72, 73–4, 77, 92, 124–7, 193, 245, 249–57
Iyalode, the, 19, 192
Iyaloja, the, 63–4

Jagun Akoka's compound, 66, 67, 68
Janes, Dr. M., 135*n*
Jaramera's compound, 67, 72, 82
Jehovah's Witnesses, 92
Jenkins, 263, 264
Jericho Residential area, 91
Johnson, 13*n*, 249, 250, 251*n*

Kingsway, 45, 129
kolanuts; *see* trade

INDEX

Rurunmi of Ijaye (Are Onakakanfo), 14*n*, 17-8, 21

Lagos, 35, 86, 95, 194, 264-5, 266; competitor with Ibadan, 7, 87, 213; trade with Ibadan, 22, 24-5, 186
Latosa (Are Onakakanfo), 21, 23, 24
leatherwork; see industries, craft
Lemanu, the, 73
Leventis, 45
Links Reservation, 51, 91

Mabolaje, the 227, 229
malams, the, 73, 121, 123, 127, 249*n*, 254
Maliki rite, 254, 255, 256
Mapo Hall, 14, 38, 46, 129
medical facilities, 7, 77, 134, 191, 206, 266-7
Methodists, 92, 239
Ministry of Economic Planning and Community Development, 83
mogaji, 5, 6, 20, 66, 213-4, 227, 254
Mokola, 8, 99, 100, 124, 160, 205*n*; market, 177-82 *pass.*
'Money Makes the Gentleman Society', 83
mukaddams, 125-6

National Council of Nigeria and the Cameroons party (N.C.N.C.), 124, 133, 227-30
National Council of Nigerian Citizens, 82
Native Aboriginal Society (Committee of Gentlemen), 222
Native Settlers' Union, 226
New Reservation, 51, 91
Nicholson Commission of Inquiry, 228
Nigerian Tobacco Company, 155
Nigerian Women's Association, 148
Northern People's Congress of the Northern Region, 229
Nupe, the, 8, 50, 99

Obisesan, Akinpelu, 221-2, 223, 225
Oderinlo, Balogun, 59-60, 81
Ogongo's compound, 62, 64, 67, 73
Ogunpa Motor Park, 179, 188, 189
Ogunsola, J. L., 223-4
oja, 173*n*
Oja Iba, 14, 38, 44-5, 81; market, 16, 37, 44-5, 59, 173-86 *pass.*, 188-9
Oje, 9, 59-83; market, 16, 175-81, *pass.*
Oje Boys and Girls Club, 83
Oje Progressive Union, 82-3

Oje Social Circle, 83
Ojuolape's compound, 62, 67, 68, 73, 81, 82
Oke Ado, 8, 90, 91, 100, 137-8, 160
Oke Bola, 90, 91, 100, 160
Oke Ibadan, cult of, 6, 18, 236, 237, 244, 246
Ola, Balogun, 220-1
Olajifin, Asaju to Bale Olugbode, 62
Oloro's compound, 63, 67, 74, 82
Oluyedun (Are Onekakanfo), 250, 251*n*
Oluyole (Bashorun), 16, 18, 59-60, 251
Oritamerin, 198-201
Ọṣẹ Meji, 235-6
Oshun Division, 134, 226
Owu, 13, 37, 65, 86
Oyewole, Bashorun, 81
Oyo, 3, 6, 11, 14, 16-7, 20, 24-5, 37, 86, 134, 159; see also Alafin of

palm kernels and oil; see agriculture
Parrinder, 249, 250, 257*n*
polygyny, 69-70, 76, 101, 120, 139-41, 241
pottery; see industries, craft
primary education; see education
printing; see industries, other
property investment; see industries, other
Provisional Council, 228, 231, 233

railway system, growth of, 7, 39, 42, 49, 87, 261, 262, 263
Regional Government, 6, 10, 148, 227-33, 264, 266, 269-71
Roman Catholic Mission, 192, 193, 239
Ross, Captain, 219-22, 263
Royal Niger Company, 99

Sabo (Sabon Gari) settlement, 99, 117-19, 120-6, 160, 179, 182
Salvation Army, the, 239
Sango cattle market, 183
Sarkin Hausawa, the, 117
secondary education; see education
Secretariat, the, 6, 131, 137
Seraphim and Cherubim sect, 92, 239, 240-2
Seriki, the, 19
Seventh Day Adventists, 92, 239
slave trade; see trade
Sodeinde, Balogun Elesin, 86

taxation, 81, 232-3, 269, 270
Tidjāniyya Order, 125-6, 254
Town Planning Authority, 56, 267, 271

INDEX

trade, 15–6, 22, 36, 40, 44–5, 85, 90–1, 102, 133; cattle, 123n, 179, 183; cloth, 16, 59, 64, 70, 85–6, 161, 175–7, 199; cooked foods, 44, 63, 70, 74–5, 102, 177, 178, 183–4; foodstuffs, 5, 16, 63, 70, 88, 102, 175, 178, 179, 181–7, 199; imported manufactured goods, 16, 64, 87, 181, 188; kolanuts, 8, 119, 123n, 179, 182–3; slave, 13, 15, 16, 86, 97; women engaged in, 63, 70–1, 74–5, 87–8, 102, 105, 106, 162

traditional deities and religious practices, 6, 63, 65, 72, 74, 76–8, 80–1, 235–9, 244, 246–7; *see also egungun* celebrations, *Oke Ibadan*, cult of

traditional political system in Ibadan, 6, 19–20, 37–8, 213–4, 262; military nature of, 18–20, 22, 36–8, 214–31; power of chief, 62, 63; among the Hausa, 124; among the Ijebu, 93–4; among the Western Ibo, 98–9

transport; *see* industries, other

transport system, 55–6, 88–9, 262, 267; *see also* railway system, growth of

unemployment among school leavers, 8, 191, 194, 197–209, 211

Unit housing, 49, 50

United Peoples' Party, 82, 133, 229–30

United States Information Service, 266

United Trading Company, 45

University of Ibadan, 7, 41, 91, 92, 100, 129–30, 133, 134, 137, 149, 191, 194, 266; Hospital, 7, 137, 267

University of Ife (Ibadan branch), 8, 91, 100, 129–30, 191, 194, 266

university, technical and further education; *see* education

Urhobo, 8, 42

Uthman b.Abu Bakr, 250–1

Ward Price, H. L., 223

Wesley College, 89, 192, 243

Wesleyan Methodist Mission, 192, 193

Western Ibo, the, 97–116

Western Ibo Union, 112–5

Western Nigerian Development Corporation, 115–6

Western Nigerian Housing Corporation, 137

Western Nigerian Printing Corporation, 155

Western Region Local Government Law, 227, 263

women, friendships of, 145–7; in the home, 70, 74–81, 102, 105–7, 140–2, 145; in prostitution, 105–6, 108, 120; in trade, 63, 70–1, 74–5, 87–8, 102, 105, 106, 162, 182, 183–4, 199, 207; opportunities for, 70–1, 134, 135–6, 141, 200–1